PENGUII

ARKAN

MEETINGS WITH RE

George Ivanovitch Gurdjieff (1877–1949) was born in Alexandropol and trained in Kars as both a priest and a physician. For some twenty years, Gurdjieff travelled in the remotest regions of Central Asia and the Middle East. These years were crucial in the moulding of his thought. On his return, he began to gather pupils in Moscow before the First World War and continued his work with a small party of followers while moving, during the year of the Russian revolution, to Essentuki in the Caucasus, and then through Tiflis, Constantinople, Berlin and London to the Château du Prieuré near Paris, where he re-opened his Institute for the Harmonious Development of Man in 1922 on a larger scale.

The story of his unremitting search for a real and universal knowledge, and the expositions of his ideas, are unfolded in his major works: *Beelzebub's Tales to His Grandson*, *Meetings with Remarkable Men*, *Life is Real Only Then, When 'I am'* and *Views from the Real World*.

Meetings With Remarkable Men

G. I. GURDJIEFF

ARKANA

PENGUIN BOOKS

ARKANA

Published by the Penguin Group
Penguin Books Ltd, 27 Wrights Lane, London W8 5TZ, England
Penguin Putnam Inc., 375 Hudson Street, New York, New York 10014, USA
Penguin Books Australia Ltd, Ringwood, Victoria, Australia
Penguin Books Canada Ltd, 10 Alcorn Avenue, Toronto, Ontario, Canada M4V 3B2
Penguin Books (NZ) Ltd, 182–190 Wairau Road, Auckland 10, New Zealand

Penguin Books Ltd, Registered Offices: Harmondsworth, Middlesex, England

First published in Great Britain by Routledge 1963
Published by Arkana 1985
11 13 15 17 19 20 18 16 14 12

Printed in England by Clays Ltd, St Ives plc

CONTENTS

WRITTEN IN RUSSIAN, THE MANUSCRIPT OF THIS BOOK
WAS BEGUN IN 1927 AND REVISED BY THE AUTHOR
OVER A PERIOD OF MANY YEARS. THE FIRST ENGLISH
TRANSLATION BY A. R. ORAGE HAS BEEN REVISED AND
REWORKED FROM THE RUSSIAN FOR THIS PUBLICATION

FOREWORD

GURDJIEFF HAD DEVOTED most of his life to teaching a system of knowledge to his pupils when, shortly before his death, he decided to publish the first of the three books in which he had expressed his ideas, *All and Everything, or Beelzebub's Tales to his Grandson*. In his own words, the aim of *Beelzebub's Tales* was 'to destroy mercilessly the beliefs and views rooted for centuries in the mind and feelings of man' by arousing in the mind of the reader a stream of unfamiliar thoughts.

Ten years after his death, his pupils decided to make known the whole body of his ideas, until then accessible only to themselves.

A second volume, which represents what Gurdjieff called the second series of his writings, was first published in France in 1960, and it is this book which is now published in English under the title *Meetings with Remarkable Men*. As Gurdjieff said, his task in this series was to furnish 'the material required to create the feeling of a new world'—a feeling which throws a different light on one's own life.

At the same time this book is written in the form of autobiography and contains the only available information about his early life and the sources of his knowledge.

Gurdjieff begins by describing the circumstances of his childhood, particularly the influence of his father, one of the last survivors of an ancient culture handed down by oral tradition. Coming as a boy under the tutelage of the dean of the Cathedral of Kars, he was given both a religious training and a modern scientific education by men who understood how to cultivate in him a taste for essential values.

As he grew up, his urge to understand the meaning of human

life became so strong that he attracted a group of 'remarkable men'—among whom were engineers, doctors, archaeologists and so on. In search of a knowledge which they were certain had existed in the past but of which almost all traces seemed to have disappeared, he set out with them to explore many countries in the Middle East and Central Asia.

With his companions, after many great and unexpected difficulties, he succeeded in finding a very few individuals and isolated communities, each time acquiring fragments of this knowledge— until the moment when the doors of a certain school opened for him, where he came to understand how to bring together all the principles of an esoteric teaching. This school he calls simply the Universal Brotherhood, without telling more.

From then on he proceeded to 'live' these principles, putting them to the test by the strictest inner disciplines till the end of his life.

Gurdjieff spoke also of a third series of his writings called *Life Is Real Only When I Am*. His aim in this series was 'to assist the arising in a man's thought and feeling of a true representation of the real world, instead of the illusory world he now perceives'.

The third book, now being prepared for publication, will consist chiefly of talks and lectures which Gurdjieff gave to his pupils. Here he shows the way towards direct work on oneself, points out the pitfalls, and provides means for a better understanding of the inner conditions which are indispensable in the self-development of man.

TRANSLATORS' NOTE[1]

THE WORK OF GURDJIEFF has many aspects. But through whatever form he expresses himself, his voice is heard as a call.

He calls because he suffers from the inner chaos in which we live.

He calls to us to open our eyes.

He asks us why we are here, what we wish for, what forces we obey. He asks us, above all, if we understand what we are.

He wants us to bring everything back into question.

And because he insists and his insistence compels us to answer, a relationship is created between him and ourselves which is an integral part of his work.

For nearly forty years this call rang with such force that people came to him from all over the world.

But to meet him was always a test. In his presence every attitude seemed artificial. Whether too deferential, or on the contrary pretentious, from the first moment it was shattered; and nothing remained but a human creature stripped of his mask and revealed for an instant as he truly was.

This was a merciless experience—and for some impossible to bear.

These people could not forgive him for having seen through them and as soon as they were out of his sight, went to great lengths to justify themselves. This was the origin of the most fantastic legends.

Gurdjieff himself was amused by these stories. He even went so far as to provoke them, at times, if only to be rid of

[1] Translated from the Note des Traducteurs in the French edition of this book, Julliard, Paris, 1960.

curiosity-seekers, incapable of understanding the meaning of his search.

As for those who knew how to approach him and for whom this meeting was a turning-point in their lives, any attempt to describe their experience seemed ridiculous. This explains why direct accounts are so rare.

The influence he exerted—and still exerts—cannot, however, be separated from Gurdjieff the man. So it is legitimate to want to know about his life, at least in its main outlines.

For this reason his pupils have felt it right to publish this book, originally intended to be read aloud to a limited circle of pupils and guests. Here Gurdjieff speaks of the least-known period of his life: his childhood, his youth and the first stages of his search.

But if Gurdjieff speaks of himself, he does so to serve his life-long purpose. It is apparent that this is not an autobiography in the strict sense of the word. For him the past is not worth re-counting except in so far as it can serve as an example. In these tales of adventure what he suggests are not models for outward imitation, but a completely new way of facing life, which touches us directly and gives us a foretaste of another order of reality.

For Gurdjieff was not, and could not be, only a writer. His task was a different one.

Gurdjieff was a master.

This idea of master, so familiar in the East, is hardly accepted at all in the West. It calls to mind nothing definite; its content is extremely vague, even suspect.

According to traditional conceptions, the function of a master is not limited to the teaching of doctrines, but implies an actual incarnation of knowledge, thanks to which he can awaken other men, and help them in their search simply by his presence.

He is there to create conditions for an experience through which knowledge can be lived as fully as possible.

This is the real key to the life of Gurdjieff.

From the time of his return to the West, he worked unceasingly to gather round him a group of people ready to share with him a life wholly turned towards the development of consciousness. He unfolded his ideas to them, sustained and gave life to their search, and brought them to the conviction that, to be complete, their experience must include at one and the same time all the aspects of a human being. And this is the very idea of the "harmonious development of man" on which he based that Institute which for many years he strove to set on its feet.

Working towards this goal, Gurdjieff had to fight a relentless battle through all the difficulties caused not only by war, revolution, and exile, but also by the indifference of some and the hostility of others.

To give the reader some idea of this struggle, and of his tireless ingenuity in carrying it on, there has been added a chapter not originally intended for this book. It is an account he gave one evening in reply to a question—seemingly very indiscreet—about the financial resources of the Institute.

This astonishing narrative, which appears under the title "The Material Question", may contribute to a better understanding of how a master's life and all his actions are subordinated to the accomplishment of his mission.

I

INTRODUCTION

EXACTLY A MONTH HAS ELAPSED since I finished the first series of my writings—just that period of the flow of time which I intended to devote exclusively to resting the parts of my common presence subordinate to my pure reason. As I wrote in the last chapter of the first series,[1] I had given myself my word that during the whole of this time I would do no writing whatsoever, but would only, for the well-being of the most deserving of these subordinate parts, slowly and gently drink down all the bottles of old calvados now at my disposal by the will of fate in the wine-cellar of the Prieuré, and specially provided the century before last by people who understood the true sense of life.

Today I have decided, and now I wish—without forcing myself at all, but on the contrary with great pleasure—to set to work at my writing again, of course with the help of all the corresponding forces and also, this time, with the help of the law-conformable cosmic results flowing in from all sides upon my person from the good wishes of the readers of the first series.

I now propose to give a form understandable for everyone to everything I have written down for the second series, in the hope that these ideas may serve as preparatory constructive material for setting up in the consciousness of creatures similar to myself a new world—a world in my opinion real, or at least one that can be perceived as real by all degrees of human thinking without the

[1] *All and Everything: Beelzebub's Tales to His Grandson,* p. 1236.

slightest impulse of doubt, instead of the illusory world which contemporary people picture to themselves.

And indeed, the mind of contemporary man, of whatever level of intellectuality, is only able to take cognizance of the world by means of data which, whenever accidentally or intentionally activated, arouse in him all sorts of fantastic impulses. And these impulses, by constantly affecting the tempo of all the associations flowing in him, gradually disharmonize the whole of his functioning, with such sorrowful results that it is impossible for any man, if he is able to isolate himself even a little from the influences of the established abnormal conditions of our ordinary life and is willing to think about it seriously, not to be terrified—as, for example, by the shortening of our life with each decade.

First of all, for the 'swing of thought', that is, for establishing a corresponding rhythm for my thinking and also for yours, I wish to follow somewhat the example of the Great Beelzebub and imitate the form of thinking of one highly respected by him and by me, and perhaps already, brave reader of my writings, by you, if of course you have had the daring to read through to the end all of the first series. That is to say, I wish to introduce at the very beginning of this writing of mine what our dear-to-all Mullah Nassr Eddin[1] would call a 'subtly philosophical question'.

I wish to do this at the very beginning because I intend to use freely, both here and in my later expositions, the wisdom of this sage, who is now recognized almost everywhere and upon whom, it is rumoured, the title of 'The One and Only' is soon to be officially conferred by the proper person.

And this subtly philosophical question may already be sensed in that sort of perplexity which is bound to arise in the consciousness of every reader of even the very first paragraph of this chapter, if he compares the many data on which his firm convictions about medical matters are based with the fact that I, the author of *Beelzebub's Tales to His Grandson*, after the accident which nearly cost me my life, with the functioning of my organism not yet fully re-established owing to the incessant active effort

[1] Mullah Nassr Eddin, a legendary figure in numerous countries of the Near East, is an embodiment of popular wisdom.

to set down my thoughts for transmission to others as exactly as possible, carried out my rest quite satisfactorily during this time chiefly by the use of immoderate quantities of alcohol, in the form of the above-mentioned old calvados and of its various full-strength virile cousins.

As a matter of fact, to give a completely true and exhaustive reply to this subtly philosophical question thus propounded impromptu, one must first reach a just verdict on my personal guilt in failing to fulfil exactly the obligation I had taken upon myself —to drink down all the remaining bottles of the said old calvados.

The point is that during this time appointed for my rest, despite all my automatic desire, I could not limit myself to the fifteen remaining bottles of old calvados which I mentioned in the last chapter of the first series, but had to combine the sublime contents of these bottles with the contents of two hundred other bottles—enchanting even to look upon—of the no less sublime liquid called old armagnac, so that this totality of cosmic substances might suffice for me personally, as well as for the whole tribe of those who have become in recent years my inevitable assistants, chiefly in these 'sacred ceremonies' of mine.

Before pronouncing this verdict on my personal guilt, one must finally take into account that from the very first day I changed my custom of drinking armagnac from what are called liqueur glasses and began drinking it from what are called tumblers. And I began to do so instinctively, it seems to me—obviously so that, in the present case also, justice might triumph.

I do not know about you, brave reader, but the rhythm of my thinking is now established, and I can begin again, without forcing myself, to wiseacre in full blast.

In this second series I intend, among other things, to introduce and elucidate seven sayings which have come down to our day from very ancient times by means of inscriptions on various monuments, which I happened to come across and deciphered during my travels—sayings in which our remote ancestors formulated certain aspects of objective truth, clearly perceptible even to contemporary human reason. I shall therefore begin with just that one saying which, besides serving as a good starting-point for the expositions which follow, will be a link with the last chapter of the first series.

This ancient saying, chosen by me for the beginning of the second series of my writings, is formulated thus:

Only he will deserve the name of man and can count upon anything prepared for him from Above, who has already acquired corresponding data for being able to preserve intact both the wolf and the sheep confided to his care.

A 'psycho-associative philological analysis' of this saying of our ancestors which was made by certain learned men of our times—of course not from among those breeding on the continent of Europe—clearly showed that the word 'wolf' symbolizes the whole of the fundamental and reflex functioning of the human organism and the word 'sheep' the whole of the functioning of a man's feeling. As for the functioning of a man's thinking, this is represented in the saying by the man himself, a man who, in the process of his responsible life, owing to his conscious labours and voluntary sufferings, has acquired in his common presence corresponding data for always being able to create conditions for a possible existence together of these two heterogeneous and mutually alien lives. Only such a man can count upon and become worthy to possess that which, as affirmed in this saying, is prepared from Above and is, in general, foreordained for man.

It is interesting to note that among the many proverbs and ingenious solutions of tricky problems habitually used by various Asiatic tribes, there is one—in which a wolf and, instead of a sheep, a goat also play their part—that corresponds very well, in my opinion, to the gist of the ancient saying I have quoted.

The question posed by this tricky problem is to find out how a man who has in his possession a wolf, a goat and, in the present case, a cabbage, can transfer them across a river from one bank to the other, if one takes into consideration, on the one hand, that his boat can carry only the load of himself and one of the three objects at a time, and on the other hand, that without his direct observation and influence the wolf can always destroy the goat, and the goat the cabbage.

And the correct answer to this popular riddle clearly shows that a man can achieve this not solely by means of the ingenuity which every normal man should have, but that in addition he must not be lazy nor spare his strength, but must cross the river an extra time for the attainment of his aim.

Returning to the meaning of the ancient saying chosen by me, and keeping in mind the gist of the correct solution of this popular riddle, then, if one thinks about it without any of the preconceptions always arising from the results of the idle thoughts usual to contemporary man, it is impossible not to admit with one's mind and agree with one's feelings that anyone calling himself a man must never be lazy, but, constantly devising all sorts of compromises, must struggle with his self-avowed weaknesses in order to attain the aim he has set himself: to preserve intact these two independent animals confided to the care of his reason, and which are, by their very essence, opposite to each other.

Having yesterday finished this, as I called it, 'wiseacring for the swing of thought', this morning I took with me the manuscript of a synopsis I had written in the first two years of my activities as a writer, which I intended to use as material for the beginning of this second series, and went into the park to sit down and work in the shade of the historic avenue of trees. After reading the first two or three pages, forgetting everything around me, I became deeply thoughtful, pondering on how to continue further; and I sat there without writing a single word until very late in the evening.

I was so wrapped up in these reflections that I did not once notice that the youngest of my nieces, the one whose task it is to see that the Arabian coffee which I usually take, particularly when doing any intensely active physical or mental work, does not become quite cold in the cup, changed it, as I afterwards learned, twenty-three times.

In order that you may understand the seriousness of this engrossed thoughtfulness of mine, and picture to yourself, if only approximately, the difficulty of my situation, I must tell you that after I had read these pages and remembered by association the entire contents of the manuscript I had intended to make use of as an introduction, it became quite clear to me that all this over which I had, as is said, 'panted' during so many sleepless nights, would now, after the changes and additions I had made in the final editing of the first series, be of no use at all.

When I understood this I experienced, for about half an hour, the state which Mullah Nassr Eddin defines by the words 'to feel oneself plunged in galoshes up to the eyebrows'; and I was ready at first to resign myself, and came to the decision to rewrite this entire chapter from beginning to end. But afterwards, continuing to recall automatically all sorts of sentences from my manuscript, I remembered, among other things, the place where, in order to explain why I took an attitude of merciless criticism towards contemporary literature, I had introduced the words of a certain intelligent, elderly Persian which I had heard in my early youth, and which, in my opinion, could not have better described the characteristics of contemporary civilization. I considered it impossible to deprive the reader either of what had been said on this subject or of all the other thoughts, so to say, artfully imbedded in this passage, thoughts which, for anyone able to decipher them, can be exceedingly valuable material for a correct understanding of what I intend to elucidate in the last two series in a form accessible to any man seeking the truth.

And so, these considerations compelled me to think out just how, without the reader being deprived of all this, it could be possible for the form of exposition I had first employed to correspond to the form now required after the great changes made in the first series.

In fact, what I had written during the first two years of this new profession of mine—which I was forced to adopt—could no longer correspond to what was now required, since I had then put down everything as a first version in the form of a synopsis understandable only to myself, intending to develop all this material in thirty-six books, devoting each book to one special question.

In the third year I had begun to give to this outline a form of exposition which might be understandable to others, at least to those specially trained in, so to say, abstract thinking. But since, little by little, I had become more adroit in the art of concealing serious thoughts in an enticing, easily grasped outer form, and in making all those thoughts which I term 'discernible only with the lapse of time' ensue from others usual to the thinking of most contemporary people, I changed the principle I had been following and, instead of seeking to achieve the aim I had set myself in writing by quantity, I adopted the principle of attaining this by quality alone. And I began to go over from the beginning everything I had written in the synopsis, with the intention now of dividing it into three series and of dividing each of these, in the final version, into several books.

And my becoming so deeply thoughtful today was perhaps also because, just yesterday, there had been freshly revived in my memory the wise ancient saying, 'always to strive that the wolf be full and the sheep intact'.

Finally, when evening drew nigh and, from below, the famous Fontainebleau dampness began to come through my 'English soles' and affect my thinking, while from above various of God's dear little creatures, called little birds, began to evoke more and more frequently a chilly sensation on my completely smooth cranium, there arose in my common presence the bold decision not to have any regard for anyone or anything but simply to insert in this first chapter of the second series, as what present-day professional writers would call a digressive development, certain polished-up fragments of this manuscript, pleasing to me personally, and only afterwards, in continuing further, to hold myself strictly to the principle I had decided upon for the writing of this series.

And this solution will be all the better both for me and for the reader, since I will thus be spared any extra new exertion of my already over-exhausted brains, and the reader, particularly if he has read through everything I have written before, will be able, owing to this digressive development, to represent to himself what kind of objectively impartial opinion is formed in the psyche of certain people, who have by chance been more or less correctly educated, concerning the results of the manifestations of the people of present-day civilization.

When this introduction was originally planned for the thirtieth book, I entitled it 'Why I Became a Writer', and described in it the impressions accumulated in me in the course of my life which are the basis of my present not very flattering opinion of the representatives of contemporary literature. In this connection, as I have already said, I introduced the speech which I had heard long ago in my youth, when I was in Persia for the first time and happened one day to be in a gathering of Persian intelligentsia where contemporary literature was being discussed.

One of those who spoke a great deal that day was the elderly, intelligent Persian whom I have mentioned—intelligent not in the European sense of the word, but in the sense in which it is understood on the continent of Asia, that is, not only by knowledge but by being.

He was very well educated and was particularly well acquainted with European culture.

He said, among other things:

'It is a great pity that the present period of culture, which we call and which people of subsequent generations will of course also call the "European civilization", is, in the whole process of the perfecting of humanity, as it were, an empty and abortive interval. And this is because, in respect of the development of the mind, that chief impeller to self-perfection, the people of our civilization cannot transmit by inheritance anything of value to their descendants.

'For example, one of the chief means for developing the mind of man is literature.

'But what has the literature of contemporary civilization to give? Nothing whatever, except the development of, so to say, "word prostitution".

'The fundamental cause of this corruption of present-day literature is, in my opinion, that the whole attention in writing has gradually, of itself, come to be concentrated not on the quality of the thought and the exactitude with which it is transmitted, but only on the striving for exterior polish or, as is otherwise said, beauty of style—thanks to which there has finally resulted what I called word prostitution.

'And in fact you can spend a whole day reading a lengthy book and not know what the writer wished to say, and only when you have nearly finished, after having wasted so much of your time—already insufficient for the fulfilment of the necessary obligations of life—do you discover that all this music was built up on an infinitesimal, almost null idea.

'All contemporary literature falls by content into three categories: the first covers what is called the scientific field, the second consists of narratives, and the third of what are called descriptions.

'The scientific books usually contain collections of all sorts of old hypotheses already obvious to everyone, but combined in different ways and applied to various new subjects.

'In the narratives or, as they are otherwise called, novels—to which bulky volumes are also devoted—for the most part there are descriptions, without sparing any details, of how some John Jones and Mary Smith attain the satisfaction of their "love"—that sacred feeling which has gradually degenerated in people, owing to their weakness and will-lessness, and has now in contemporary man turned completely into a vice, whereas the possibility of its natural manifestation was given to us by our Creator for the salvation of our souls and for the mutual moral support necessary for a more or less happy life together.

'The third category of books gives descriptions of travels, of adventures, and of the flora and fauna of the most diverse countries. Works of this kind are generally written by people who have never been anywhere and have never in reality seen anything, by people who, as is said, have never crossed their own doorsteps; with very few exceptions, they simply give rein to their imagination or copy various fragments from books written by others, former fantasists just like themselves.

'With this puny understanding of the responsibility and significance of literary works, the writers of today, in striving ever more and more for beauty of style, sometimes even invent an incredible hodge-podge in verse, in order to obtain what in their opinion is beauty of consonance, and thereby even further destroy the already feeble sense of everything they write.

'Strange as it may seem to you, in my opinion a great deal of harm to contemporary literature has been brought about by grammars, namely, the grammars of the languages of all the peoples who take part in what I call the "common malphonic concert" of contemporary civilization.

'The grammars of their different languages are, in most cases, constructed artificially, and have been composed and continue to be altered chiefly by a category of people who, in respect of understanding real life and the language evolved from it for mutual relations, are quite "illiterate".

'On the other hand, among all the peoples of past epochs, as ancient history very definitely shows us, grammar was always formed gradually by life itself, according to the different stages of their development, the climatic conditions of their chief place of existence and the predominant means of obtaining food.

'In present-day civilization the grammars of certain languages so greatly distort the meaning of what the writer wishes to transmit, that the reader, especially if he is a foreigner, is deprived of the last possibility of grasping even the few minute thoughts which, if expressed differently, that is, without this grammar, might perhaps still be understood.

'In order to make clearer what I have just said,' this elderly, intelligent Persian continued, 'I will give as an example an episode which took place in my own life.

'As you know, of all the persons near to me by blood, the only one still living is my nephew on the paternal side, who a few years ago, having inherited an oil well situated in the environs of Baku, was obliged to move there.

'And so I go from time to time to that town, because my nephew, being always very occupied with his numerous commercial affairs, is seldom able to leave and visit me, his old uncle, here at our birthplace.

'The district where these oils wells are located, and also the town of Baku, belong at the present time to Russia, which as one of the large nations of contemporary civilization produces an abundance of literature.

'Almost all the inhabitants of the town of Baku and its environs are of diverse races having nothing in common with the Russians, and in their own households they speak their native languages, but for outer mutual relations they are compelled to use Russian.

'During my visits there I came in contact with all kinds of people, and, having to speak with them for various personal needs, I decided to learn this language.

'I had had to learn so many languages in my lifetime that the learning of Russian did not present any great difficulty for me. Before very long I was able to speak it quite fluently but of course, like all the local inhabitants, with an accent, and only after a fashion.

'As one who has now become to some degree a "linguist", I consider it necessary to remark here, by the way, that it is never possible to think in a foreign language, even though knowing it to perfection, if one continues to speak one's native language or some other language in which one is accustomed to thinking.

'And therefore when I began to speak Russian, continuing all the while to think in Persian, I was searching mentally for words in the Russian language to correspond to my Persian thoughts.

'And it was then that I became aware of various incongruities—at first quite inexplicable to me—in this contemporary civilized language, on account of which it was sometimes impossible to transmit exactly the simplest and most ordinary expressions of our thoughts.

'Becoming interested in this, and being free of all life obligations, I began to study Russian grammar, and later the grammars of several other modern languages. I then understood that the cause of the incongruities I had noticed lay precisely in these artificially composed grammars of theirs, and there began to be formed in me the firm conviction which I have just expressed to you: that the grammars of the languages in which contemporary literature is written are invented by people who, in respect of true knowledge, are on a lower level than ordinary simple people.

'As a concrete illustration of what I have just said, I shall point out, among the many incongruities in the Russian language which I noticed at the very beginning, the one that led me to make a detailed study of this question.

'Once, when I was conversing in Russian and, as usual, was translating my thoughts, which formed themselves Persian fashion, I found it necessary to use an expression which we Persians often employ in conversation, *myan-diaram*, which means in French *je dis* and in English "I say". But try as I might, searching my memory for a corresponding word in Russian, I could not find one, in spite of my knowing by this time almost all the words of this language used either in literature or for the ordinary mutual relations of people of all levels of intellectuality.

'Not finding a corresponding word for this simple expression so often used by us, I of course at first decided that I simply did not yet know it, and I began to search in my numerous dictionaries and to inquire of certain people who were considered authorities, for some Russian word which would correspond to this Persian meaning of mine. However, it turned out that in modern Russian there is no such word at all, but instead a word is used, namely, *yah gohvahriou*, which means in Persian *myan-soïl-yaram*, in French *je parle* and in English "I speak".

'Since you Persians have the same sort of thinking faculty as I have for digesting the meaning conveyed by words, I therefore ask you: could I, or any other Persian, on reading in contemporary Russian literature a word corresponding to the meaning of *soïl-yaram*, accept it without instinctive disturbance as having the same meaning as the word *diaram*? Of course not: *soïl-yaram* and *diaram*—or "speak" and "say"—are two quite different "experienced actions".

'This very minor example is characteristic of thousands of other incongruities to be found in all the languages of the peoples who represent the so-called flower of contemporary civilization. And it is these incongruities which prevent the literature of today from serving as the basic means for developing the minds of those peoples who are considered representatives of this civilization and also of those peoples who at the present time—obviously for reasons already suspected by certain persons with common sense

—are somehow deprived of the good fortune of being considered civilized and are therefore, as historical data bear witness, usually called backward.

'Owing to all these incongruities of language existing in contemporary literature, any man—particularly a man from races not included among the representatives of contemporary civilization —who has a more or less normal thinking faculty and is able to give words their real meaning, will of course, on hearing or reading any word used in an incorrect sense, as in the example just given, perceive the general thought of a sentence according to this incorrectly employed word, and as a result will grasp something quite different from what the sentence was intended to express.

'Although the ability to grasp the meaning contained in words differs in different races, the data for sensing the repeated experienced actions which are already well established in the process of the life of people are formed in all of them alike by life itself.

'The very absence, in the present-day Russian language, of a word exactly expressing the meaning of the Persian word *diaram*, which I have taken as an example, can serve to confirm my seemingly unfounded statement that the illiterate upstarts of our time, who call themselves grammarians, and what is worse, are considered such by those round them, have succeeded in transforming even the language elaborated by life itself into, so to say, German *ersatz*.

'I must tell you here that when I began to study Russian grammar and also the grammars of several other modern languages in order to determine the causes of these numerous incongruities, I decided, being in general attracted to philology, to acquaint myself also with the history of the origins and development of the Russian language.

'And my study of its history proved to me that formerly it had contained exactly corresponding words for all the experienced actions already fixed in the process of the life of people. And it was only when this language, having reached a relatively high degree of development in the course of centuries, became in its turn an object for the "sharpening of the beaks of ravens", that is to say, an object of wiseacring for various illiterate upstarts, that many words were distorted or even entirely ceased to be used, merely because their consonance did not answer to the requirements of civilized grammar. Among these latter was the very word I searched for, which exactly corresponded to our *diaram*, and which was then pronounced *skaʒivaïou*.

'It is interesting to notice that this word has been preserved even up to the present time, but is used, and in the sense exactly corresponding to its meaning, only by people who, although they belong to the Russian nation, happen to be isolated from the effects of present-day civilization, that is to say, by people of various country districts situated far from any centre of culture.

'This artificially invented grammar of the languages of today, which the younger generation everywhere is now compelled to learn, is in my opinion one of the fundamental causes of the fact that, among contemporary European people, only one of the three independent data necessary for obtaining a sane human mind has developed—namely, their so-called thought, which tends to predominate in their individuality; whereas without feeling and instinct, as every man with a normal reason must know, the real understanding accessible to man cannot be formed.

'To sum up everything that has been said about the literature of our times, I cannot find better words to describe it than the expression "it has no soul".

'Contemporary civilization has destroyed the soul of literature, as of everything else to which it has turned its gracious attention.

'I have all the more grounds for criticizing so mercilessly this result of modern civilization, since according to the most reliable historical data which have come down to us from remote antiquity we have definite information that the literature of former civilizations had indeed a great deal to assist the development of the mind of man; and the results of this development, transmitted from generation to generation, could still be felt even centuries later.

'In my opinion, the quintessence of an idea can sometimes be very well transmitted to others by means of certain anecdotes and proverbs formed by life.

'So, in the present case, in order to show the difference between the literature of former civilizations and the contemporary, I wish to make use of an anecdote very widely known among us in Persia, entitled "The Conversation of the Two Sparrows".

'In this anecdote it is said that once upon a time on the cornice of a high house sat two sparrows, one old, the other young.

'They were discussing an event which had become the "burning question of the day" among the sparrows, and which had resulted from the mullah's housekeeper having just previously thrown out of a window, on to a place where the sparrows gathered to play, something looking like left-over porridge, but which turned out to be chopped cork; and several of the young and as yet inexperienced sparrows had sampled it, and almost burst.

'While talking about this the old sparrow, suddenly ruffling himself up, began with a pained grimace to search under his wing for the fleas tormenting him, and which in general breed on underfed sparrows; and having caught one, he said with a deep sigh:

' "Times have changed very much—there is no longer a living to be had for our fraternity.

' "In the old days we used to sit, just as now, somewhere upon a roof, quietly dozing, when suddenly down in the street there would be heard a noise, a rattling and a rumbling, and soon after an odour would be diffused, at which everything inside us would begin to rejoice; because we felt fully certain that when we flew down and searched the places where all that had happened, we would find satisfaction for our essential needs.

' "But nowadays there is plenty and to spare of noise and rattlings, and all sorts of rumblings, and again and again an odour is also diffused, but an odour which it is almost impossible to endure; and when sometimes, by force of old habit, we fly down during a moment's lull to seek something substantial for ourselves, then search as we may with tense attention, we find nothing at all except some nauseous drops of burned oil."

'This tale, as is surely evident to you, refers to the old horse-drawn vehicles and to the present-day automobiles; and although these latter, as the old sparrow said, produce even more noise, rumblings, rattlings, and smell than the former, in spite of all this they have no significance whatever for the feeding of sparrows.

'And without food, as you yourself will understand, it is difficult even for sparrows to bring forth a healthy posterity.

'This anecdote seems to me an ideal illustration of what I wished to point out about the difference between contemporary civilization and the civilization of past epochs.

'In the present civilization, as in former civilizations, literature exists for the purpose of the perfecting of humanity in general, but in this field also—as in everything else contemporary—there is nothing substantial for our essential aim. It is all exterior: all only, as in the tale of the old sparrow, noise, rattling, and a nauseous smell.

'For any impartial man this viewpoint of mine can be conclusively confirmed by observing the difference between the degree of development of feeling in people who are born and spend their whole lives on the continent of Asia, and in people born and educated in the conditions of contemporary civilization on the continent of Europe.

'It is a fact, noted by a great many people, that among all the present-day inhabitants of the continent of Asia who, owing to geographical and other conditions, are isolated from the effects of modern civilization, feeling has reached a much higher level of development than among any of the inhabitants of Europe. And since feeling is the foundation of common sense, these Asiatic people, in spite of having less general knowledge, have a more correct notion of any object they observe than those belonging to the very *tzimuss* of contemporary civilization.

'A European's understanding of an object observed by him is formed exclusively by means of an all-round, so to say, "mathematical informedness" about it, whereas most of the people of Asia grasp the essence of the object observed by them sometimes with their feelings alone and sometimes even solely by instinct.'

At this point in his speech about contemporary literature, this intelligent, elderly Persian, among other things, touched on a question which at the present time is interesting many European, as they are called, 'propagators of culture'.

He then said:

Introduction

'The people of Asia were at one time greatly interested in European literature but, soon feeling all the emptiness of its content, they gradually lost interest in it, and now it is scarcely read there at all.

'In the weakening of their interest in European literature, the chief part, in my opinion, was played by that branch of modern writing known by the name of novels.

'These famous novels of theirs consist mainly, as I have already said, of long descriptions, in various forms, of the course of a malady which has arisen among contemporary people and which, owing to their weakness and will-lessness, lasts rather a long time.

'The Asiatic people, who are not as yet so far removed from Mother Nature, recognize with their consciousness that this psychic state which arises in both men and women is unworthy of human beings in general, and is particularly degrading for a man —and instinctively, they assume an attitude of contempt toward such people.

'And as regards the other branches of European literature, such as the scientific, the descriptive, and other forms of instructive exposition, the Asiatic, having lost to a lesser degree the ability to feel, that is to say, standing closer to nature, half-consciously feels and instinctively senses the writer's complete lack of any knowledge of reality and of any genuine understanding of the subject he is writing about.

'And so because of all this the Asiatic people, after first manifesting a great interest in European literature, gradually stopped paying any attention to it, and at the present time disregard it completely; whereas among the European peoples, the shelves of their public and private libraries and bookshops are groaning from the daily increasing number of new books.

'The question must doubtless arise in many of you as to how what I have just said can be reconciled with the fact that an overwhelming majority of the people of Asia are illiterate in the strict sense of the word.

'To this I will answer that nevertheless the real cause of the lack of interest in contemporary literature lies in its own shortcomings. I myself have seen how hundreds of illiterate people will gather

17

round one literate man to hear a reading of the sacred writings or of the tales known as the "Thousand and One Nights". You will of course reply that the events described, particularly in these tales, are taken from their own life, and are therefore understandable and interesting to them. But that is not the point. These texts—and I speak particularly of the "Thousand and One Nights"—are works of literature in the full sense of the word. Anyone reading or hearing this book feels clearly that everything in it is fantasy, but fantasy corresponding to truth, even though composed of episodes which are quite improbable for the ordinary life of people. The interest of the reader or listener is awakened and, enchanted by the author's fine understanding of the psyche of people of all walks of life round him, he follows with curiosity how, little by little, a whole story is formed out of these small incidents of actual life.

'The requirements of contemporary civilization have engendered yet another quite specific form of literature called journalism.

'I cannot pass by in silence this new form of literature, since, aside from the fact that it offers nothing whatsoever for the development of the mind, it has, from my point of view, become the fundamental evil in the life of people today because of the poisonous influence it exerts on their mutual relations.

'This form of literature has become very widespread in recent times because, according to my unshakeable conviction, it answers more completely than anything else to the weaknesses and demands which lead to the ever-increasing will-lessness of man. It thus accelerates in people the atrophy of even their last possibilities for acquiring those data which formerly still gave them a certain relative cognizance of their own individuality, which alone leads to what we call "remembering oneself"—that absolutely necessary factor in the process of self-perfecting.

'Besides, owing to this unprincipled daily literature, the thinking function of people has come to be even further separated from their individuality; and thereby conscience, which was occasionally awakened in them, has now ceased to participate in this thinking of theirs. They are thus deprived of those factors which formerly gave people a more or less tolerable life, if only in respect of their mutual relations.

'To our common misfortune, this journalistic literature, which is becoming more widespread in the life of people year by year, weakens the already weakened mind of man still more by laying it open without resistance to all kinds of deceit and delusion, and leads it astray from relatively well-founded thinking, thus stimulating in people, instead of sane judgement, various unworthy properties, such as incredulity, indignation, fear, false shame, hypocrisy, pride and so on and so forth.

'In order to portray to you more concretely all the maleficence for people of this new form of literature, I will tell you about several events which took place on account of newspapers, the reality of which was for me beyond all doubt, as by chance I had personally taken part in them.

'In Teheran I had a certain close friend, an Armenian, who some time before his death had made me his executor.

'He had a son, no longer young, who on account of his business lived with his numerous family in a large European city.

'One sad evening after having eaten their supper, he and the members of his family all fell ill, and died before morning. As executor for the family, I was obliged to go to the place where this tragic event had occurred.

'I found out that just before this event the father of this unfortunate family had read long articles for several days in succession, in one of the various newspapers he received, about a butcher shop where, according to these articles, special sausages were made from genuine products in some particular way.

'At the same time he kept coming across large advertisements of this new butcher shop in all the newspapers.

'Finally all this so tempted him that, although neither he nor his family cared for sausages very much, as all of them had been raised in Armenia where sausages are not eaten, he went and bought some. And having had these sausages for supper that same evening, all the family were mortally poisoned.

'My suspicions having been aroused by this extraordinary occurrence, I succeeded a little later, with the co-operation of an agent of the "private secret police", in bringing to light the following:

'Some large firm had acquired, at a low price from an export concern, an enormous consignment of sausages originally destined for a foreign country, which had been rejected owing to a delay in shipment. To get rid of the entire consignment as quickly as possible, this firm spared no expense on reporters, to whom it entrusted this maleficent campaign in the newspapers.

'Another occurrence:

'During one of my stays in Baku I myself, for several days in succession, read in the local newspapers obtained by my nephew lengthy articles, taking up nearly half the entire paper, which went into ecstasies about the marvels performed by some famous actress.

'So much was written about her and in such a handsome way that even I, an old man, was, as is said, fired by it all, and one evening, putting off everything I had to do and changing my established evening régime, I went to the theatre to see this wonder.

'And what do you think I saw? Something corresponding, even in the slightest, to what had been written about her in these articles which filled up half the paper? . . . Nothing of the sort.

'I had seen, in my day, many representatives of this art, both the good and the bad, and without exaggeration I can say that for some time I had been considered a great authority on these matters. But even without taking into consideration my personal views on art in general, and speaking merely from an ordinary standpoint, I must confess that in all my life I had never seen anybody to compare with this celebrity for lack of talent and absence of even the most elementary notions of the principles of playing a role.

'In all her manifestations on the stage there was such a complete lack of any kind of presence that I personally, even if aroused to altruism, would not have permitted such a wonder to fill the role of kitchenmaid in my kitchen.

'As I afterwards learned, one of the typical oil refiners of Baku, who had happened to make a fortune, had paid several reporters a good round sum as a bribe, promising to double it if they should succeed in making a celebrity of his private lady-love, who up till then had been chambermaid in the house of a Russian engineer, and whom he had seduced, taking advantage of business appointments with this engineer.

'One more example:

'In a widely circulated German newspaper I read, from time to time, lofty panegyrics glorifying a certain painter, and owing to these articles I formed the opinion that in contemporary art this painter was simply a phenomenon.

'My nephew, having just built a house in the town of Baku, had decided, in preparation for his wedding, to decorate the interior very richly. Since twice that year he had unexpectedly struck oil with signs of increasing output, which would assure him a considerable fortune, I advised him not to spare his money but to send for that famous painter to superintend the decoration of the house and to paint some frescoes on the walls. In this way his expenditures, already very great, would at least be of benefit to his posterity, who would inherit these frescoes and other works by the hand of this incomparable master.

'And my nephew did so; he even went himself to invite this great European painter. And soon afterwards the painter arrived, bringing with him a whole train of assistants, artisans and even, it seemed to me, his own harem, of course in the European sense of the word; and without the slightest hurry he finally set to work.

'The result of the work of this celebrity was that, firstly, the day of the wedding had to be postponed and, secondly, no little money had to be spent to bring everything back to its original state, so that simple Persian artisans might decorate, paint and embellish everything in a way more corresponding to genuine artistry.

'In the present case—to give them their due—the reporters participated in building up the career of this mediocre painter almost disinterestedly, simply as comrades and modest side-line workers.

'As a last example, I will tell you a sad story of misunderstanding, which was due this time to a "big shot" of this contemporary, especially pernicious literature.

'One day, when I was living in the town of Khorasan, I met at the house of mutual acquaintances a young European couple and soon got to know them rather well.

'They came to Khorasan several times, but each time only for a short stay.

'Travelling with his young wife, this new friend of mine was collecting all kinds of information, in many countries, and making analyses to determine the effects of the nicotine in various kinds of tobacco on the human organism and psyche.

'After collecting the data he needed on this question in several Asiatic countries, he returned with his wife to Europe, where he began to write a long book on the results of his research.

'But since his young wife, obviously owing to her youth and inexperience as regards the necessity of preparing for what are called rainy days, had spent all their resources during these travels of theirs, she was compelled, in order to give her husband the possibility of finishing his book, to take employment as a typist in the office of a large publishing house.

'There often came to this office a certain literary critic who met her there, and having, as is said, fallen in love with her, tried, simply for the satisfaction of his lust, to get on intimate terms with her; but she, an honourable wife who knew her duty, would not yield to his advances.

'But while, in this "faithful wife of a European husband", morality continued to triumph, there was nourished in this loathsome contemporary type, in proportion to the non-satisfaction of his lust, the desire for vengeance usual in such people; and by all sorts of intrigues he succeeded in getting her dismissed from her employment for no reason whatsoever. Then, when her husband, my young friend, had finished his book and published it, this specific ulcer of our times, because of his resentment, began to write in the newspaper to which he contributed, and also in other newspapers and periodicals, a whole series of articles containing all sorts of false statements, which discredited the book so completely that it was a total failure—that is to say, no one became interested in it or bought it.

'And so, thanks to one of these unconscionable representatives of this unprincipled literature, things came to such a pass that this honest worker and his beloved wife, having spent their last resources and not having even the wherewithal to buy bread, by mutual pact, hanged themselves.

'From my point of view, these literary critics, owing to the influence of their authority as writers on the general mass of naïve and easily suggestible people, are a thousand times more pernicious than all the slobbering boy-reporters.

'I myself knew a music critic who had never once in his life touched a musical instrument, and therefore had no practical understanding of music: he did not even know what sound was in general, or the difference between the notes "do" and "re" But, owing to the established abnormalities of contemporary civilization, he somehow occupied the responsible post of music critic, and thus became an authority for all the readers of a well-established and widely circulated newspaper. And it was, of course, according to his quite illiterate indications that unshakeable opinions were formed in all his readers on the question of music—that question which should in reality be like a beacon light for the correct understanding of one of the aspects of truth.

'The public never knows who is writing; it knows only the newspaper itself, which belongs to a group of experienced business men.

'What the person writing in these papers really knows, or what is going on behind the scenes in the newspaper office, the readers never know, but take everything written in the papers at its face value.

'According to my conviction, which has finally become as fir. as a rock—and anyone thinking more or less impartially will come to the same conclusion—it is chiefly owing to this journalistic literature that any man who tries to develop by the means available in contemporary civilization acquires a thinking faculty adequate, at the very most, for "the first invention of

Edison", and in respect of emotionality develops in himself, as Mullah Nassr Eddin would say, "the fineness of feeling of a cow".

'The leaders of contemporary civilization themselves, standing on a very low level of moral and psychic development, are incapable, like children playing with fire, of knowing the force and significance of the effect of such literature on the mass of the people.

'According to my impression obtained from the study of ancient history, the leaders of former civilizations would never have allowed such an abnormality to continue for so long.

'This opinion of mine may be confirmed by authentic information which has come down to us about the serious attitude towards daily literature taken by the rulers of our country not so long ago, in the period when it was considered one of the greatest nations, namely, when Great Babylon belonged to us and was the sole centre of culture recognized by everyone on earth.

'According to this information, a daily press also existed there, in the form of what are called printed papyri, although of course in an incomparably smaller quantity than now. But at that time those who participated in such literary organs were only elderly and qualified persons, known to all for their serious merits and honourable lives; and there was even an established rule for appointing such men to these positions under oath, and they were therefore called sworn collaborators, just as now there are sworn juries, sworn experts and so on.

'But nowadays any whipper-snapper can be a journalist, so long as he knows how to express himself prettily and, as is said, literarily.

'I became particularly well acquainted with the psyche, and could in general evaluate the being, of these products of contemporary civilization who fill the newspapers and periodicals with their various wiseacrings, when for three or four months, in that same town of Baku, I happened to be present every day at their gatherings and to exchange opinions with them.

'This occurred in the following circumstances:

'Once, when I had gone to Baku with the intention of staying all winter with my nephew, several young persons came to him and asked his permission for their "New Society of Literati and Journalists" to hold meetings in one of the large rooms on the ground floor of his house, in which he had originally intended to establish a restaurant. My nephew at once gave his consent, and from the next day on these young people assembled, chiefly in the evenings, for their, as they called them, general meetings and learned debates.

'Outsiders were admitted to these meetings and I often went to listen to their discussions, as I was quite free in the evenings and my quarters were very near the room where they assembled. Soon several of them began to converse with me and friendly relations were gradually established between us.

'Most of them were still quite young, weak and effeminate, and the faces of some showed clearly that their parents must have been drunkards or had suffered from other passions through will-lessness, or that the possessors themselves of these faces had various bad habits concealed from others.

'Although Baku is only a small town in comparison with most of the large cities of today, and although the contemporary types who were assembled there represented, at the most, "low-flying birds", I have no hesitation in generalizing about all their colleagues everywhere. And I feel I have the right to do this, because later, when travelling in Europe, I often happened to come in contact with the representatives of this modern literature, and they all made the same impression on me, resembling one another like peas in a pod.

'The only difference between them was in the degree of their importance, depending upon which literary organs they contributed to, that is, depending upon the reputation and circulation of the newspaper or periodical in which their wiseacrings found a place, or upon the soundness of the commercial firm which owned both the given organ and all of them—the literary workmen.

'Many of them, for some reason or other, are called poets. At

the present time anywhere in Europe anyone who writes even a
short piece of nonsense—of the order of

> *Green roses*
> *Purple mimosas*
> *Divine are her poses*
> *Like hanging memories*

and so on—is awarded the appellation of poet by those around
him; and some of them even engrave this title on their visiting-
cards.

'Among these contemporary journalists and writers, *esprit de
corps* is somehow highly developed, and they strongly support and
immoderately extol one another on all occasions.

'It seems to me that this feature of theirs is the chief cause of
their spreading sphere of influence and of their false authority
over the masses, and also of the unconscious and servile adulation
with which the crowd bows down before these nullities, as with
a clear conscience one can call them.

'At the meetings in Baku which I have mentioned, one of them
would go on to the platform and begin to read something of the
order of the verses I have just quoted, or speak about why the
minister of some nation had expressed himself during a banquet
concerning some question or other in such a way and not otherwise; and then the lecturer would in most cases finish his speech
by making an announcement more or less as follows:

' "I now yield the platform to an incomparable luminary of the
learning of our time, Mr. So-and-so, who by chance has come to
our city on particularly important business and has been so kind
as not to refuse to come to our meeting today. We will now have
the privilege of listening to his enchanting voice with our own
ears."

'And when this celebrity would appear on the platform he
would begin his speech with these words:

' "My dear ladies and gentlemen, my colleague has been so
modest as to call me a celebrity." (It must be said here that he
could not have heard what his colleague had said, since he had
come in from another room to which the door had been closed,

26

and he had opened it himself when he came in, and I knew very well the accoustics in that house and the solidity of the doors.)

'Then he would continue:

' "As a matter of fact, in comparison with him I am not worthy even to sit in his presence.

' "The celebrity is not I, but he—he is known not only everywhere in all our great Russia, but throughout the whole civilized world. Posterity will pronounce his name with palpitation, and no one will ever forget what he has done for learning and the future welfare of mankind.

' "This god of truth is at present in this insignificant town not by chance, as it may appear to us, but doubtless for very important reasons known only to himself.

' "In reality his place is not among us but beside the ancient gods of Olympus", and so on and so forth.

'And only after such a preamble would this new celebrity pronounce several absurdities, as for example on the theme: Why the Sirikitsi Made War on the Parnakalpi.

'After these learned sessions, suppers were always served, with two bottles of cheap wine; and many hid in their pockets some bit of hors-d'œuvre, either a piece of sausage or a herring with a piece of bread, and if by chance anyone else noticed this they would usually say: "This is for my dog—the rascal already has the habit—always expects something when I return home late."

'On the day after these suppers an account of the meeting always appeared in all the local papers, written in an incredibly pompous style; and the speeches were more or less accurately quoted, but of course no mention was made of the modesty of the supper or of the making-off with a piece of sausage for the dog.

'Such are the people who write in the papers about all sorts of "truths" and scientific discoveries, and the naïve reader, who does not see them or know their lives, draws his conclusions about events and ideas from the empty words of these writers, who are neither more nor less than ill, inexperienced and "illiterate", as far as human life is concerned.

'In all the cities of Europe, with very few exceptions, the writers of books or newspaper articles are just such immature scatter-brains, who have become what they are owing chiefly to their heredity and their specific weaknesses.

'From my point of view there can be no doubt whatsoever that of all the causes of the many abnormalities of contemporary civilization, the principal and most obvious one is this same journalistic literature, owing to its demoralizing and pernicious effect on the psyche of people. It astonishes me extremely that not a single government, among all the peoples of contemporary civilization, has ever become aware of this, and that not one of them, although expending more than half of what are called the government revenues on the maintenance of police, prisons, judicial establishments, churches, hospitals, etc., and on paying numerous civil employees, such as priests, physicians, agents of the secret police, public prosecutors, propagandists, and the like, for the sole purpose of maintaining the fidelity and morality of its citizens, spends a single cent on undertaking something or other in order to destroy at its root this obvious cause of many crimes and misunderstandings.'

Thus ended the speech of this elderly, intelligent Persian.

And so, my brave reader, who is perhaps already standing with one foot in galoshes, as I have finished with this speech—which I tacked on here only because, from my point of view, the ideas expressed in it could be very instructive and useful, especially for those adorers of contemporary civilization who naïvely consider it immeasurably higher than former civilizations in respect of the perfecting of human reason—I can now conclude this intro-duction and pass on to the reworking of the material intended for this series of my writings.

In beginning to rewrite this material with the intention of giving it a form as understandable as possible and accessible to all, the thought has arisen in me that this work of mine should also be carried out in accordance with a very sensible counsel for living often employed by our great Mullah Nassr Eddin and expressed by him thus: 'Always and in everything strive to attain at the same time what is useful for others and what is pleasant for oneself.'

As regards carrying out the first half of this very sensible counsel of our wise teacher, I have nothing to be concerned about, since the ideas I intend to introduce in this series will themselves abundantly fulfil it. But as regards what is pleasant for myself, this I wish to attain by giving to the pre-designated material a form of exposition which, from now on, will make my existence in some respects more bearable among the people who meet me than the one I had before my activity as a writer.

In order that you may understand what I wish to convey by the expression 'bearable existence', it must be said that, after all my travels in those countries of the continents of Asia and Africa which for some reason or other in the last fifty years have come to interest many people, I have long been reputed to be a sorcerer and an expert in 'questions of the beyond'.

And in consequence of this, everyone who met me considered that he had the right to disturb me for the satisfaction of his idle curiosity concerning these questions of the beyond, or to compel me to relate something or other of my personal life or some incident of my travels.

And no matter how tired I might be, I was obliged to answer something, as otherwise people became offended, and feeling ill-disposed towards me, would always, whenever my name was mentioned, say something to harm my activities and belittle my significance.

That is why, in revising the material destined for this series, I have decided to present it in the form of separate independent tales, and to insert in them various ideas which can serve as answers to all the questions often put to me, so that if I should again have to deal with these shameless idlers, I may simply refer them to this or that chapter, whereby they can satisfy their automatic curiosity. And this, at the same time, will give me the possibility of conversing with some of them merely by the flow of associations, as is habitual to them, and will also sometimes provide a necessary breathing-space for my active thinking which

is inevitably required in the conscious and conscientious fulfilment of my life obligations.

Of the questions often put to me by people of various classes
and different degrees of 'informedness', the following, as I recall,
recurred most frequently:

What remarkable men have I met?

What marvels have I seen in the East?

Has man a soul and is it immortal?

Is the will of man free?

What is life, and why does suffering exist?

Do I believe in the occult and spiritualistic sciences?

What are hypnotism, magnetism, and telepathy?

How did I become interested in these questions?

What led me to my system, practised in the Institute bearing
my name?

So I shall now arrange this series in separate chapters, serving
as answers to the first of the enumerated questions, namely, 'What
remarkable men have I met?' I will distribute in the separate
tales about these meetings, according to a principle of logical
sequence, all the ideas and thoughts that I intend to make
known in this series in order that they may serve as preparatory
constructive material, and at the same time I will answer all the
other questions often asked me. Furthermore, I shall arrange
these separate tales in such an order that, among other things,
there may stand out distinctly the outline of my, as it were,
autobiography.

Before going further, I consider it necessary to explain exactly
the expression 'a remarkable man', since like all expressions for
definite notions it is always understood among contemporary
people in a relative, that is a purely subjective, sense.

For example, a man who does tricks is for many people a

remarkable man, but even for them he ceases to be remarkable as soon as they learn the secret of his tricks.

As a definition of who may be considered and called remarkable, I will simply say, for the present, to cut a long story short, to what men I personally apply this expression.

From my point of view, he can be called a remarkable man who stands out from those around him by the resourcefulness of his mind, and who knows how to be restrained in the manifestations which proceed from his nature, at the same time conducting himself justly and tolerantly towards the weaknesses of others.

Since the first such man I knew—whose influence left its trace on the whole of my life—was my father, I shall begin with him.

II

MY FATHER

MY FATHER WAS WIDELY KNOWN, during the final decades of the last century and the beginning of this one, as an *ashokh*, that is, a poet and narrator, under the nickname of 'Adash'; and although he was not a professional *ashokh* but only an amateur, he was in his day very popular among the inhabitants of many countries of Transcaucasia and Asia Minor.

Ashokh was the name given everywhere in Asia and the Balkan peninsula to the local bards, who composed, recited or sang poems, songs, legends, folk-tales, and all sorts of stories.

In spite of the fact that these people of the past who devoted themselves to such a career were in most cases illiterate, having not even been to an elementary school in their childhood, they possessed such a memory and such alertness of mind as would now be considered remarkable and even phenomenal.

They not only knew by heart innumerable and often very lengthy narratives and poems, and sang from memory all their various melodies, but when improvising in their own, so to say, subjective way, they hit upon the appropriate rhymes and changes of rhythm for their verses with astounding rapidity.

At the present time men with such abilities are no longer to be found anywhere.

Even when I was very young, it was being said that they were becoming scarcer and scarcer.

I personally saw a number of these *ashokhs* who were

considered famous in those days, and their faces were strongly impressed on my memory.

I happened to see them because my father used to take me as a child to the contests where these poet *ashokhs*, coming from various countries, such as Persia, Turkey, the Caucasus and even parts of Turkestan, competed before a great throng of people in improvising and singing.

This usually proceeded in the following way:

One of the participants in the contest, chosen by lot, would begin, in singing an improvised melody, to put to his partner some question on a religious or philosophical theme, or on the meaning and origin of some well-known legend, tradition or belief, and the other would reply, also in song, and in his own improvised subjective melody; and these improvised subjective melodies, moreover, had always to correspond in their tonality to the previously produced consonances as well as to what is called by real musical science the 'ansapalnianly flowing echo'.

All this was sung in verse, chiefly in Turko-Tartar, which was then the accepted common language of the peoples of these localities, who spoke different dialects.

These contests would last weeks and sometimes even months, and would conclude with the award of prizes and presents— provided by the audience and usually consisting of cattle, rugs and so on—to those singers who, according to the general verdict, had most distinguished themselves.

I witnessed three such contests, the first of which took place in Turkey in the town of Van, the second in Azerbaijan in the town of Karabakh, and the third in the small town of Subatan in the region of Kars.

In Alexandropol and Kars, the towns where my family lived during my childhood, my father was often invited to evening gatherings to which many people who knew him came in order to hear his stories and songs.

At these gatherings he would recite one of the many legends or poems he knew, according to the choice of those present, or he would render in song the dialogues between the different characters.

The whole night would sometimes not be long enough for finishing a story and the audience would meet again on the following evening.

On the evenings before Sundays and holidays, when we did not have to get up early the following morning, my father would tell stories to us children, either about ancient great peoples and wonderful men, or about God, nature and mysterious miracles, and he would invariably conclude with some tale from the 'Thousand and One Nights', of which he knew so many that he could indeed have told us one whole tale for each of the thousand and one nights.

Among the many strong impressions from these various stories of my father's, which left their mark on my whole life, there was one that served for me in later years, perhaps no less than five times, as a 'spiritualizing factor' enabling me to comprehend the incomprehensible.

This strong impression, which later served for me as a spiritualizing factor, became crystallized in me while, one evening, my father was reciting and singing the legend of the 'Flood before the Flood' and there arose between him and a certain friend of his a discussion on this subject.

This took place at the period when, owing to the dictates of life circumstances, my father was compelled to become a professional carpenter.

This friend of his often dropped in to see him at his workshop, and sometimes they would sit all night long pondering on the meaning of the ancient legends and sayings.

His friend was no other than Dean Borsh of Kars Military Cathedral, the man who was soon to become my first tutor, the founder and creator of my present individuality, and, so to say, the 'third aspect of my inner God'.

On the night when this discussion took place, I too was in the workshop, as well as my uncle, who had come to town that evening from a neighbouring village where he had large market-gardens and vineyards.

My uncle and I sat together quietly on the soft shavings in the corner and listened to the singing of my father, who was chanting the legend of the Babylonian hero Gilgamesh and explaining its meaning.

The discussion arose when my father had finished the twenty-first song of the legend, in which a certain Ut-Napishtim relates to Gilgamesh the story of the destruction by flood of the land of Shuruppak.

After this song, when my father paused to fill his pipe, he said that in his opinion the legend of Gilgamesh came from the Sumerians, a people more ancient than the Babylonians, and that undoubtedly just this same legend was the origin of the account of the Flood in the Hebrew Bible and served as a basis of the Christian world view; only the names and some details had been changed in certain places.

The father dean began to object, bringing forward many data to the contrary, and the argument became so heated that they even forgot about sending me off to bed as they usually did on such occasions.

And my uncle and I also became so interested in their controversy that, without moving, we lay on the soft shavings until daybreak, when at last my father and his friend ended their discussion and parted.

This twenty-first song was repeated in the course of that night so many times that it was engraved on my memory for life.

In this song it is said:

> *I will tell thee, Gilgamesh,*
> *Of a mournful mystery of the Gods:*
> *How once, having met together,*
> *They resolved to flood the land of Shuruppak.*
> *Clear-eyed Ea, saying nothing to his father, Anu,*
> *Nor to the Lord, the great Enlil,*
> *Nor to the spreader of happiness, Nemuru,*
> *Nor even to the underworld prince, Enua,*
> *Called to him his son Ubara-Tut;*
> *Said to him: 'Build thyself a ship;*
> *Take with thee thy near ones,*

And what birds and beasts thou wilt;
Irrevocably have the Gods resolved
To flood the land of Shuruppak.'

The data formed in me, during my childhood, thanks to the strong impressions I received during this discussion on an abstract theme between these two persons who had lived their lives to old age relatively normally, led to a beneficent result for the formation of my individuality which I first became aware of only much later, namely, just before the general European war;[1] and from then on it began to serve for me as the above-mentioned spiritualizing factor.

The initial shock for my mental and feeling associations, which brought about this awareness, was the following:

One day I read in a certain magazine an article in which it was said that there had been found among the ruins of Babylon some tablets with inscriptions which scholars were certain were no less than four thousand years old. This magazine also printed the inscriptions and the deciphered text—it was the legend of the hero Gilgamesh.

When I realized that here was that same legend which I had so often heard as a child from my father, and particularly when I read in this text the twenty-first song of the legend in almost the same form of exposition as in the songs and tales of my father, I experienced such an inner excitement that it was as if my whole future destiny depended on all this. And I was struck by the fact, at first inexplicable to me, that this legend had been handed down by *ashokhs* from generation to generation for thousands of years, and yet had reached our day almost unchanged.

After this occurrence, when the beneficent result of the impressions formed in my childhood from the narratives of my father finally became clear to me—a result that crystallized in me a spiritualizing factor enabling me to comprehend that which usually appears incomprehensible—I often regretted having begun too late to give the legends of antiquity the immense significance that I now understand they really have.

---

[1] The First World War.

My Father

There was another legend I had heard from my father, again about the 'Flood before the Flood', which after this occurrence also acquired for me a quite particular significance.

In this legend it was said, also in verse, that long, long ago, as far back as seventy generations before the last deluge (and a generation was counted as a hundred years), when there was dry land where now is water and water where now is dry land, there existed on earth a great civilization, the centre of which was the former island Haninn, which was also the centre of the earth itself.

As I elucidated from other historical data, the island of Haninn was approximately where Greece is now situated.

The sole survivors of the earlier deluge were certain brethren of the former Imastun[1] Brotherhood, whose members had constituted a whole caste spread all over the earth, but whose centre had been on this island.

These Imastun brethren were learned men and, among other things, they studied astrology. Just before the deluge, they were scattered all over the earth for the purpose of observing celestial phenomena from different places. But however great the distance between them, they maintained constant communication with one another and reported everything to the centre by means of telepathy.

For this, they made use of what are called pythonesses, who served them, as it were, as receiving apparatuses. These pythonesses, in a trance, unconsciously received and recorded all that was transmitted to them from various places by the Imastuns, writing it down in four different agreed directions according to the direction from which the information reached them. That is to say, they wrote from top to bottom communications coming from localities lying to the east of the island; from right to left those from the south; from bottom to top those which came from the west (from the regions where Atlantis was and where America is now); and from left to right communications transmitted from the place now occupied by Europe.

As I have happened, in the logical course of the exposition of

[1] The word *imastun* in ancient Armenian means 'wise man', and it was also the title given to all remarkable historical personages. For example, this word is still placed before the name of King Solomon.

37

this chapter devoted to the memory of my father, to mention his friend, my first tutor, Dean Borsh, I consider it indispensable to describe a certain procedure established between these two men who had lived normally to old age, and who had taken upon themselves the obligation of preparing me, an unconscious boy, for responsible life and deserve now, by their conscientious and impartial attitude towards me, to represent for my essence 'two aspects of the divinity of my inner God'.

This procedure, as was evident when I later understood it, was an extremely original means for development of the mind and for self-perfecting.

They called it *kastousilia*, a term derived, it seems to me, from the ancient Assyrian, and which my father evidently took from some legend.

This procedure was as follows:

One of them would unexpectedly ask the other a question, apparently quite out of place, and the other, without haste, would calmly and seriously reply with logical plausibility.

For instance, one evening when I was in the workshop, my future tutor entered unexpectedly and, as he walked in, asked my father: 'Where is God just now?'

My father answered most seriously, 'God is just now in Sari Kamish.'

Sari Kamish is a forest region on the former frontier between Russia and Turkey, where unusually tall pine-trees grow, renowned everywhere in Transcaucasia and Asia Minor.

Receiving this reply from my father, the dean asked, 'What is God doing there?'

My father answered that God was making double ladders there and on the tops of them he was fastening happiness, so that individual people and whole nations might ascend and descend.

These questions and answers were carried on in a serious and quiet tone—as though one of them were asking the price of potatoes today and the other replying that the potato crop was very poor this year. Only later did I understand what rich thoughts were concealed beneath such questions and answers.

They very often carried on conversations in this same spirit, so that to a stranger it would have seemed that here were two old men out of their senses, who were at large only by mistake instead of being in a mad-house.

Many of these conversations which then seemed to me meaningless grew to have a deep meaning for me later when I came across questions of the same kind, and it was only then that I understood what a tremendous significance these questions and answers had for these two old men.

My father had a very simple, clear and quite definite view on the aim of human life. He told me many times in my youth that the fundamental striving of every man should be to create for himself an inner freedom towards life and to prepare for himself a happy old age. He considered that the indispensability and imperative necessity of this aim in life was so obvious that it ought to be understandable to everyone without any wiseacring. But a man could attain this aim only if, from childhood up to the age of eighteen, he had acquired data for the unwavering fulfilment of the following four commandments:

First— To love one's parents.

Second—To remain chaste.

Third— To be outwardly courteous to all without distinction, whether they be rich or poor, friends or enemies, power-possessors or slaves, and to whatever religion they may belong, but inwardly to remain free and never to put much trust in anyone or anything.

Fourth—To love work for work's sake and not for its gain.

My father, who loved me particularly as his first-born, had a great influence on me.

My personal relationship to him was not as towards a father, but as towards an elder brother; and he, by his constant conversations with me and his extraordinary stories, greatly assisted the arising in me of poetic images and high ideals.

My father came of a Greek family whose ancestors had emigrated from Byzantium, having left their country to escape the persecution by the Turks which followed their conquest of Constantinople.

At first they settled in the heart of Turkey, but later, for certain reasons, among which was the search for more suitable climatic conditions and better pasturage for the herds of domestic cattle forming a part of the enormous riches of my ancestors, they moved to the eastern shores of the Black Sea, to the environs of the town now called Gumush Khaneh. Still later, not long before the last big Russo-Turkish war, owing to repeated persecutions by the Turks, they moved from there to Georgia.

In Georgia my father separated from his brothers and moved to Armenia, settling in the town of Alexandropol, the name of which had just been changed from the Turkish name of Gumri.

When the family possessions were divided, there fell to my father's share what was considered, at that time, great riches, including several herds of domestic cattle.

A year or two after he had moved to Armenia, all this wealth that my father had inherited was lost, as a result of a calamity independent of man.

This happened owing to the following circumstances:

When my father settled in Armenia with all his family, his shepherds and his herds, he was the richest cattle owner of the district and the poorer families soon gave into his charge—as was the custom—their own small number of horned and other domestic cattle, in exchange for which they were to receive from him during the season a certain quantity of butter and cheese. But just when his herd had been increased in this way by several thousand head of other people's cattle, a cattle plague came from Asia and spread all over Transcaucasia.

This mass pestilence among the cattle then raged so violently that in a couple of months or so almost all the animals perished; only an insignificant number survived, and these were merely skin and bones.

As my father, in accepting the care of these cattle, had taken upon himself, as was then also the custom, their insurance against all kinds of accidents—even against their seizure by wolves, which happened rather frequently—he not only lost all his own cattle by this misfortune, but was forced to sell almost all his remaining possessions to pay for the cattle belonging to others.

And in consequence my father, from having been very well off, suddenly found himself a pauper.

Our family then consisted of only six persons, namely, my father, my mother, my grandmother, who had wished to end her days with her youngest son, and three children—myself, my brother and my sister—of whom I was the eldest. I was then about seven years old.

Having lost his fortune, my father had to take up some business, since the maintenance of such a family, and, what is more, a family which until then had been pampered by a life of wealth, cost a good deal. So, having collected the remnants of his former large and grandly maintained household, he began by opening a lumber-yard and with it, according to local custom, a carpenter's shop for making all kinds of wooden articles.

But from the very first year, owing to the fact that my father had never before in his life been engaged in commerce and had in consequence no business experience, the lumber-yard was a failure.

He was finally compelled to liquidate it and to limit himself to the workshop, specializing in the production of small wooden articles.

This second failure in my father's affairs occurred in the fourth year after his first big calamity. Our family lived in the town of Alexandropol all this time, which happened to coincide with the period of rapid reconstruction by the Russians of the near-by fortress-town of Kars which they had taken.

The opening up of good prospects for making money in Kars, and the added persuasions of my uncle, who already had his business there, induced my father to transfer his workshop to Kars. He first went there alone, and later took his whole family.

By this time our family had already increased by three more 'cosmic apparatuses for the transformation of food', in the form of my three then really charming sisters.

Having settled in Kars, my father first sent me to the Greek school, but very soon transferred me to the Russian municipal school.

As I was very quick at my studies, I wasted very little time on the preparation of lessons, and in all my spare time I helped my father in his workshop. Very soon I even began to have my own circle of customers, first among my comrades, for whom I made various things such as guns, pencil-boxes and so on; and later, little by little, I passed on to more serious work, doing all kinds of small repairs in people's houses.

In spite of the fact that I was then still only a boy, I very well remember this period of our family life down to the smallest detail; and in this setting there stands out in my memory all the grandeur of my father's calm and the detachment of his inner state in all his external manifestations, throughout the misfortunes which befell him.

I can now say for certain that in spite of his desperate struggle with the misfortunes which poured upon him as though from the horn of plenty, he continued then as before, in all the difficult circumstances of his life, to retain the soul of a true poet.

Hence it was, in my opinion, that during my childhood, in spite of great want, there constantly reigned in our family unusual concord, love and the wish to help one another.

Owing to his inherent capacity for finding inspiration in the beauty of the details of life, my father was for us all, even in the most dismal moments of our family life, a source of courage; and, infecting us all with his freedom from care, he engendered in us the above-mentioned happy impulses.

In writing about my father, I must not pass by in silence his views on what is called the 'question of the beyond'. Concerning this he had a very particular and at the same time simple conception.

I remember that, the last time I went to see him, I asked him one of the stereotyped questions by means of which I had carried on, during the last thirty years, a special inquiry or quest in my meetings with remarkable people who had acquired in themselves data for attracting the conscious attention of others. Namely, I asked him, of course with the preliminary preparation which had become customary to me in these cases, to tell me, very simply and without any wiseacring and philosophizing, what personal opinion he had formed during his life about whether man has a soul and whether it is immortal.

'How shall I put it?' he answered. 'In that soul which a man supposedly has, as people believe, and of which they say that it exists independently after death and transmigrates, I do not believe; and yet, in the course of a man's life "something" does form itself in him: this is for me beyond all doubt.

'As I explain it to myself, a man is born with a certain property and, thanks to this property, in the course of his life certain of his experiencings elaborate in him a certain substance, and from this substance there is gradually formed in him "something or other" which can acquire a life almost independent of the physical body.

'When a man dies, this "something" does not disintegrate at the same time as the physical body, but only much later, after its separation from the physical body.

'Although this "something" is formed from the same substance as the physical body of a man, it has a much finer materiality and, it must be assumed, a much greater sensitivity towards all kinds of perceptions. The sensitivity of its perception is in my opinion such as—you remember, when you made that experiment with the half-witted Armenian woman, Sando?'

He had in mind an experiment I had made in his presence many years before, during a visit in Alexandropol, when I brought people of many different types into various degrees of hypnosis, for the purpose of elucidating for myself all the details of the phenomenon which learned hypnotists call the exteriorization of sensitivity or the transference of sensations of pain at a distance.

I proceeded in the following way:

I made from a mixture of clay, wax and very fine shot a figure roughly resembling the medium I intended to bring into the hypnotic state, that is, into that psychic state of man which, in a branch of science which has come down to our day from very ancient times, is called loss of initiative and which, according to the contemporary classification of the School of Nancy, would correspond to the third stage of hypnosis. I then thoroughly rubbed some part or other of the body of the given medium with an ointment made of a mixture of olive and bamboo oil, then scraped this oil from the body of the medium and applied it to the corresponding part on the figure, and thereupon proceeded to elucidate all the details that interested me in this phenomenon.

What greatly astonished my father at the time was that when I pricked the oiled place on the figure with a needle, the corresponding place on the medium twitched, and when I pricked more deeply a drop of blood appeared on the exactly corresponding place of the medium's body; and he was particularly amazed by the fact that, after being brought back to the waking state and questioned, the medium remembered nothing about it and insisted that she had felt nothing at all.

And so my father, in whose presence this experiment had been carried out, now said, in referring to it:

'So, in the same way, this "something", both before a man's death and afterwards until its disintegration, reacts to certain surrounding actions and is not free from their influence.'

My father had in connection with my education certain definite, as I have called them, 'persistent pursuits'.

One of the most striking of these persistent pursuits of his, which later produced in me an indisputably beneficent result, acutely sensed by me and noticeable also to those with whom I came in contact during my wanderings in the various wilds of the earth in the search for truth, was that during my childhood, that is, at the age when there are formed in man the data for the impulses he will have during his responsible life, my father took measures on every suitable occasion so that there should be formed in me, instead of data engendering impulses such as fastidiousness, repulsion, squeamishness, fear, timidity and so on, the data for an attitude of indifference to everything that usually evokes these impulses.

I remember very well how, with this aim in view, he would sometimes slip a frog, a worm, a mouse, or some other animal likely to evoke such impulses, into my bed, and would make me take non-poisonous snakes in my hands and even play with them, and so forth and so on.

Of all these persistent pursuits of his in relation to me, I remember that the one most worrying to the older people round me, for instance my mother, my aunt and our oldest shepherds, was that he always forced me to get up early in the morning, when a child's sleep is particularly sweet, and go to the fountain and splash myself all over with cold spring water, and afterwards to run about naked; and if I tried to resist he would never yield, and although he was very kind and loved me, he would punish me without mercy. I often remembered him for this in later years and in these moments thanked him with all my being.

If it had not been for this, I would never have been able to overcome all the obstacles and difficulties that I had to encounter later during my travels.

He himself led an almost pedantically regular life, and was merciless to himself in conforming to this regularity.

For instance, he was accustomed to going to bed early so as to begin early the next morning whatever he had decided upon beforehand, and he made no exception to this even on the night of his daughter's wedding.

I saw my father for the last time in 1916. He was then eighty-two years old, still full of health and strength. The few recent grey hairs in his beard were hardly noticeable.

His life ended a year later, but not from natural causes.

This event, sorrowful and grievous for all who knew him, and especially so for me, occurred during the last great periodic human psychosis.

At the time of the Turkish attack on Alexandropol, when the family had to flee, he was unwilling to leave his homestead to the mercy of fate; and while protecting the family property he was wounded by the Turks. He died soon after, and was buried by some old men who had happened to remain there.

The texts of the various legends and songs he had written or dictated, which, in my opinion, would have been his most fitting memorial, were lost—to the misfortune of all thinking people—during the repeated sackings of our house; yet perhaps, by some miracle, a few hundred of the songs he sang, recorded on phonograph rolls, may still be preserved among the things I left in Moscow.

It will be a great pity for those who value the old folklore if these records cannot be found.

The individuality and intellectuality of my father can, in my opinion, be very well pictured in the mind's eye of the reader if I quote here a few of his many favourite 'subjective sayings', which he often used in conversation.

In this connection, it is interesting to remark that I, as well as many others, noticed that when he himself used these sayings in conversation, it always seemed to every hearer that they could not have been more apt or better put, but that if anyone else made use of them, they seemed to be entirely beside the point or improbable nonsense.

Some of these subjective sayings of his were as follows:

Without salt, no sugar.

Ashes come from burning.

The cassock is to hide a fool.

He is deep down, because you are high up.

If the priest goes to the right, then the teacher must without fail turn to the left.

If a man is a coward, it proves he has will.

A man is satisfied not by the quantity of food, but by the absence of greed.

Truth is that from which conscience can be at peace.

No elephant and no horse—even the donkey is mighty.

In the dark a louse is worse than a tiger.

If there is 'I' in one's presence, then God and Devil are of no account.

Once you can shoulder it, it's the lightest thing in the world.

A representation of Hell—a stylish shoe.

My Father

Unhappiness on earth is from the wiseacring of women.

He is stupid who is 'clever'.

Happy is he who sees not his unhappiness.

The teacher is the enlightener; who then is the ass?

Fire heats water, but water puts out fire.

Genghis Khan was great, but our policeman, so please you, is still greater.

If you are first, your wife is second; if your wife is first, you had better be zero: only then will your hens be safe.

If you wish to be rich, make friends with the police.

If you wish to be famous, make friends with the reporters.

If you wish to be full—with your mother-in-law.

If you wish to have peace—with your neighbour.

If you wish to sleep—with your wife.

If you wish to lose your faith—with the priest.

To give a fuller picture of my father's individuality, I must say something about a tendency of his nature rarely observed in contemporary people, and striking to all who knew him well. It was chiefly on account of this tendency that from the very beginning, when he became poor and had to go into business, his affairs went so badly that his friends and those who had business dealings with him considered him unpractical and even not clever in this domain.

And indeed, every business that my father carried on for the purpose of making money always went wrong and brought none of the results obtained by others. However, this was not because he was unpractical or lacked mental ability in this field, but only because of this tendency.

This tendency of his nature, apparently acquired by him when still a child, I would define thus: 'an instinctive aversion to deriving personal advantage for himself from the naïveté and bad luck of others'.

47

In other words, being highly honourable and honest, my father could never consciously build his own welfare on the misfortune of his neighbour. But most of those round him, being typical contemporary people, took advantage of his honesty and deliberately tried to cheat him, thus unconsciously belittling the significance of that trait in his psyche which conditions the whole of Our Common Father's commandments for man.

Indeed, there could be ideally applied to my father the following paraphrase of a sentence from sacred writings, which is quoted at the present time by the followers of all religions everywhere, for describing the abnormalities of our daily life and for giving practical advice:

Strike—and you will not be struck.
But if you do not strike—they will beat you to death, like Sidor's goat.

In spite of the fact that he often happened to find himself in the midst of events beyond the control of man and resulting in all sorts of human calamities, and in spite of almost always encountering dirty manifestations from the people round him—manifestations recalling those of jackals—he did not lose heart, never identified himself with anything, and remained inwardly free and always himself.

The absence in his external life of everything that those round him regarded as advantages did not disturb him inwardly in the least; he was ready to reconcile himself to anything, provided there were only bread and quiet during his established hours for meditation.

What most displeased him was to be disturbed in the evening when he would sit in the open looking at the stars.

I, for my part, can only say now that with my whole being I would desire to be able to be such as I knew him to be in his old age.

Owing to circumstances of my life not dependent on me, I have not personally seen the grave where the body of my dear father lies, and it is unlikely that I will ever be able, in the future, to visit his grave. I therefore, in concluding this chapter devoted to my father, bid any of my sons, whether by blood or in spirit, to seek out, when he has the possibility, this solitary grave, abandoned by force of circumstances ensuing chiefly from that human scourge called the herd instinct, and there to set up a stone with the inscription:

I AM THOU,

THOU ART I,

HE IS OURS,

WE BOTH ARE HIS.

SO MAY ALL BE

FOR OUR NEIGHBOUR.

III

MY FIRST TUTOR

AS I HAVE ALREADY MENTIONED in the previous chapter, my first tutor was Dean Borsh. He was at that time dean of the Kars Military Cathedral and was the highest spiritual authority for the whole of that region conquered not long before by Russia.

He became for me, through quite accidental life circumstances, so to say, a 'factor for the secondary stratum of my present individuality'.

While I was attending the Kars municipal school, choristers for the choir of the fortress cathedral were being chosen from among the pupils of this school and I, having then a good voice, was one of those chosen. From then on I went to this Russian cathedral for singing and practices.

The fine-looking old dean, who was interested in the new choir chiefly because the melodies of the various sacred canticles to be sung that year were of his own composition, often came to our practices; and, loving children, he was very kind to us little choristers.

Soon, for some reason or other, he began to be especially kind to me, perhaps because for a child I had an exceptionally good voice, which stood out even in a big choir when I sang second voice, or perhaps simply because I was very mischievous and he liked such rascals. In any case, he began to show an increasing interest in me and soon even began to help me prepare my school lessons.

Towards the end of the year, I did not come to the cathedral for a whole week, because of having contracted trachoma. Learning of this, the father dean himself came to our house, bringing with him two military physicians who were eye-specialists.

My father was at home when he came, and after the doctors had examined me and left (having decided to send an assistant to give me a copper sulphate cauterization twice a day and apply golden ointment every three hours), these two men, who had lived their lives to old age relatively normally—with almost identical convictions, in spite of having received their preparation for responsible age in entirely different conditions—talked with each other for the first time.

From this very first meeting they took to each other, and afterwards the old dean often came to see my father in the workshop, where, sitting on the soft shavings at the back of the shop and drinking coffee made there by my father, they would converse for hours on all sorts of religious and historical subjects. I remember how especially animated the dean would become when my father said anything about Assyria, about the history of which my father knew a great deal, and which for some reason or other at that time greatly interested Father Borsh.

Father Borsh was then seventy years old. He was tall, thin, with a fine-looking face, of delicate health but strong and firm in spirit. He was a man distinguished by the depth and breadth of his knowledge, and his life and views were quite different from those of the people round him, who in consequence considered him peculiar.

And indeed, his outer life gave grounds for such an opinion, if it were only for the fact that, although he was very well off and received a large allowance and the right to special quarters, he occupied only one room and a kitchen in the guard's house at the cathedral, whereas his assistant priests, who received much less than he, lived in quarters of from six to ten rooms with every kind of comfort.

He led a very secluded life, mixing very little with those round him and paying no visits to acquaintances. And at that time he allowed no one access to his room except myself and his orderly—who was not, however, allowed to enter it in his absence.

Conscientiously fulfilling his obligations, he gave all his spare time to science, especially to astronomy and chemistry; and sometimes, for a rest, he worked at music, playing the violin or composing sacred canticles, some of which came to be very well known in Russia.

Several of these canticles, which had been composed in my presence, I happened to hear many years later on the gramophone, for example, 'O Thou Almighty God', 'Calm Light', 'Glory to Thee', and others.

The dean often came to see my father, usually in the evenings when they were both free from their duties.

In order, as he said, 'not to lead others into temptation', he tried to make these visits inconspicuously, since he occupied a very eminent position in the town and almost everyone knew him by sight, whereas my father was only a simple carpenter.

During one of the talks which took place before me in my father's workshop, the dean began to talk about me and my studies.

He said that he saw in me a very capable boy and that he considered it senseless for me to stay in school and drag out the eight-year period, merely in order to receive at the end a three-class certificate.

And, in fact, the arrangement of the municipal schools was then quite absurd. The school consisted of eight grades and one was compelled to attend each grade for a year, receiving a final certificate equivalent only to the first three classes in a higher school.

That is why Father Borsh advised my father so convincingly to take me away from school and have me taught at home, promising to give me some of the lessons himself. He said that, if I should need a certificate later on, I could simply take, in any school, the examination for the corresponding class.

After a family council this was settled. I left school and from then on Father Borsh undertook my education, teaching me some subjects himself and also providing other teachers for me.

At first these teachers were the candidates for the priesthood, Ponomarenko and Krestovsky, graduates of the Theological Seminary who were serving as deacons at the cathedral while waiting for posts as army chaplains. A physician, Sokolov, also gave me lessons.

Ponomarenko taught me geography and history; Krestovsky, Scripture and Russian; Sokolov, anatomy and physiology; mathematics and other subjects were taught me by the dean himself.

I began to study very hard.

Although I was very capable and learning came very easily to me, I nevertheless scarcely found time to prepare so many lessons and rarely had a single moment free.

A great deal of time was spent in going and coming from the house of one teacher to that of another, as they lived in different districts; particularly long was the walk to Sokolov, who lived at the military hospital at Fort Chakmak, three or four miles from the town.

My family had at first intended me for the priesthood, but Father Borsh had a quite particular conception of what a real priest should be.

According to his notion a priest should not only care for the souls of the members of his flock but should know all about their bodily diseases and how to cure them.

As he conceived it, the duties of a priest should be combined with those of a physician. He said: 'Just as a physician who does not have access to the soul of his patient cannot be of any real help to him, so also one cannot be a good priest without being at the same time a physician, because the body and soul are interconnected and it is often impossible to cure the one when the cause of the illness lies in the other.'

He was in favour of my having a medical education, though not in the ordinary sense but as he understood it, that is, with the aim of becoming a physician for the body and a confessor for the soul.

I myself, however, was drawn towards quite another way of life. Having had from my early childhood an inclination for making all sorts of things, I dreamed of technical specialization.

As at first it was not definitely decided which way I was to go,

I began at the same time to prepare myself to be a priest and a physician, the more so since there were certain subjects necessary in both cases.

Afterwards things continued by themselves and I, being capable, was able to progress in both directions. I even found time to read a great many books on various subjects, either given to me by Father Borsh or which fell into my hands.

The father dean worked intensively with me in the subjects he had undertaken to teach me. Often after the lessons he let me stay with him, gave me tea, and sometimes asked me to sing some canticle he had just composed, to verify the transcription for the voices.

During these frequent and extended visits he would have long conversations with me, either on the subjects of the lessons I had just finished or on quite abstract questions; and little by little such a relationship was formed between us that he began to talk to me as to an equal.

I soon got used to him and the feeling of shyness I at first had towards him disappeared. Retaining all my respect for him, I nevertheless sometimes forgot myself and began to argue with him—which did not in the least offend him but, as I now understand, even pleased him.

In his conversations with me he often spoke about the question of sex.

Concerning sexual desire, he once told me the following:

'If a youth but once gratify this lust before reaching adulthood, then the same would happen to him as happened to the historical Esau, who for a single mess of pottage sold his birthright, that is, the welfare of his whole life; because if a youth yields to this temptation even once, he will lose for the rest of his life the possibility of being a man of real worth.

'The gratification of lust before adulthood is like pouring alcohol into Mollavallian *madjar*.[1]

'Just as from *madjar* into which even a single drop of alcohol has been poured only vinegar is obtained and never wine, so the

---

[1] Mollavalli is a small place in the south of the Kars region and *madjar* is a very new, not yet fermented wine (must).

gratification of lust before adulthood leads to a youth's becoming a monstrosity. But when the youth is grown up, then he can do whatever he likes; just as with *madjar*—when it is already wine you can put as much alcohol in it as you like; not only will it not be spoiled but you can obtain whatever strength you please.'

Father Borsh had a very original idea of the world and of man.

His views on man and the aim of man's existence differed completely from those of the people round him and from everything I had heard or gathered from my reading.

I will mention here certain thoughts of his which may serve to illustrate the understanding he had of man and what he expected of him.

He said:

'Until adulthood, man is not responsible for any of his acts, good or bad, voluntary or involuntary; solely responsible are the people close to him who have undertaken, consciously or owing to accidental circumstances, the obligation of preparing him for responsible life.

'The years of youth are for every human being, whether male or female, the period given for the further development of the initial conception in the mother's womb up to, so to say, its full completion.

'From this time on, that is, from the moment the process of his development is finished, a man becomes personally responsible for all his voluntary and involuntary manifestations.

'According to laws of nature elucidated and verified through many centuries of observation by people of pure reason, this process of development is finished in males between the ages of twenty and twenty-three, and in females between the ages of fifteen and nineteen, depending on the geographical conditions of the place of their arising and formation.

'As elucidated by wise men of past epochs, these age periods have been established by nature, according to law, for the acquisition of independent being with personal responsibility for all one's manifestations, but unfortunately at the present time they are hardly recognized at all. And this, in my opinion, is owing chiefly to the negligent attitude in contemporary education towards the question of sex, a question which plays the most important role in the life of everyone.

'As regards responsibility for their acts, most contemporary people who have reached or even somewhat passed the age o adulthood, strange as it may seem at first glance, may prove to be not responsible for any of their manifestations; and this, in my opinion, can be considered conforming to law.

'One of the chief causes of this absurdity is that, at this age, contemporary people in most cases lack the corresponding type of the opposite sex necessary, according to law, for the completion of their type, which, from causes not dependent upon them but ensuing, so to say, from Great Laws, is in itself a "something not complete".

'At this age, a person who does not have near him a corresponding type of the opposite sex for the completion of his incomplete type, is nonetheless subject to the laws of nature and so cannot remain without gratification of his sexual needs. Coming in contact with a type not corresponding to his own and, owing to the law of polarity, falling in certain respects under the influence of this non-corresponding type, he loses, involuntarily and imperceptibly, almost all the typical manifestations of his individuality.

'That is why it is absolutely necessary for every person, in the process of his responsible life, to have beside him a person of the opposite sex of corresponding type for mutual completion in every respect.

'This imperative necessity was, among other things, providentially well understood by our remote ancestors in almost all past epochs and, in order to create conditions for a more or less normal collective existence, they considered it their chief task to be able to make as well and as exactly as possible the choice of types from opposite sexes.

'Most of the ancient peoples even had the custom of making these choices between the two sexes, or betrothals, in the boy's seventh year with a girl one year old. From this time on the two families of the future couple, thus early betrothed, were under the mutual obligation of assisting the correspondence in both children of all the habits inculcated in the course of growth, such as inclinations, enthusiasms, tastes and so on.'

I also very well remember that on another occasion the father dean said:

'In order that at responsible age a man may be a real man and not a parasite, his education must without fail be based on the following ten principles.

'From early childhood there should be instilled in the child:

Belief in receiving punishment for disobedience.

Hope of receiving reward only for merit.

Love of God—but indifference to the saints.

Remorse of conscience for the ill-treatment of animals.

Fear of grieving parents and teachers.

Fearlessness towards devils, snakes and mice.

Joy in being content merely with what one has.

Sorrow at the loss of the goodwill of others.

Patient endurance of pain and hunger.

The striving early to earn one's bread.'

To my great distress, I did not happen to be present during the last days of this worthy and, for our time, remarkable man, in order to pay the last debt of earthly life to him, my unforgettable tutor, my second father.

One Sunday, many years after his death, the priests and congregation of the Kars Military Cathedral were much astonished and interested when a man quite unknown in the neighbourhood requested the full funeral service to be held over a lonely and forgotten grave, the only one within the grounds of the cathedral. And they saw how this stranger with difficulty held back his tears and, having generously recompensed the priests and without looking at anyone, told the coachman to drive to the station.

Rest in peace, dear Teacher! I do not know whether I have justified or am justifying your dreams, but the commandments you gave me I have never once in all my life broken.

IV

BOGACHEVSKY

BOGACHEVSKY, OR FATHER EVLISSI, is still alive and well, and has the good fortune to be an assistant to the abbot of the chief monastery of the Essene Brotherhood, situated not far from the shores of the Dead Sea.

This brotherhood was founded, according to certain surmises, twelve hundred years before the Birth of Christ; and it is said that in this brotherhood Jesus Christ received his first initiation.

I met Bogachevsky, or Father Evlissi, for the first time when he was a very young man and when, having finished his course at the Russian Theological Seminary, he was waiting to be ordained to the priesthood and was a deacon at the military cathedral of Kars.

Soon after his arrival in Kars he consented, at the request of my first tutor, Dean Borsh, to become my teacher in place of Krestovsky, another candidate for the priesthood, who several weeks before had received a post as chaplain to a regiment somewhere in Poland. Bogachevsky had then taken his place at the cathedral.

Bogachevsky turned out to be a very sociable and kindly man; he soon won the confidence of all the cathedral clergy, even of Ponomarenko, who was also a candidate, but crude and, in the full sense of the word, a boor, and not on good terms with anyone. With Bogachevsky, however, he got along so well that they even shared the same lodgings, taking rooms together near the public gardens close to the military fire-brigade.

Bogachevsky

Although I was then still very young, my relationship with Bogachevsky soon became very friendly. I often went to see him in my spare time, and when I had afternoon lessons I would often stay after they were finished, either to prepare other lessons or to listen to his conversations with Ponomarenko and with the acquaintances who were always visiting them. Sometimes I helped them in their simple household.

Among those who often came to see them was an army engineer, Vseslavsky, who was a fellow-countryman of Bogachevsky, and an artillery officer and pyrotechnical expert named Kouzmin. Seated around the samovar, they would discuss anything and everything.

I would always listen very attentively to Bogachevsky and his friends, as, reading at that time a large number of books on the most varied subjects in Greek, Armenian and Russian, I was interested in many questions; but because of my youth I naturally never joined in their conversation. Their opinions were authoritative for me, and at that time I had a great veneration for these men on account of their advanced education.

It was, by the way, all the conversations and discussions of these men, who gathered at my teacher Bogachevsky's to kill time in the monotonous life of the remote and very boring town of Kars, which awakened my ever-continuing interest in abstract questions.

Since this interest played an important part in my life, leaving a definite mark on my entire subsequent existence, and since the events which stimulated this interest occurred during the period to which belong my memories of Bogachevsky, I will dwell upon them a little longer.

Once, during one of these conversations, a lively discussion arose about spiritualism and, among other things, about table-turning, which at that time was a subject of absorbing interest everywhere.

The army engineer asserted that this phenomenon occurs through the participation of spirits. The others denied this, attributing it to other forces of nature, such as magnetism, the law of attraction, auto-suggestion and so forth; but nobody denied the existence of the fact itself.

I, as usual, listened attentively and every opinion that was expressed deeply interested me. Although I had already read a great deal of 'anything and everything', this was the first time I heard about these matters.

This discussion about spiritualism made a particularly strong impression on me because of the recent death of my favourite sister and my grief over it, from which I had not yet recovered. In those days I often thought about her and involuntarily questions arose in my mind about death and life beyond the grave. What was said that evening seemed to be in response to the thoughts and questions which had unconsciously arisen in me and were demanding a solution.

As a result of their discussion they decided to make an experiment with a table. For this a table with three legs was necessary, and there was one in the corner of the room; but the specialist in these experiments, the army engineer, would not use it because there were nails in it. He explained that the table had to be without iron, and so they sent me to a neighbouring photographer to ask whether he had such a table. Finding that he had one, I brought it back with me.

It was evening. Having closed the doors and turned down the light, we all sat down round the table and, placing our hands on it in a certain way, began to wait.

Sure enough, in about twenty minutes our table did begin to move, and when the engineer asked it the age of each one present it tapped out the numbers with one leg. How and why it was tapping was incomprehensible to me; I did not even try to explain anything to myself, so strong was the impression of the vast, unknown fields opening up before me.

What I had heard and seen agitated me so profoundly that when I went home I thought about these questions all that night and the next morning, and even decided to ask Father Borsh about them during my lessons. This I did, and told him about the conversation and experiment of the previous evening.

'All that is nonsense,' replied my first tutor. 'Don't think and bother about such things, but learn what is necessary for you to know for leading a tolerable existence.'

And he could not resist adding: 'Come, you little garlic-head' —that was his favourite expression—'think! If spirits can really tap with the leg of a table, it means that they have some physical force. And if they have, why should they resort to such an idiotic and moreover complicated means of communicating with people as tapping with the leg of a table? Surely they could transmit whatever they wished to say either by touch or by some other means!'

Much as I valued the opinion of my old tutor, I could not accept his categorical reply without criticism, the more so since it seemed to me that my younger instructor and his friends, who had been through the seminary and other higher educational institutions, might know more about some things than the old man who had studied in the days when science was not so advanced.

So, in spite of all my respect for the old dean, I doubted his views on certain problems concerning higher mattters.

My question was thus left unanswered. I tried to solve it by reading books given me by Bogachevsky, the dean and others. My studies, however, did not allow me to think very long about anything extraneous, and after a time I forgot about this question and thought no more about it.

Time passed. I studied very hard with all my teachers, including Bogachevsky, and only occasionally, during the holidays, went to visit my uncle in Alexandropol, where I had many friends. I went there also to earn money. I always needed money for personal expenses, for clothes, books and so on, and also now and then for helping some member or other of my family, which at that time was in great want.

I went to Alexandropol to earn money, firstly, because everyone knew me there as a 'master of all trades' and I was always asked to make or repair something. One person wanted a lock repaired, another a watch mended, a third a special stove hewn out of the local stone, and another a cushion embroidered for a trousseau or for decorating the parlour. In short, I had a large

clientele there and plenty of work and, for those times, I was very
well paid. I also went to Alexandropol because in Kars I mixed
with people of the 'learned' and 'superior' circles, according to
my youthful understanding, and I did not wish them to know me
as an artisan or to suspect that my family was in need and that I
was compelled to earn money for my own expenses as a simple
craftsman. At that time all this deeply wounded my self-love.

And so at Easter that year I went as usual to Alexandropol,
which was only about sixty miles from Kars, to stay with the
family of my uncle, to whom I was much attached and whose
favourite I had always been.

On the second day of this visit, at dinner, my aunt said to me,
among other things: 'Listen, take care not to have an accident.'

I was astonished. What could possibly happen to me? I asked
her what she meant.

'I don't quite believe it myself,' said she, 'but something that
was foretold about you has already come true, and I am afraid
that the rest of it might also come true.' And she told me the
following:

At the beginning of the winter the half-witted Eoung-Ashokh
Mardiross came to Alexandropol, as he did each year, and for
some reason or other my aunt took it into her head to summon
this fortune-teller and ask him to foretell my future. He had pre-
dicted many things awaiting me and, according to her, some of
them had already occurred. She then pointed out certain things
which had indeed happened to me during this time. 'But thank
God,' she continued, 'there are two things which have not yet
happened to you: one, that you will have a large sore on your
right side; the other, that you are in danger of a serious accident
from a fire-arm. You should, therefore, be very cautious wherever
shooting is going on,' concluded my aunt, stating that, although
she did not believe this lunatic, it was in any case better to be
careful.

I was very much astonished by what she told me, because two
months before a carbuncle had indeed appeared on my right side,
which I had had to have treated for a month, going to the military
hospital almost every day to have it dressed. But I had not spoken

of it to anyone, and even at home no one knew about it, so how could my aunt, who lived far away, have possibly known anything about it?

However, I did not attach any great importance to my aunt's story, since I did not believe at all in any of this fortune-telling, and I soon quite forgot about this prediction.

In Alexandropol I had a friend named Fatinov. He had a friend, Gorbakoun, the son of a company commander in the Baku regiment, which was stationed not far from the Greek quarter.

About a week after my aunt's story this Fatinov came and asked me to go with him and his friend to shoot wild duck. They were going to Lake Alagheuz at the foot of the mountain of the same name.

I agreed to join them, thinking it would be a good opportunity for a rest. I was really very tired, as I had been working hard studying certain absorbing books on neuropathology. Moreover, I had been very fond of shooting since early childhood.

Once, when I was only six years old, I had taken my father's rifle without permission and had gone out to shoot sparrows, and although the first shot knocked me down this not only did not discourage me but even added zest to my love of shooting. Of course they at once took the rifle away from me, and hung it so high that I could not possibly reach it; but out of old cartridge shells I made myself another one, which shot the cardboard bullets I had for my toy gun. This rifle, loaded with small lead shot, hit the mark no worse than a real one and became so sought after among my comrades that they began to order such fire-arms from me; and besides passing for an excellent 'gunsmith', I began to earn a good income.

And so, two days later, Fatinov and his friend called for me and we went off to shoot. We had to walk about fifteen miles, so we started at daybreak in order to arrive by evening, without hurrying, and be ready early the next morning for the ducks to rise.

There were four of us—a soldier, the orderly of commander Gorbakoun, had joined us. We all brought guns, and Gorbakoun even had a service rifle. Arriving at the lake as planned, we made a fire, had supper, built a hut, and went to sleep.

Rising before dawn, we divided the shores of the lake between us and began to wait for the birds to fly. On my left was Gorbakoun with his service rifle. He fired at the first duck that rose while it was still very low, and the bullet hit me right in the leg. Fortunately it passed clean through, missing the bone.

Of course this spoiled the shooting-party. My leg was bleeding profusely and began to be painful, and as I was unable to walk, my comrades had to carry me all the way home on an improvised litter made with the rifles.

I stayed at home and the wound soon healed, as only the flesh had been injured; but I limped for a long time afterwards.

The coincidence of this accident with the prediction of the local oracle made me think a great deal. On a later visit at my uncle's house I heard that Eoung-Ashokh Mardiross had returned to the district and I asked my aunt to send for him.

The fortune-teller came. He was tall and thin, with very faded eyes and the nervous, disordered movements of a half-wit. He shuddered from time to time and smoked incessantly. He was certainly a very sick man.

His way of telling fortunes was as follows:

Sitting between two lighted candles, he held his thumb up before him and stared for a long time at his thumb-nail until he fell into a doze. Then he began to tell what he saw in the nail, first of all saying what the person was wearing and then what would happen to him in the future. If he were telling the fortune of someone absent, he would first ask for his name, the details of his face, the general direction of the place where he lived, and if possible his age.

On this occasion he again made predictions about me. And one day, without fail, I will relate how these predictions were fulfilled.

That summer, also in Alexandropol, I met with another phenomenon for which I could not then find any explanation.

Across from my uncle's house was some vacant land, in the middle of which was a little grove of poplars. I liked this spot and used to go there with a book or with work of some sort.

Children were always playing there, gathered from all parts of the town—children of all colours and different races. There were Armenians and Greeks, Kurds and Tartars, and their games made an incredible noise and commotion—which, however, never disturbed my work.

One day I was sitting under the poplars, busy with some work ordered by a neighbour for his niece's wedding the following day. My task was to draw a monogram on a shield—to be hung over the door of his house—a monogram combining his niece's initials with those of the man she was to marry. I had also to find space on the shield for the day of the month and the year.

Certain strong impressions somehow deeply imprint themselves on one's memory. I remember even now how I racked my brains to find the best way to fit in the figures of the year 1888. I was deep in my work when suddenly I heard a desperate shriek. I jumped up, certain that an accident had happened to one of the children during their play. I ran and saw the following picture:

In the middle of a circle drawn on the ground stood one of the little boys, sobbing and making strange movements, and the others were standing at a certain distance laughing at him. I was puzzled and asked what it was all about.

I learned that the boy in the middle was a Yezidi, that the circle had been drawn round him and that he could not get out of it until it was rubbed away. The child was indeed trying with all his might to leave this magic circle, but he struggled in vain. I ran up to him and quickly rubbed out part of the circle, and immediately he dashed out and ran away as fast as he could.

This so dumbfounded me that I stood rooted to the spot for a long time as if bewitched, until my usual ability to think returned. Although I had already heard something about these Yezidis, I had never given them any thought; but this astonishing incident, which I had seen with my own eyes, now compelled me to think seriously about them.

Looking round and seeing that the boys had gone back to their games, I returned to my place, full of my thoughts, and continued the work on the monogram, which was not going well but had to be finished at all costs that same day.

The Yezidis are a sect living in Transcaucasia, mainly in the regions near Mount Ararat. They are sometimes called devil-worshippers.

Many years after the incident just described, I made a special experimental verification of this phenomenon and found that, in fact, if a circle is drawn round a Yezidi, he cannot of his own volition escape from it. Within the circle he can move freely, and the larger the circle, the larger the space in which he can move, but get out of it he cannot. Some strange force, much more powerful than his normal strength, keeps him inside. I myself, although strong, could not pull a weak woman out of the circle; it needed yet another man as strong as I.

If a Yezidi is forcibly dragged out of a circle, he immediately falls into the state called catalepsy, from which he recovers the instant he is brought back inside. But if he is not brought back into the circle, he returns to a normal state, as we ascertained, only after either thirteen or twenty-one hours.

To bring him back to a normal state by any other means is impossible. At least my friends and I were not able to do so, in spite of the fact that we already possessed all the means known to contemporary hypnotic science for bringing people out of the cataleptic state. Only their priests could do so, by means of certain short incantations.

Having somehow finished and delivered the shield that evening, I set off to the Russian quarter, where most of my friends and acquaintances lived, in the hope that they might help me understand this strange phenomenon. The Russian quarter of Alexandropol was where all the local intelligentsia lived.

It should be mentioned that from the age of eight, owing to chance circumstances, my friends in Alexandropol as well as in Kars were much older than I and belonged to families who were considered socially higher than mine. In the Greek part of Alexandropol, where my parents formerly lived, I had no friends at all. They all lived on the opposite side of the town in the Russian quarter, and were the children of officers, officials and clergymen. I often went to see them, and getting to know their families, gradually gained the entrée into almost all the houses of the quarter.

I remember that the first person I spoke to about the phenomenon which had so greatly astonished me was my good friend Ananiev, who was also much older than I. He did not even listen until I finished, but authoritatively stated:

'These boys simply played on your credulity. They were pulling your leg and have made an ass of you. But look, how smart this is!' he added, running to the next room and putting on, as he came back, his brand new uniform. (He had recently been appointed a postal-telegraph official.) He then asked me to go with him to the public gardens. I made the excuse of not having time and went off to see Pavlov, who lived in the same street.

Pavlov, who was a treasury official, was a very good fellow but a great drinker. At his house were the deacon of the fortress church, Father Maxim, an artillery officer called Artemin, Captain Terentiev, the teacher Stolmakh and two others whom I hardly knew. They were drinking vodka, and when I came in they asked me to join them and offered me a drink.

It must be said that that year I had already begun to drink, not much, it is true, but when I was invited to do so, as sometimes happened, I did not refuse. I had begun to drink owing to an incident in Kars. One morning, being very tired from studying all night long, I was about to go to bed when suddenly a soldier came to call me to come to the cathedral. That day a service was to be held at a certain fort—I do not remember in honour of what—and at the last minute it was decided to have the choir for it, so the attendants and orderlies were sent to all parts of the town to call the choristers.

Having had no sleep all night, I was so exhausted by the walk up the steep hill to the fort and by the service itself that I could hardly stand on my feet. After the service a dinner had been prepared at the fort for the people invited and a special table had been laid for the choristers. The choir-master, a hearty drinker, seeing how weak I was, persuaded me to drink a small glass of vodka. When I had drunk it I did in fact feel much better, and after taking a second glass all my weakness disappeared. After that whenever I was very tired or nervous I took one or two, or sometimes even three, small glasses.

On this evening also I took a glass of vodka with my friends, but, however much they tried to persuade me, I refused a second one. The company was not yet drunk, as they had only just begun drinking. But I knew how things usually went in this gay crowd. The first one to get tipsy was always the father deacon. When only slightly intoxicated he would, for some reason or other, begin to intone a prayer for the repose of the soul of that true believer, etc., the late Alexander I. . . . But seeing that he was still sitting there glum, I could not resist telling him what I had seen that day. I did not, however, speak so seriously about it as I did to Ananiev, but instead spoke somewhat jokingly.

Everybody listened to me attentively and with great interest, and when I finished my story they began to express their opinions. The first to speak was the captain, who said that he himself had recently seen some soldiers draw a circle on the ground round a Kurd who begged them almost in tears to rub it away. Not until he, the captain, had ordered a soldier to erase a part of the circle, was the Kurd able to get out of it. 'I think,' added the captain, 'that they take some vow never to go out of a closed circle, and they do not go out of it, not because they cannot, but because they do not wish to break their vow.'

The deacon said: 'They are devil-worshippers and under ordinary circumstances the devil does not touch them, as they are his own. But as the devil himself is only a subordinate and is obliged by his office to impose his authority on everyone, he therefore, as you might say, for the sake of appearances, has limited the Yezidis' independence in this way so that other people should not suspect that they are his servants. It's exactly like Philip.'

Philip was a policeman who stood at the street-corner and whom these fellows, having no one else available, sometimes sent for cigarettes and drinks. The police service there at that time, as is said, 'even made the cat laugh'.

'Now if I,' the deacon continued, 'make a row, let's say, in the street, this Philip is obliged without fail to take me to the police-station, and for appearances' sake, so that it should not seem strange to others, he will of course do so, but as soon as we turn the corner he will let me go, not forgetting to say, "Please, a little tip . . ."

'Well, the Unclean One is just the same, you might say, with his servants, the Yezidis.'

I do not know whether he invented this episode on the spur of the moment, or whether it had really taken place.

The artillery officer said that he had never heard about such a phenomenon and that, in his opinion, nothing of the sort could exist. He much regretted that we, intelligent people, should believe in such marvels and, still more, rack our brains about them.

Stolmakh, the teacher, retorted that on the contrary he firmly believed in supernatural phenomena and that, if there were much that positive science could not explain, he was fully convinced that, with the present rapid progress of civilization, contemporary science would soon prove that all mysteries of the metaphysical world could be fully explained by physical causes. 'In regard to the fact you are now talking about,' he continued, 'I think it is one of those magnetic phenomena which are now being investigated by scientists at Nancy.'

He was going to say something more but Pavlov interrupted him, exclaiming: 'The devil take them and all the devil-worshippers! Give them each a half-bottle of vodka and then no devil will hold them back. Let's drink to the health of Isakov!' (Isakov was the proprietor of the local vodka distillery.)

These discussions not only did not calm my thoughts, but on the contrary on leaving Pavlov's I began to think all the more, and at the same time began to have doubts about people whom I had until then considered educated.

The next morning I met by chance the chief physician of the 39th Division, Dr. Ivanov. He had been called to see a sick Armenian neighbour of ours and I was asked to come and serve as interpreter. Dr. Ivanov had a good reputation among the townspeople and had a very large practice. I knew him well as he was often at my uncle's.

After his visit to the sick man, I said to him: 'Your Excellency,' (he had the rank of a general) 'please explain to me why Yezidis cannot get out of a circle.'

'Ah, you mean those devil-worshippers?' he asked. 'That is simply hysteria.'

'Hysteria?' I queried.

'Yes, hysteria . . .' and then he rattled off a long rigmarole about hysteria, and all I could gather from it was that hysteria is hysteria. This I already knew myself, as there was not a single book on neuropathology and psychology in the library of the Kars military hospital that I had not read, and read very attentively, carefully going over almost every line in my intense desire to find, through these branches of science, an explanation of the phenomenon of table-turning. Therefore I already well understood that hysteria is hysteria, but I wished to know something more.

The more I realized how difficult it was to find a solution, the more I was gnawed by the worm of curiosity. For several days I was not myself and did not wish to do anything. I thought and thought of one thing only: 'What is true? What is written in books and taught by my teachers, or the facts I am always running up against?'

Soon another incident occurred and this time I was completely bewildered.

Five or six days after the incident of the Yezidis, while going one morning to the fountain to wash—it was the custom there to wash in spring water every morning—I saw a group of women at the corner talking excitedly. I went up to them and learned the following:

That night in the Tartar quarter a *gornakh* had appeared. This was the name there of an evil spirit which used the bodies of people who had recently died and appeared in their shape to do all sorts of villainies, especially to the enemies of the dead person.

This time one of these spirits had appeared in the body of a Tartar who had been buried the day before, the son of Mariam Batchi.

I knew about the death and burial of this man, as his house was next to our old house, where our family had lived before our departure for Kars and where I had gone the day before to collect the rent from the tenants. I had also called on several Tartar neighbours and had seen the body of the dead man being carried out.

He was a young man who had recently joined the police guard, and he used to visit us. I had known him very well.

Several days before, during a *dzhigitovka* contest, he had fallen from his horse and, as they said, had twisted his intestines. Although a military doctor, named Koulchevsky, had given him a full glass of mercury to 'readjust his intestines', the poor man had died and, according to the Tartar custom, was buried very soon.

Then this evil spirit, it seems, entered his body and tried to drag it back home, but someone, happening to see this, raised an outcry and rang the alarm, and to prevent the spirit from doing any great harm the good neighbours quickly cut the throat of the body and carried it back to the cemetery.

It is believed there among the followers of the Christian religion that these spirits enter exclusively the bodies of Tartars because, according to the Tartar custom, the coffin is not deeply buried at first but only lightly covered with earth, and food is often put inside. It is difficult for spirits to go off with the bodies of Christians buried deep in the earth, and that is why they prefer Tartars.

This incident completely stupefied me. How could I explain it to myself? What did I know? I looked round me. Gathered at the corner were my uncle, the esteemed Giorgi Mercourov, and his son, who had nearly finished school, and a police official, all talking about this. All were generally respected; all had lived much longer than I and surely knew many things that I had not even dreamed of. Did I see in their faces indignation, grief or astonishment? No; they even seemed to be glad that somebody had succeeded this time in punishing the evil spirit and warding off its mischief.

I gave myself up again to reading books, hoping that through them I could satisfy the worm which was gnawing me.

Bogachevsky helped me very much, but unfortunately he soon went away, because two years after his arrival in Kars he was appointed chaplain of the garrison in a town of the Transcaspian region.

While he lived in Kars and was my teacher, he introduced into our relationship a certain peculiarity, namely, although he was not yet a priest, he confessed me every week. When he left he bade me, among other things, write out my confession each week and send it to him in a letter, promising that he would sometimes reply. We agreed that he would send his letters through my uncle, who would forward them to me.

A year later in the Transcaspian region, Bogachevsky gave up his duties as chaplain and became a monk. At the time it was said that the cause of his action was that his wife seemed to be having an affair with some officer, and Bogachevsky had turned her out and had not wished to remain in the town or even to hold office in the church.

Soon after Bogachevsky's departure from Kars I went to Tiflis. At this time I received two letters from Bogachevsky through my uncle, after which I had no news of him for several years.

Once, much later, I met him quite by accident in the town of Samara as he was leaving the house of the local bishop. He was then wearing the monk's habit of a well-known monastery. He did not immediately recognize me, as I had by then grown up and changed a good deal, but when I told him who I was he was very glad to see me, and for several days we saw each other often, until both of us left Samara.

After this meeting I never saw him again. I heard later that he had not wished to remain in his monastery in Russia and had soon left for Turkey, then for Holy Athos, where he also did not stay long. He had then renounced his monastic life and had gone to

Jerusalem. There he chanced to become friends with a vendor of rosaries who traded near the Lord's Temple.

This trader was a monk of the Essene Order who, having gradually prepared Bogachevsky, introduced him into his brotherhood. Owing to his exemplary life, Bogachevsky was appointed warden and, a few years later, prior in one of the branches of this brotherhood in Egypt; and later, on the death of one of the assistants to the abbot of the chief monastery, Bogachevsky was appointed in his place.

Of his extraordinary life during this period I learned much, when I was in Broussa, from the tales of a certain friend of mine, a Turkish dervish who had often met Bogachevsky. Before this time I had received another letter from him, again sent through my uncle. In addition to the few words of blessing, there were enclosed a small photograph of him in the dress of a Greek monk and several views of holy places in the environs of Jerusalem.

When he was in Kars, still only a candidate for the priesthood, Bogachevsky had very original views on morality. He then said and taught me that on earth there are two moralities: one objective, established by life in the course of thousands of years, and the other subjective, pertaining to individuals as well as to whole nations, kingdoms, families, groups of people and so forth.

'Objective morality,' he said, 'is established by life and by the commandments given us by the Lord God Himself through His prophets, and it gradually becomes the basis for the formation in man of what is called conscience. And it is by this conscience that objective morality, in its turn, is maintained. Objective morality never changes, it can only broaden in the course of time. As for subjective morality, it is invented by man and is therefore a relative conception, differing for different people and different places and depending upon the particular understanding of good and evil prevailing in the given period.

'For example, here in Transcaucasia,' said Bogachevsky, 'if a woman does not cover her face and if she speaks with a guest, everyone will regard her as immoral, spoiled and badly brought up. But in Russia, on the contrary, if a woman does cover her face and if she does not welcome a guest and entertain him with conversation, everyone will consider her badly brought up, rude, disagreeable and so forth.

'Another example: if a man here in Kars does not go once a week, or at least once in two weeks, to the Turkish bath, everyone round him will dislike him and be disgusted by him, and even find that he has a bad odour, which he may not have at all. But in St. Petersburg it is just the opposite: if a man even mentions going to the baths, he is considered uneducated, unintelligent, boorish and so on; and if by chance he should actually go, he will hide the fact from others so that such a low taste should not be attributed to him.

'As a very good illustration of the relative understanding of so-called morality or honour,' continued Bogachevsky, 'let us take the two incidents which occurred here in Kars last week among the officers and which made a great stir.

'The first was the trial of Lieutenant K and the second the suicide of Lieutenant Makarov.

'Lieutenant K was tried by the military court for having struck a shoemaker, Ivanov, in the face so brutally that he lost an eye. The court acquitted him, after having found out on investigation that the shoemaker had caused Lieutenant K much annoyance and had spread insulting rumours about him.

'Having become very interested in this case, I decided, disregarding the evidence of the court, to question the family and acquaintances of the unfortunate shoemaker, so as to ascertain for myself the real reasons for the conduct of Lieutenant K.

'This lieutenant, as I learned, had ordered first one pair and then two more pairs of boots from the shoemaker Ivanov and had promised to send him the money on the twentieth of the month, when he would receive his pay. When the lieutenant did not send the money on the twentieth, Ivanov went to his house to ask for what was due to him. The officer promised to pay the next day, but the next day he again put him off till the next, and in short, fed him for a long time, as is said, on "tomorrows". Ivanov, however, went to him time after time to ask for the money, as it represented for him a very large sum. It was almost all he possessed—consisting of the entire savings of his wife, a laundress, who for many years had put it away kopek by kopek, and had given it to her husband to buy material for the lieutenant's boots. Besides, Ivanov kept coming for his money because he had six small children to feed.

'At last Lieutenant K grew annoyed at Ivanov's insistence and told his orderly to say he was not at home; then he simply had him driven off, and threatened to have him sent to prison. Finally the lieutenant told his orderly to give Ivanov a good thrashing if he came again.

'The orderly, a kindly man, did not beat Ivanov, as his master had ordered, but, wanting to persuade him in a friendly way not to annoy the lieutenant with his repeated visits, invited him into the kitchen to talk. Ivanov sat down on a stool, and the orderly began to pluck a goose for roasting. Seeing this, Ivanov remarked: "So! Our lords and masters eat roast goose every day and do not pay their debts, and meanwhile my children go hungry!"

'At this moment Lieutenant K happened to come into the kitchen and, overhearing what Ivanov had said, grew so furious that he took a large beetroot from the table and struck Ivanov in the face so hard that he knocked his eye out.

'The second incident,' continued Bogachevsky, 'was, so to speak, the reverse of the first one: a certain Lieutenant Makarov could not pay his debt to a certain Captain Mashvelov, and so he shot himself.

'It must be said that this Mashvelov was an inveterate gambler and also a great card-sharper. Not a day passed without his fleecing someone; it was obvious to all that he played a crooked game.

'A short time ago Lieutenant Makarov was playing cards with some officers, among them Mashvelov, and he lost not only all his own money, but also a sum borrowed from this Mashvelov on the promise to return it to him in three days. As the sum was a large one, Lieutenant Makarov could not raise it in three days, and, being unable to keep his word, decided to shoot himself rather than stain his honour as an officer.

'Both these events occurred on account of debts. In one case, the creditor has his eye knocked out by the debtor, and in the other case, the debtor shoots himself. Why? Simply because everyone round Makarov would have severely condemned him for not paying his debt to the sharper Mashvelov, whereas in the case of Ivanov, the shoemaker, even if all his children were to starve to death—that would be quite in the order of things, for the code of honour of an officer is not concerned with the payment of his debts to a shoemaker.

'And in general, I repeat, acts of this kind occur simply because people stuff their children, while the future man is still being formed in them, with all sorts of conventions, and so prevent Nature herself from developing in them that conscience which has taken form over thousands of years of struggle by our ancestors against just such conventions.'

Bogachevsky often urged me not to adopt any conventions, either those of my immediate circle or those of any other people.

He said: 'From the conventions with which one is stuffed subjective morality is formed, but for real life objective morality is needed, which comes only from conscience.

'Conscience is everywhere the same. As it is here, so it is in St. Petersburg, America, Kamchatka, and in the Solomon Islands. Today you happen to be here, but tomorrow you may be in America; if you have a real conscience and live according to it, it will always be well with you wherever you may be.

'You are still quite young; you have not yet begun life. Everybody here may now call you badly brought up; you may not know how to bow correctly, or to say the right thing in the proper manner, but this does not matter if only when you grow up and begin to live you have in yourself a real conscience, that is, the foundation of objective morality.

'Subjective morality is a relative conception, and if you are filled with relative conceptions, then when you are grown up you will always and everywhere act and judge other people according to the conventional views and notions you have acquired. You must learn not what people round you consider good or bad, but to act in life as your conscience bids you. An untrammelled conscience will always know more than all the books and teachers put together. But for the present, until your own conscience is formed, live according to the commandment of our Teacher Jesus Christ: "Do not do to others what you would not wish them to do to you." '

Father Evlissi, who is now an aged man, happened to become one of the first persons on earth who has been able to live as our Divine Teacher Jesus Christ wished for us all.

May his prayers be an aid to all those who wish to be able to live according to the Truth!

V

MR. X OR CAPTAIN POGOSSIAN

SARKIS POGOSSIAN, or as he is now called, Mr. X, is at the present time the owner of several ocean steamers, one of which, cruising among his favourite places, between the Sunda and Solomon Islands, he commands himself.

By race an Armenian, he was born in Turkey, but spent his childhood in Transcaucasia, in the town of Kars.

I met Pogossian and became friends with him when he was still a young man, finishing his studies at the Theological Seminary of Echmiadzin and preparing for the priesthood.

Before I met him I had already heard about him through his parents, who lived in Kars not far from our house and often came to see my father. I knew that they had an only son who had formerly studied at the 'Temagan Dprotz' or Theological Seminary of Erivan, and was now at the Theological Seminary of Echmiadzin.

Pogossian's parents were natives of Turkey, from the town of Erzerum and had moved to Kars soon after it was taken by the Russians. His father was by profession a *poïadji*[1] and his mother an embroideress in gold, specializing in breast-pieces and belts for *djuppays*.[2] Living very simply themselves, they spent all they had to give their son a good education.

[1] A *poïadji* is a dyer. A person of this profession can always be recognized by his arms, which are blue to the elbows from the dye that can never be washed off.

[2] A *djuppay* is the special costume of the Armenian women of Erzerum.

Sarkis Pogossian rarely came to see his parents and I never had an opportunity to see him in Kars. My first meeting with him took place the first time I was in Echmiazdin. Before going there I returned to Kars for a short time to see my father, and the parents of Pogossian, learning that I would soon be leaving for Echmiadzin, asked me to take their son a small parcel of linen.

I was going to Echmiadzin for the purpose—as always—of seeking an answer to the question of supernatural phenomena, in which my interest not only had not diminished but had grown even stronger.

I must say here, as I mentioned in the previous chapter, that having become extremely interested in supernatural phenomena, I had plunged into books and also applied to men of science for explanations of these phenomena. But failing to find answers that satisfied me either in books or from the people I turned to, I began to seek them in religion. I visited various monasteries and went to see men about whose piety I had heard, read the Holy Scriptures and the Lives of the Saints, and was even for three months an acolyte of the famous Father Yevlampios in the monastery of Sanaïne; and I also made pilgrimages to most of the holy places of the many different faiths in Transcaucasia.

During this period I happened again to witness a whole series of phenomena which were unquestionably real, but which I could in no way explain. This left me more bewildered than ever.

For example, once when I went with a company of pilgrims from Alexandropol for a religious festival to a place on Mount Djadjur, known among the Armenians by the name of Amena-Pretz, I witnessed the following incident:

A sick man, a paralytic, from the small village of Paldevan was being taken there on a cart, and on the road we fell into conversation with the relatives who were accompanying the invalid and talked with them as we went along.

This paralytic, who was barely thirty years old, had been ill for the past six years, but before that he had been in perfect health and had even done military service. He had fallen ill after his return home from service, just before his wedding, and had lost all use of the left side of his body. In spite of various treatments by doctors and healers, nothing helped. He had even been specially taken for treatment to Mineralne Vodi in the Caucasus, and now his relatives were bringing him here, to Amena-Pretz, hoping against hope that the saint would help him and alleviate his sufferings.

On the way to this holy place we made a special stop, as all pilgrims usually do, at the village of Diskiant to pray at the miraculous icon of Our Saviour, which was in the house of a certain Armenian family. As the invalid also wished to pray, he was taken into the house, I myself helping to carry the poor man in.

Soon afterwards we came to the foot of Mount Djadjur, on the slopes of which the little church with the miraculous tomb of the saint is situated. We halted at the place where the pilgrims usually leave their carts, wagons and vans, at the end of the carriage road. From there the further ascent of a quarter of a mile must be made on foot, and many walk barefoot, according to the custom there, while others even do this distance on their knees or in some other special way.

When the paralytic was lifted from the cart to be carried to the top, he suddenly resisted, wishing to try to crawl up by himself as best he could. He was put on the ground and he started dragging himself along on his healthy side. He did this with such difficulty that it was pitiable to watch him; but he still refused all help. Resting often on the way, he finally, after three hours, reached the top, crawled to the tomb of the saint, which was in the centre of the church, and having kissed the tombstone, immediately lost consciousness.

His relatives, with the help of the priests and myself, tried to revive him. We poured water into his mouth and bathed his head. And it was just as he came to himself that a miracle occurred. His paralysis was gone.

At first the man was stupefied; but when he realized that he could move all his limbs, he sprang up and almost began to dance; then, all of a sudden recollecting himself, with a loud cry he flung himself prone and began to pray.

All the people there, with the priest at their head, immediately fell on their knees and began to pray also. Then the priest stood up, and amidst the kneeling worshippers, held a service of thanksgiving to the saint.

Another incident, which puzzled me no less, took place in Kars. That year there was terrible heat and drought in the whole province of Kars; almost all the crops had been scorched; a famine threatened, and the people were becoming agitated.

That same summer there arrived in Russia from the patriarchate of Antioch an archimandrite with a miraculous icon—I do not remember whether of St. Nicholas the Miracle-worker or of the Virgin—to collect money for the relief of the Greeks who suffered in the Cretan War. He travelled with this icon chiefly to places in Russia with a Greek population, and he also came to Kars.

I do not know whether politics or religion was at the bottom of it all, but the Russian authorities in Kars, as elsewhere, took part in organizing an impressive welcome and in according him all kinds of honours.

When the archimandrite arrived in any town, the icon was carried from church to church, and the clergy, coming to meet it with banners, welcomed it with great solemnity.

The day after the archimandrite arrived in Kars, the rumour spread that a special service for rain would be held before this icon, by all the clergy, at a place outside the town. And indeed, just after twelve o'clock on that same day, processions set out from all the churches, with banners and icons, to join in the ceremony at the appointed place.

In this ceremony there took part the clergy of the old Greek church, of the recently rebuilt Greek cathedral, the military cathedral, the church of the Kuban regiment, and also of the Armenian church.

It was a day of particularly intense heat. In the presence of almost the entire population, the clergy, with the archimandrite at their head, held a solemn service, after which the whole procession marched back towards the town.

And then something occurred to which the explanations of contemporary people are absolutely inapplicable. Suddenly the sky became covered with clouds, and before the people had time to reach the town there was such a downpour that everyone was drenched to the skin.

In explanation of this phenomenon, as of others similar to it, one might of course use the stereotyped word 'coincidence', which is such a favourite word among our so-called thinking people; but it cannot be denied that this coincidence was almost too remarkable.

The third incident occurred in Alexandropol, when my family had returned there for a short period and we were living again in our old house. Next door to us was my aunt's house. One of the lodgings in her house had been let to a Tartar who worked for the local district government either as a clerk or a secretary. He lived with his old mother and his little sister and had recently married a handsome girl, a Tartar from the neighbouring village of Karadagh.

Everything went well at first. Forty days after her marriage the young wife, according to the Tartar custom, went to visit her parents. But there, either she caught cold or something else happened to her, for when she returned she did not feel well, had to go to bed, and gradually became very ill.

They gave her the best of care, but in spite of being treated by several doctors, among whom, I remember, were the town doctor, Resnik, and the former army doctor Keeltchevsky, the condition of the sick woman went from bad to worse. An acquaintance of mine, a doctor's assistant, went every morning, by order of Dr. Resnik, to give her an injection. This doctor's assistant, whose name I do not remember—I only remember that he was unbelievably tall—often dropped in to see us when I was at home.

One morning he came in while my mother and I were drinking tea. We invited him to join us at the table and in the course of the conversation I asked him, among other things, how our neighbour was getting on.

'She is very sick,' he replied. 'It is a case of galloping consumption and doubtless it will soon be "all over" with her.'

While he was still sitting there, an old woman, the mother-in-law of the sick woman, came in and asked my mother's permission to gather some rose-hips in our little garden. In tears she told us how Mariam Ana—as the Tartars call the Virgin—had appeared that night to the sick woman in a dream and bade her gather rose-hips, boil them in milk, and drink; and in order to calm her the old woman wished to do this. Hearing this, the doctor's assistant could not help laughing.

My mother of course gave her permission and even went to help her. When I had seen the assistant off I also went to help.

What was my astonishment when, the next morning on my way to the market, I met the invalid with the old woman coming out of the Armenian church of Sev-Jiam, where there is a miraculous icon of the Virgin; and a week later I saw her washing the windows of her house. Dr. Resnik, by the way, explained that her recovery, which seemed a miracle, was a matter of chance.

These indubitable facts, which I had seen with my own eyes, as well as many others I had heard about during my searchings—all of them pointing to the presence of something supernatural—could not in any way be reconciled with what common sense told me or with what was clearly proved by my already extensive knowledge of the exact sciences, which excluded the very idea of supernatural phenomena.

This contradiction in my consciousness gave me no peace, and was all the more irreconcilable because the facts and proofs on both sides were equally convincing. I continued my searchings, however, in the hope that sometime, somewhere, I would at last find the real answer to the questions constantly tormenting me.

And it was this aim which took me, among other places, to Echmiadzin, the centre of one of the great religions, where I hoped to find at least some slight clue leading to the solution of these inescapable questions.

Echmiadzin, or, as it is also called, Vagarshapat, is for the

Armenians what Mecca is for the Moslems and Jerusalem for the Christians. Here is the residence of the Catholicos of all Armenians, and here also is the centre of Armenian culture. Every year in the autumn big religious festivals are held, to which come many pilgrims not only from all parts of Armenia but from all over the world. A week before the beginning of such a festival all the surrounding roads are filled with pilgrims, some travelling on foot, others in carts and wagons and still others on horses and asses.

I travelled on foot, in company with other pilgrims from Alexandropol, having put my belongings in the wagon of the Molokan sect.

On reaching Echmiadzin I went directly, as was the custom, to worship at all the holy places. I then went into the town to look for a lodging, but it was impossible to find one, since all the inns (hotels did not exist then) were full and more than full; and so I decided to do as many others did—simply establish myself outside the town under a cart or wagon. But as it was still early, I decided first of all to do my errand, that is, find Pogossian and give him the parcel.

He lived not far from the main inn in the house of a distant relative, the Archimandrite Surenian. I found him at home. He was about the same age as I, dark, of medium height, and had a small moustache. His eyes were very sad, but at times they burned with an inner fire. The right eye was slightly crossed. At that time he seemed to be very frail and shy.

He began asking me about his parents, and having learned in the course of the conversation that I had not succeeded in finding lodgings, he ran off and, returning almost immediately, proposed that I should share his room.

I of course accepted, and went at once and brought back all my paraphernalia from the wagon. And I had just finished arranging a bed for myself with Pogossian's help, when we were called to take supper with Father Surenian, who greeted me affably and asked me about Pogossian's family and about things in general in Alexandropol.

After supper I went with Pogossian to see the town and the

sacred relics. It must be said that during the festival there is a great deal of movement all night in the streets of Echmiadzin, and all the cafés and *askhani* are open.

That whole evening and all the days following were spent with Pogossian. He took me everywhere, as he knew all the ins and outs of the town. We went to places where ordinary pilgrims do not have access and even to the Kanzaran, where the treasures of Echmiadzin are kept and where one is very rarely admitted.

During our talks we discovered that the questions which were agitating me also interested him; both of us had much material to share on these questions, and little by little our talks became more intimate and heart-to-heart, and a strong tie was gradually formed between us.

Pogossian was nearing the end of his studies at the Theological Seminary and in two years was to be ordained a priest, but his inner state did not correspond to this at all. Religious as he was, he was none the less extremely critical of his environment and strongly averse to living among priests whose mode of life seemed to him to run entirely counter to his own ideals.

When we had become friends, he told me a great deal about the hidden side of the life of the clergy there; and the thought that on becoming a priest he would have to live in this environment made him suffer inwardly and feel deeply distressed.

After the holidays I stayed on in Echmiadzin for three more weeks, living with Pogossian at the house of the Archimandrite Surenian; and thus I had the opportunity more than once of talking about the subjects which agitated me with the archimandrite himself, and also with other monks to whom he introduced me.

But during my stay in Echmiadzin I did not find what I was looking for and, having spent enough time to realize that I could not find it there, I went away with a feeling of deep inner disillusionment.

Pogossian and I parted great friends. We promised to write to each other and to share our observations on the questions which interested us both.

One fine day, two years later, Pogossian arrived in Tiflis and came to stay with me.

He had graduated from the seminary and had been in Kars for a short time with his parents. Now he had only to marry in order to obtain a parish. His family had even found a bride for him, but he was in a state of complete indecision and did not know what to do. He would spend days on end reading all kinds of books that I had, and in the evenings, on my return home from work as a stoker at the Tiflis railway station we would go together to the Moushtaïd and, walking along the deserted paths, we would talk and talk.

Once, while walking in the Moushtaïd, I jokingly proposed that he should come to work with me at the railway station, and I was greatly astonished when the next day he insisted that I should help him get a place there. I did not try to dissuade him, but sent him with a note to my good friend the engineer Yaroslev, who at once gave him a letter of introduction to the station-master, who took him on as assistant locksmith.

So it continued until October. We were still engrossed in abstract questions and Pogossian had no thought of returning home.

Once at the house of Yaroslev I made the acquaintance of another engineer, Vasiliev, who had just arrived in the Caucasus to survey the route of the proposed railway between Tiflis and Kars. After we had met several times, he proposed one day that I should go with him on the survey as overseer and interpreter. The salary offered was very tempting—almost four times as much as I was earning. I was already tired of my job, which was beginning to interfere with my main work, and as it also became clear that I should have much free time, I accepted. I proposed to Pogossian that he should go with me in some capacity or other, but he refused, as he had become interested in his work as a locksmith and wished to continue what he had begun.

I travelled with this engineer for three months in the narrow valleys between Tiflis and Karaklis and managed to earn a great deal, having besides my official salary several unofficial sources of income of a rather questionable character.

Knowing beforehand which villages and little towns the railway was to go past, I would send someone to the power-possessors of these villages and towns, offering to 'arrange' for the railway to be laid through these places. In most cases my offer was accepted and I would receive for my trouble a private remuneration, at times in the form of a rather large amount of money.

When I returned to Tiflis I had collected, including what remained from my previous earnings, quite a substantial sum, so I did not look for work again but devoted myself entirely to the study of the phenomena which interested me.

Pogossian had meanwhile become a locksmith and also found time to read a great many books. He had recently become especially interested in ancient Armenian literature, of which he procured a large quantity from the same booksellers as I.

By this time Pogossian and I had come to the definite conclusion that there really was 'a certain something' which people formerly knew, but that now this knowledge was quite forgotten. We had lost all hope of finding any guiding clue to this knowledge in contemporary exact science, in contemporary books or from people in general, and so we directed all our attention to ancient literature. Having chanced to come across a whole collection sel ancient Armenian books, Pogossian and I became inteny of interested in them and decided to go to Alexandropol to look for a quiet place where we could give ourselves up entirely to study.

Arriving in Alexandropol, we chose as such a place the isolated ruins of the ancient Armenian capital, Ani, which is thirty miles from Alexandropol, and having built a hut among the ruins we settled there, getting our food from the neighbouring villages and from shepherds.

Ani became the capital of the Bagratid kings of Armenia in the year 962. It was taken by the Byzantine Emperor in 1046, and at that time was already called the 'City of a Thousand Churches'. Later it was conquered by the Seljuk Turks; between 1125 and 1209 it was taken five times by the Georgians; in 1239 it was taken by the Mongols, and in 1313 it was completely destroyed by earthquake.

Among the ruins there are, by the way, the remains of the Patriarchs' Church, finished in the year 1010, the remains of two churches also of the eleventh century, and of a church which was completed about 1215.

At this point in my writings I cannot pass by in silence a fact which, in my opinion, may be of interest to certain readers, namely, that these historical data which I have just cited concerning the ancient Armenian capital Ani are the first, and I hope the last, that I have taken from information officially recognized on earth; that is to say, it is the first instance since the beginning of my writing activities in which I have had recourse to an encyclopedia.

About the city Ani there still exists one very interesting legend, explaining why, after being called the City of a Thousand Churches for a long time, it came to be called the City of a Thousand and One Churches.

This legend is as follows:

Once the wife of a certain shepherd complained to her husband about the shocking misbehaviour in the churches. She said that there was no place for quiet prayer and, wherever one went, the churches were as crowded and noisy as beehives. And the shepherd, heeding her just indignation, began building a church especially for his wife.

In former times the word 'shepherd' did not have the same meaning as it has now. Formerly a shepherd himself was the owner of the flocks he grazed; and shepherds were considered among the richest people of the country; some of them even possessed several flocks and herds.

When he had finished building the church, this shepherd called it the 'Church of the Shepherd's Pious Wife', and from then on the city of Ani was called the City of a Thousand and One Churches. Other historical data assert that, even before the shepherd built this church, there were many more than a thousand churches in the city, but it is said that during recent excavations a stone was found confirming the legend of the shepherd and his pious wife.

Living among the ruins of this city and spending our days

reading and studying, we sometimes, for a rest, made excavations in the hope of finding something, as there are many underground passages in the ruins of Ani.

Once, Pogossian and I, while digging in one of these underground passages, noticed a place where the consistency of the ground had changed, and on digging further we discovered a new passage, which turned out to be a narrow one, blocked at the end with fallen stones. We cleared the stones away and before us appeared a small room with arches crumbling with age. Everything indicated that it had been a monastic cell. There was nothing left in this cell but broken pottery and pieces of rotten wood, doubtless the remains of furniture; but in a kind of niche in the corner lay a pile of parchments.

Some of the parchments were turning to dust, others were more or less preserved. With the utmost care we took them to our hut, and tried to decipher them. They were written in a language which appeared to be Armenian but was unknown to us. I knew Armenian well, to say nothing of Pogossian; nevertheless we could not understand any of this writing, as it was a very ancient Armenian, very different from that of today.

This discovery interested us so much that we left everything else and returned that same day to Alexandropol, where we spent many days and nights trying to decipher at least a few words. Finally, after a great deal of difficulty and much questioning of experts, it became clear that these parchments were simply letters written by one monk to another monk—a certain Father Arem.

We were especially interested in one letter in which the writer referred to information he had received concerning certain mysteries. This parchment, however, was one of those which had been most damaged by time, and there were a number of words that we could only guess at; but we nevertheless succeeded in reconstructing the letter.

What interested us most was not the beginning but the end of this letter. It began with a long greeting, and went on about the ordinary small happenings in the life of a certain monastery where, as could be inferred, this Father Arem had formerly lived.

Towards the end one passage particularly attracted our attention. It said:

'Our worthy Father Telvant has at last succeeded in learning the truth about the Sarmoung Brotherhood. Their *ernos*[1] actually did exist near the town of Siranoush, and fifty years ago, soon after the migration of peoples, they also migrated and settled in the valley of Izrumin, three days journey from Nivssi. . . .' Then the letter went on about other matters.

What struck us most was the word Sarmoung, which we had come across several times in the book called *Merkhavat*. This word is the name of a famous esoteric school which, according to tradition, was founded in Babylon as far back as 2500 B.C., and which was known to have existed somewhere in Mesopotamia up to the sixth or seventh century A.D.; but about its further existence one could not obtain anywhere the least information.

This school was said to have possessed great knowledge, containing the key to many secret mysteries.

Many times had Pogossian and I talked of this school and dreamed of finding out something authentic about it, and now suddenly we found it mentioned in this parchment! We were greatly excited.

But apart from its name being mentioned, we discovered nothing else from this letter. We knew no more than before when and how this school arose, where it had existed or whether it might even still exist.

After several days of laborious research, we were able to establish only the following:

About the sixth or seventh century the descendants of the Assyrians, the Aïsors, were driven by the Byzantines out of Mesopotamia into Persia, and probably it was in this period that these letters were written.

And when we were able to verify that the present city of Mosul, the former capital of the country of Nievi, had once been called Nivssi, the city mentioned in the parchment, and that at the present time the population round about this city consisted

---

[1] An *ernos* was a kind of corporation.

chiefly of Aïsors, we concluded that in all probability the letter referred precisely to these Aïsors.

If such a school had really existed and had moved somewhere during that period, then it could only have been an Aïsorian school, and if it should still exist, then it must be among the Aïsors and, taking into consideration the indicated three days' journey from Mosul, it must now be situated somewhere between Urmia and Kurdistan, and it should not be too difficult to find out where it was. We therefore decided to go there and try at any cost to find out where the school was situated and then enter it.

The Aïsors, who, as I have said, are descended from the Assyrians, are now scattered all over the earth. There are many of them in Transcaucasia, north-western Persia and eastern Turkey, and one finds groups of them throughout the whole of Asia Minor. It is estimated that in all there are about three million of them. Most of them are Nestorians, that is, they do not acknowledge the divinity of Christ. The minority consists of Jacobites, Maronites, Catholics, Gregorians and others; among them are also Yezidis, or devil-worshippers, though not in great number.

Missionaries of various religions have recently manifested great zeal in converting the Aïsors to their different faiths, and one must give the Aïsors their due in that they have no less zealously 'converted themselves', outwardly changing their faith and even deriving from these conversions so much material benefit that this has become proverbial. In spite of all the differences of faith, almost the entire race is under the authority of the patriarchate of the East Indies.

The Aïsors live mostly in little villages ruled by priests; several villages, or a certain district, constitute a clan which is ruled over by a prince or, as they call him, a melik. All the meliks are subordinate to the patriarch, whose office is hereditary, passing from uncle to nephew, and is said to derive originally from Simon, the Brother of the Lord.

It must be said that the Aïsors suffered very much in the last war,[1] having been a pawn in the hands of Russia and England, with the result that half of them perished from the vengeance of

[1] The First World War.

the Kurds and the Persians; and if the rest survived, it was only thanks to the American consul, Dr. Y, and his wife. The Aïsors, particularly those in America—and there are many of them there —ought, in my opinion, if Dr. Y is still living, to organize and permanently maintain at his door an Aïsorian guard of honour, and, if he is dead, without fail to erect a monument to him at his birthplace.

Just in that year when we decided to set out on our expedition there was a great nationalist movement among the Armenians, and on everyone's lips were the names of the heroes who had fought for freedom, especially the name of young Andronik, who later became a national hero.

Everywhere, among the Turkish and Persian Armenians, as among the Russian Armenians, various parties and committees were being formed; attempts at unity were made even while sordid quarrels kept breaking out among the different factions; in short, a violent political explosion was taking place, such as recurs from time to time in Armenia, with the usual train of consequences.

Early one morning in Alexandropol, I was on my way, as usual, to the river Arpa Chai to bathe. Half-way, at the place called Karakuli, Pogossian overtook me, quite out of breath, and told me that the day before in conversation with the priest Z he had learned that the Armenian Committee wished to choose several volunteers from the members of the party to send to Moush on a special mission.

'When I got home,' Pogossian continued, 'it suddenly occurred to me that we could make use of this opportunity for our purpose, that is, for trying to find traces of the Sarmoung Brotherhood; so I got up at sunrise and came to talk it over with you, but as I missed you I ran to catch up with you.'

I interrupted him and said that in the first place we were not members of the party, and in the second place . . .

He did not let me finish but announced that he had already thought everything out and knew how it could be arranged, and all he now needed to know was whether I would agree to such a plan.

Mr. X or Captain Pogossian

I answered that I wished at any cost to get to the valley which was once named Izrumin and that it was all the same to me how I got there, whether on the devil's back or even arm-in-arm with the priest Vlakov. (Pogossian knew that this Vlakov was the man I most disliked and whose presence exasperated me a mile away.)

'If you say you can arrange it,' I continued, 'then do whatever you please and as circumstances demand, and I agree beforehand to everything, if only as a result we get to the place I have set as my goal.'

I do not know what Pogossian did or with whom or how he talked, but the result of his efforts was that several days later, provided with a considerable sum of Russian, Turkish and Persian money and a great many letters of introduction to people living in the different places along our proposed route, we set out from Alexandropol in the direction of Kaghyshman.

In two weeks we arrived at the banks of the river Arax, which is the natural frontier between Russia and Turkey, and crossed it with the aid of some Kurds who had been sent to meet us. It seemed to us that we had now surmounted the greatest difficulties, and we hoped that from there on everything would go smoothly and successfully.

We travelled mostly on foot, staying either with shepherds or with people recommended to us in the villages already passed through, or with those persons to whom we had letters from Alexandropol.

It must be confessed that although we had undertaken certain obligations and attempted, as far as possible, to carry them out, we never lost sight of our real purpose for the journey, the itinerary of which did not always coincide with the places of our commissions; on such occasions we did not hesitate to leave them unfulfilled and, truth to tell, did not experience on this account any great remorse of conscience.

When we had passed the Russian frontier, we decided to go over Mount Egri Dagh, even though it was the most difficult way, because it gave us a better chance of avoiding the numerous bands of Kurds and the Turkish detachments who were pursuing the Armenians. Having crossed over the pass, we turned south towards Van, leaving on our right the region of the sources of the great rivers Tigris and Euphrates.

During our journey, we had thousands of adventures which I will not describe, but there is one that I cannot pass by in silence. Although it happened so many years ago, I still cannot recall this incident without laughing, and without at the same time re-experiencing the sensation I had then—of instinctive fear combined with a presentiment of imminent catastrophe.

Many times after this incident I found myself in very critical situations. For example, more than once I was surrounded by scores of dangerous enemies; I have had to cross the path of a Turkestan tiger; and several times I was taken literally at the point of a gun; but never did I have such a feeling as I experienced on this occasion, however comical it may seem now, after the event.

Pogossian and I were calmly walking along. He was humming some march and swinging his stick. Suddenly, as if from nowhere, a dog appeared, then another, and another, and still another—in all about fifteen sheep-dogs, who began barking at us. Pogossian imprudently flung a stone at them and they immediately sprang at us.

They were Kurd sheep-dogs, very vicious, and in another moment they would have torn us to pieces if I had not instinctively pulled Pogossian down and made him sit beside me on the road. Just because we sat down the dogs stopped barking and springing at us; surrounding us, they also sat down.

Some time passed before we came to ourselves; and when we were able to take stock of the situation we burst out laughing. As long as we remained sitting the dogs also sat, peaceably and still, and when we threw them bread from our knapsacks, they ate it with great pleasure, some of them even wagging their tails in gratitude. But when, reassured by their friendliness, we tried to stand up, then, 'Oh no, you don't!'—for they instantly jumped up and, baring their teeth, made ready to spring at us; so we were compelled to sit down once more. When we again tried to get up, the dogs showed themselves so viciously hostile that we did not risk trying a third time.

In this situation we remained sitting for about three hours. I do not know how much longer we would have had to sit there if a young Kurd girl had not chanced to appear in the distance with an ass, gathering *keesiak* in the fields.

Making various signs to her, we finally managed to attract her attention, and when she came closer and saw what the trouble was, she went off to fetch the shepherds to whom the dogs belonged, who were not far away behind a hill. The shepherds came and called off the dogs, but only when they were at some distance did we risk standing up; and all the time they were moving away the rascals kept an eye on us.

As it turned out, we had been most naïve in assuming that after crossing the river Arax we would have left the greatest difficulties and troubles behind us; as a matter of fact, it was only there that they began.

The greatest difficulty was that after crossing this frontier river and going over Mount Egri Dagh, we could no longer pass for Aïsors, as we had until the encounter with the dogs, because we now found ourselves in places populated by genuine Aïsors. To travel as Armenians, in regions where at that time they were being persecuted by all the other races, was quite out of the question. It was also dangerous to go as Turks or Persians. It would have been preferable to pass ourselves off as Russians or Jews, but neither Pogossian's appearance nor mine would permit this.

At that time great care had to be taken if one wished to conceal one's real nationality, because to be found out in any disguise would have been very dangerous. The natives were not then over-particular in their choice of means for getting rid of undesirable foreigners. For instance, it was rumoured from authentic sources that several Englishmen had recently been flayed alive by Aïsors, for having attempted to make copies of certain inscriptions.

After long deliberation, we decided to disguise ourselves as

Caucasian Tartars. Somehow or other we made the appropriate changes in our dress, and continued on our journey.

Exactly two months after crossing the river Arax, we finally came to the town of Z, beyond which we had to go through a certain pass in the direction of Syria. In this pass, before reaching the famous waterfall of K, we were to turn off towards Kurdistan and it was somewhere along this road that we expected to find the place which was the chief objective of our journey.

In our further peregrinations, since we had by this time sufficiently adapted ourselves to surrounding conditions, everything went along fairly smoothly—until one unexpected accident changed all our intentions and plans.

One day we were sitting by the roadside eating our bread and the *tarekh*[1] we had brought with us. Suddenly Pogossian jumped up with a shout and I saw darting away from under him a big yellow phalanga. I at once understood the cause of his cry and, springing up, killed the phalanga and rushed to Pogossian. He had been bitten in the leg. I knew that the bite of this insect—a kind of tarantula—is often fatal, and so I instantly tore away the clothes to suck the wound. But seeing he had been bitten in the fleshy part of the leg and knowing that sucking the wound would be dangerous if there were the slightest scratch in one's mouth, I took the lesser risk for both of us, seized my knife, and quickly cut away a piece of my comrade's calf—but in my haste I cut away too much.

Obviating in this way all danger of fatal poisoning, I felt less anxious and immediately began washing the wound and bandaging it as best I could. As the wound was large and Pogossian had lost much blood and all kinds of complications were to be feared, it was not possible for the time being to think of continuing the journey we had mapped out. We had to decide at once what was to be done.

Having talked it over together, we decided to spend the night there on the spot, and in the morning to find some means of reaching the town of N, thirty miles away, where we had a letter

[1] *Tarekh* is a strongly salted fish, quite popular in those regions and caught only in Lake Van.

to deliver to a certain Armenian priest—a commission we had not carried out as this town was not on the route we had planned before the accident.

The next day, with the help of an old Kurd who happened to be passing and who turned out to be quite friendly, I hired in a little village near by a kind of cart harnessed to two oxen, which was used for carting manure, and putting Pogossian in it, set out in the direction of N.

It took us almost forty-eight hours to cover this short distance, stopping every four hours to feed the oxen. We finally arrived at N and went straight to the Armenian priest, to whom we had a letter of introduction as well as the letter to be delivered. He received us most amiably, and when he learned what had happened to Pogossian, he immediately offered him a room in his house, which of course we most gratefully accepted.

While still on the road Pogossian's temperature had risen and, although it went down on the third day, the wound had festered and had to be treated with great care. That is how we came to accept the hospitality of this priest for almost a whole month.

Living so long under the same roof with this priest and frequently talking with him about anything and everything, very close relations were gradually established between us. Once, in the course of conversation, he told me, by the way, about a certain object he possessed and the story connected with it.

It was an ancient parchment with some kind of map on it. It had been in his family a long time, and had been passed down to him by inheritance from his great-grandfather.

'The year before last,' said the priest, 'a man who was quite unknown to me came and asked me to show him the map. How he could have known that I had it I have no idea. It all seemed to me suspicious, and not knowing who he was, I did not at first wish to show it to him and even denied that I had it; but when he persisted in asking me about it, I thought, "Why should I not let him see it?" and I did show it to him.

'He had hardly looked at the parchment when he asked me whether I would sell it to him and immediately offered me two hundred Turkish pounds for it. Although the sum was large, I did not wish to sell it, not being in need of the money and not wishing to part with something I was accustomed to having and which I cherished as a remembrance.

'This stranger, it appeared, was staying with our bey. The next day the bey's servant came to me, on behalf of their newly-arrived guest, with an offer to buy the parchment for five hundred pounds.

'I must say that from the moment the stranger had left my house many things had seemed to me suspicious: first of all, this man had apparently come a long way specially for this parchment; then, the incomprehensible means by which he had learned that it was in my possession; and finally, the intense interest he showed while looking at it.

'All this taken together proved to me that this thing must be very valuable. So when he offered such a sum as five hundred pounds, although inwardly tempted by the offer, I feared to let the thing go too cheaply and, deciding to be cautious, again refused.

'In the evening the stranger came to see me again, this time accompanied by the bey himself. When he renewed his offer to pay me five hundred pounds for the parchment, I flatly refused to sell at all. But as he had come with our bey, I invited them both in as my guests. They came in and we drank coffee and talked about one thing and another.

'In the course of conversation it transpired that my visitor was a Russian prince. He told me, among other things, that he was interested in antiques and, as this parchment fitted so well into his collection, he, being a connoisseur, wished to buy it and had offered a sum far above the value of the article. But he considered it would be foolish to pay more and regretted that I refused to sell it.

'The bey, who had been listening attentively to our conversation, became interested in the parchment and expressed a wish to see it. When I brought the parchment and they were both looking at it, the bey was obviously astonished that such a thing was worth so much.

'During the conversation the prince suddenly asked me how

much I would take to let him make a copy of my parchment. I hesitated, not knowing what to answer, as, speaking frankly, I was afraid that I had lost a good customer. He then offered me two hundred pounds to let him make a copy, and this time I felt ashamed to bargain as, in my opinion, he was giving me this sum for nothing.

'Just think, for permission merely to make a copy of the parchment I was receiving as much as two hundred pounds! Without thinking longer about it, I agreed to the prince's offer, telling myself that, after all, the parchment would remain with me and I would always be able to sell it if I wished.

'The next morning the prince returned. We spread the parchment out on the table, and the prince added water to some powdered alabaster he had brought with him; after covering the parchment with oil he spread the alabaster over it. Several minutes later he removed the alabaster, wrapped it up in a piece of old *djedjin* I gave him, paid me two hundred pounds, and went away. Thus did God send me two hundred pounds for nothing, and I have the parchment to this day.'

The priest's story interested me greatly, but I gave no sign of it and simply asked him, as though out of curiosity, to show me what it was for which he had been offered such a large sum of money. The priest went to a chest and took out a roll of parchment. When he unrolled it I could not at first make out what it was, but when I looked at it more closely . . . My God! What I experienced at that moment! I shall never forget it.

I was seized with violent trembling, which was all the more violent because I was inwardly trying to restrain myself and not show my excitement. What I saw—was it not precisely what I had spent long months of sleepless nights thinking about!

It was a map of what is called 'pre-sand Egypt'.

With great effort, I continued trying to look as though I were not particularly interested in this thing and spoke of something else.

The priest rolled up the parchment and put it back in the chest. I was no Russian prince to pay two hundred pounds for making a copy, yet this map was perhaps no less necessary to me than to him. I therefore decided, then and there, that at any cost I must have a copy, and at once began to think how it could be obtained.

By this time Pogossian was feeling so much better that we used to take him out on the terrace, where he would sit for long hours in the sun. I arranged that he would let me know when the priest went out on his business and the next day, on hearing from him that the priest had left the house, I went stealthily into his room to fit a key to his heirloom chest. The first time I was not able to note all the details of the key, and it was not until the third attempt, after numerous filings, that I succeeded in making one fit.

One evening, two days before our departure, while the priest was absent, I got into his room again and took the parchment from the chest. I took it to our room and throughout the night Pogossian and I traced all the details of the map, after having covered it with oiled paper. The next day I put the parchment back in its place.

From the moment I had this treasure—so full of mystery and promise—securely and unnoticeably sewn in the lining of my clothes, it was as if all my other interests and intentions evaporated. An eagerness which was not to be restrained arose in me to reach at any cost and without delay the places where, with the aid of this treasure, I could at last appease that desire for knowledge which during the past two or three years had given me no rest, gnawing me within like a worm.

After this perhaps justifiable, but nevertheless—whatever way one regards it—culpable treatment of the hospitality of the Armenian priest, I talked things over with my still half-sick comrade Pogossian. I persuaded him not to spare his lean financial resources but to buy two good local saddle-horses, of the kind we had noticed during our stay there and whose peculiar, quick, ambling trot we had admired, so that we could set off as soon as possible in the direction of Syria.

The gait of the horses bred in that locality is indeed so smooth that one can ride on them almost at the speed of the flight of a large bird, holding in one's hand a glassfull of water without spilling a single drop.

I will not describe here all the ups and downs of our journey, nor the unforeseen circumstances which forced us frequently to change our route. I will only say that exactly four months after we took leave of that hospitable and kindly Armenian priest, we reached the town of Smyrna, where, on the evening of our arrival, we had an adventure which happened to be a turning-point in the subsequent destiny of Pogossian.

That evening we went to a small Greek restaurant for a little diversion after the period of difficulty and strain we had just been through. We were leisurely drinking the famous *douẓiko* and helping ourselves to this and that, as is the local custom, from the numerous small saucers piled with all kinds of hors-d'œuvres, from dried mackerel to salted chick peas.

Besides ourselves, there were several groups of people in the restaurant, most of them sailors from the foreign ships anchored in the harbour. They were rather rowdy and it was evident that they had already visited more than one tavern and had got themselves, as is said, 'pretty well soaked'.

Between the sailors of different nationalities sitting at separate tables, squabbles arose from time to time, which were at first confined to an interchange of noisy epithets in a peculiar jargon, mostly a mixture of Greek, Italian and Turkish—and then suddenly, without warning, an explosion occurred.

I do not know how the gunpowder was ignited, but all at once a rather large group of sailors sprang up in a body and, with threatening gestures and shouts, threw themselves upon some other sailors sitting not far from us. The latter also sprang up and in the twinkling of an eye a free fight was in full swing.

Pogossian and I, also somewhat excited by the fumes of the *douẓiko*, rushed to help the smaller group of sailors. We had no idea what it was all about—or even who was getting the best and who the worst of it.

When the other people in the restaurant and the military patrol, which happened to be passing, had separated us, scarcely a single one of those in the fight had come out unscathed: one had a broken nose, another was spitting blood, and so on, while I stood in the middle of them decorated with an enormous black left eye, and Pogossian, cursing all the time in Armenian, groaned and gasped, complaining of an unbearable pain under the fifth rib.

When, as the sailors would have said, the storm abated, Pogossian and I, finding that we had had enough for one evening and had been sufficiently diverted by these good people—and not even by request—dragged ourselves home to sleep.

It cannot be said that we were very talkative on the way home; my eye kept shutting involuntarily and Pogossian was groaning and cursing himself for not minding his own business.

The next morning at breakfast, reviewing our physical condition and our rather idiotic behaviour of the previous evening, we decided not to postpone the trip to Egypt we had planned, as we calculated that the long voyage on the boat and the pure sea air would cure our wounds of battle completely by the time we arrived there. So we went at once to the port to find out if there were a ship to suit our pockets which would soon be going to Alexandria.

We discovered that there was a Greek sailing-vessel in the harbour about to leave for Alexandria, and we hurried off to the office of the steamship company to which this ship belonged to get the necessary information. Just at the door of this office a sailor ran up to us and, jabbering something or other in broken Turkish, began warmly and excitedly shaking hands with both of us.

At first we did not understand anything, but it soon became clear that he was an English sailor, one of the group in whose defence we had fought the previous evening. Gesturing to us to wait, he hurried off and a few minutes later returned accompanied by three comrades, one of whom, as we afterwards learned, was an officer. All of them thanked us warmly for what we had done the day before and insisted that we go to a Greek restaurant near by to have a glass of *douziko* with them.

After three rounds of the miraculous *douziko*—that worthy offspring of the beneficent *mastikhe* of the ancient Greeks—we began to talk more and more noisily and freely, of course thanks to the ability we had all inherited of making ourselves understood by 'ancient Greek mimicry' and 'ancient Roman gesticulation', as well as with the help of words taken from all the seaport languages on earth. When they learned that we wished to get somehow or other to Alexandria, then the beneficent effect of that worthy offspring of the invention of the ancient Greeks did not fail to make itself manifest in a most striking manner.

The sailors, as though they had forgotten our existence, began talking among themselves, and whether they were quarrelling or joking we could not tell. Suddenly two of them, finishing their drinks in one gulp, went off in a great hurry, while the two who were left vied with each other, in a tone of benevolent concern, to assure and reassure us of something or other.

At last we began to guess what it was all about and, as it afterwards turned out, our guess was almost correct: those two comrades of theirs who had suddenly left had gone to put in a word for us in the proper quarter, so that we might go on their ship, which was sailing the next day for Piraeus, from there to Sicily, and from Sicily to Alexandria, where it would stop for about two weeks before sailing to Bombay.

The sailors took a long time to come back, and while waiting for them we did justice to the magnificent offspring of *mastikhe*, to the accompaniment of strong words from all languages.

In spite of this pleasant way of passing the time waiting for favourable news, Pogossian, evidently remembering his fifth rib, suddenly lost patience and started to insist that we should not wait any longer but should return home at once; moreover, he assured me with great earnestness that my other eye was also beginning to look black.

Considering that Pogossian had not entirely recovered from the phalanga bite, I could not refuse and, without going into any explanations with our chance companions in the consumption of *douziko*, I obediently got up and went off after him.

Astonished by the unexpected and silent departure of their defenders of the day before, the sailors got up too and came along after us. We had rather a long way to go. Each of us entertained himself in his own way; one sang, another gesticulated, as if to prove something to somebody, another was whistling some military march. . . .

As soon as we arrived Pogossian lay down at once, without even undressing, and I, giving up my bed to the elder sailor, simply stretched out on the floor, making a sign to the other to do the same.

Waking up in the night with a terrible headache and recalling in snatches everything that had happened the day before, I remembered, among other things, the sailors who had come home with us; but when I looked round the room I discovered that they had gone.

I went back to sleep and it was already late when I was awakened by the clatter of dishes made by Pogossian preparing tea and by his singing, as he did every morning, the special Armenian morning prayer, '*Lusatsav lusn pareen yes avadam zair ghentaneen*'. Neither Pogossian nor I wanted tea that morning; we wanted something very sour. We drank only some cold water and, without exchanging a single word, went back to bed.

We were both very depressed and felt wretched in every way. In addition, I had a sensation in my mouth as though at least a dozen cossacks, with their horses and harness, had spent the night there.

While we were still lying in this condition, each of us thinking his own thoughts in silence, the door was suddenly pushed open and three English sailors burst into the room. Only one of them had been with us the day before; the other two we saw for the first time. Interrupting each other constantly, they tried to tell us something. By asking questions and racking our brains, we finally understood that they wanted us to get up, dress quickly and go with them to their ship, as they had received permission from the authorities to take us with them as extra ship's hands.

While we were dressing, the sailors continued talking among themselves gaily, as was clear from their faces; then suddenly, much to our astonishment, all of them jumped up together and began packing our belongings. By the time we had finished dressing, called the *ustabash* of the caravanserai and paid our bill, our things were already neatly packed and the sailors, dividing them among themselves, made signs to us to follow them.

We all went out into the street and walked towards the harbour.

When we got there, we saw a small boat at the wharf with two sailors in it who were evidently waiting for us. We stepped into the boat and after being rowed along for half an hour, with the English sailors singing all the time, we came alongside a fairly large warship.

It was obvious that we were expected on board, for no sooner did we reach the deck than some sailors standing at the gangway quickly took our things and led us to a small cabin, which had been assigned to us and made ready beforehand in the hold near the galley.

When we had somehow settled ourselves in this stuffy but, as it seemed to us, very cosy corner of the warship, we went out on the upper deck, accompanied by one of the sailors for whom we had fought in the restaurant. We sat down on some coils of rope and soon we were surrounded by almost all the crew—both ordinary sailors and junior officers.

All of them, irrespective of their rank, seemed to have a marked feeling of friendliness towards us. Every one of them felt obliged to shake hands with us and, taking our ignorance of English into account, tried, with the aid of gestures and what words they knew in various languages, to say something obviously pleasant.

During this very original conversation in many languages, one of the sailors, who spoke tolerable Greek, suggested that during the voyage each one present should set himself the task of learning every day at least twenty words—we in English, they in Turkish.

This proposal was approved by all with noisy applause, and two sailors, from among our friends of the day before, at once began choosing and writing down those English words which they thought we ought to learn first, and Pogossian and I made a list of Turkish words for them.

When the launch with the senior officers came alongside and the hour of sailing drew near, all the crew went off to carry out their duties, and Pogossian and I at once set to work to memorize the first twenty English words, which were written phonetically in Greek characters.

We were so absorbed in learning these twenty words and in

trying to pronounce correctly the unaccustomed sounds, so foreign to our ear, that we did not notice that evening had come and the ship was under way. We broke off our occupation only when a sailor came towards us, swaying to the measured rolling of the ship, and, explaining with a very expressive gesture that it was time to eat, took us to our cabin near the galley.

During the meal we discussed matters between ourselves and, after consulting the sailor who spoke tolerable Greek, we decided to ask permission—which was granted that very evening—for me to begin the next morning cleaning the metal-work on the ship and for Pogossian to work in some capacity or other in the engine-room.

I will not dwell on the events during the remainder of our voyage on that warship.

On arriving at Alexandria I warmly took leave of the hospitable sailors, and left the ship with the burning determination to reach Cairo as soon as possible. But Pogossian, who had become friends with several of the sailors during the voyage and was enthusiastic about his work in the engine-room, wished to stay on the ship and go further. We agreed to keep in touch with each other.

As I later learned, Pogossian, after we had parted, continued to work in the engine-room of this English warship, acquired a passion for mechanics, and became very close friends with several of the sailors and younger officers.

From Alexandria he went with this ship to Bombay, and then, after calling at various Australian ports, finally landed in England. There, in the city of Liverpool, persuaded by these new English friends of his and through their influence, he entered a technical institute of marine engineering where, along with intensive technical studies, he perfected himself in the English language. At the end of two years he became a qualified mechanical engineer.

In concluding this chapter devoted to the first comrade and friend of my youth, Pogossian, I wish to mention a certain highly original feature of his general psyche which was apparent from his earliest years and was very characteristic of his individuality.

Pogossian was always occupied; he was always working at something.

He never sat, as is said, with folded arms, and one never saw him lying down, like his comrades, reading diverting books which give nothing real. If he had no definite work to do, he would either swing his arms in rhythm, mark time with his feet or make all kinds of manipulations with his fingers.

I once asked him why he was such a fool as not to rest, since no one would pay him anything for these useless exercises.

'Yes, indeed,' he replied, 'for the present no one will pay me for these foolish antics of mine—as you and all those pickled in the same barrel of brine think they are—but in the future either you yourself or your children will pay me for them. Joking apart, I do this because I like work, but I like it not with my nature, which is just as lazy as that of other people and never wishes to do anything useful. I like work with my common sense.

'Please bear in mind,' he added, 'that when I use the word "I", you must understand it not as the whole of me, but only as my mind. I love work and have set myself the task of being able, through persistence, to accustom my whole nature to love it and not my reason alone.

'Further, I am really convinced that in the world no conscious work is ever wasted. Sooner or later someone must pay for it. Consequently, if I now work in this way, I achieve two of my aims. First, I shall perhaps teach my nature not to be lazy, and secondly, I will provide for my old age. As you know, I cannot expect that when my parents die they will leave me an ample inheritance to suffice for the time when I will no longer have the strength to earn a living. I also work because the only real satisfaction in life is to work not from compulsion but consciously; that is what distinguishes man from a Karabakh ass, which also works day and night.'

This reasoning of his has been fully justified by facts. Although he spent his whole youth—the time most valuable to a man for securing his old age—in, as it were, useless wanderings and never concerned himself with making money for his later life, and although he did not go into a serious business until the year 1908, he is now one of the richest men on earth. As for his honesty in earning his wealth, that cannot be questioned.

He was right when he said that no conscious labour is ever wasted. He did indeed work consciously and conscientiously, day and night, like an ox, all his life, in all circumstances and under all conditions.

May God grant him now, at last, his well-earned rest.

VI

ABRAM YELOV

AFTER POGOSSIAN, ABRAM YELOV WAS THE NEXT
of those remarkable people whom I happened to meet during my
preparatory age and who, voluntarily and involuntarily, served
as 'vivifying factors' for the complete formation of one or another
aspect of my individuality.

I first met him a short time after I had lost all hope of discover-
ing from contemporary people anything real concerning those
questions in which I was wholly absorbed, and when, on returning from Echmiadzin to Tiflis, I had buried myself in the reading
of ancient literature.

I returned to Tiflis chiefly because I could obtain there any
book I wanted. In this city, both then and the last time I stopped
there, it was very easy to find any rare book in any language,
especially in Armenian, Georgian and Arabic.

When I arrived in Tiflis, I went to live in the district called
Didoubay and from there I used to go nearly every day to the
Soldiers' Bazaar, to one of the streets along the west side of the
Alexander Gardens, where most of the shops of the Tiflis booksellers were situated. On this same street in front of the permanent
bookstores, small traders, or book pedlars, used to spread out
their books and pictures on the ground, especially on market
days.

Among these small traders was a certain young Aïsor who
bought and sold or handled on commission all kinds of books.

This was Abrashka Yelov, as he was called in his youth—an artful dodger if there ever was one, but for me an irreplaceable friend.

He was even then a walking catalogue, for he knew innumerable titles of books in almost all languages, the names of the authors, and also the date and place of publication of any book, and where it could be obtained.

In the beginning I bought books from him, and later I exchanged or returned those I had already read and he used to help me find whatever other books I needed. We soon became friends.

At that time Abram Yelov was preparing himself to enter the Cadet School and spent almost all his free time cramming for this; but nevertheless, being much attracted to philosophy, he also managed to read a great many books on this subject.

It was owing to his interest in philosophical questions that our close friendship began, and we often used to meet in the evening in the Alexander Gardens, or in the Moushtaïd, and discuss philosophical themes. We often rummaged together through stacks of old books, and I even began helping him, on market days, in his trading.

Our friendship was further strengthened by the following occurrence:

On market days, there was a certain Greek who used to set his stall next to where Yelov traded. This Greek traded in various plaster-of-Paris wares, such as statuettes, busts of famous people, figures of Cupid and Psyche, a shepherd and shepherdess, and all kinds of money-boxes of all sizes, in the form of cats, dogs, pigs, apples, pears, and so forth—in short, in all the rubbish with which it was at one time fashionable to decorate tables, chests of drawers and special what-nots.

One day, during a lull in the trading, Yelov nodded in the direction of these wares and, in his singular way of expressing himself, said:

'There's someone making a pile of money, whoever it is that's making that junk. They say it's some dirty Italian, a newcomer that makes the trash in his dirty hovel; and those idiots, hawkers like that Greek, stuff his pockets full of the money laboriously earned by the fools who buy these horrors to decorate their idiotic homes. And here we stick all day on one spot, suffering in the cold, so that in the evening we can choke ourselves on a piece of stale maize bread to just barely keep body and soul together; and the next morning we come here again and go through the same cursed grind.'

Soon after this I went up to the Greek hawker and learned from him that these wares were indeed made by an Italian, who guarded the secrets of his manufacture in every possible way.

'And twelve of us hawkers,' added the Greek, 'are hardly enough to sell these wares all over Tiflis.'

His story and Yelov's indignation stirred me up, and then and there I thought of trying to steal a march on this Italian, the more so since at that time I had to consider beginning some business or other means of earning, as my money was already going like the exodus of the Israelites.

I first of all spoke with the Greek hawker, of course intentionally arousing his feelings of patriotism; then, having composed in my mind a plan of action, I went with him to the Italian and asked for work. To my good fortune it turned out that just previously a boy who had been working for him had been discharged for stealing tools, and the Italian needed someone to pour the water for him during the stirring of the plaster. As I was willing to work for any pay, I was immediately taken on.

According to my plan, I pretended from the very first day to be a blockhead. I worked very hard, almost as much as three men, but in other respects behaved stupidly. For this the Italian very soon even took a liking to me and no longer hid his secrets from this young fellow, who was so foolish and harmless, as carefully as he did from others.

In two weeks I already knew how many of the things were made. My employer would call me to hold the glue, to stir the mixture, and so on, and I thus penetrated to his holy of holies and soon learned all the little but, in this work, very important secrets. And in this sort of work they are indeed very important; for example, when the plaster is dissolved, one must know how many drops of lemon juice should be added so that the plaster will not have bubbles and the articles will come out smooth; otherwise the fine extremities of the statuettes, such as the nose, ear, and so on, may have ugly hollows. It is also important to know the right proportions of glue, gelatine and glycerine for making the moulds; a little more or a little less of anything, and everything goes wrong. Knowing only the procedures without these secrets would not enable one to obtain good results.

In a word, a month and a half later there appeared on the market similar wares of my making. To the forms which the Italian had, I added several comic heads which were filled with small shot and served as penholders; I also put up for sale special money-boxes which sold in great numbers and were christened by me 'The Invalid in Bed'. I do not think there was a single house in Tiflis at that time that did not have one of my money-boxes.

Later I had several workmen working for me and six Georgian girls as apprentices. Yelov, with great delight, helped me in everything, and even stopped trading in books on week-days. At the same time, Yelov and I continued our own work: the reading of books and the study of philosophical questions.

After several months, when I had amassed a fair sum of money and was growing weary of my workshop, I sold it, while it was in full swing, to two Jews for a good price. As I had to vacate my rooms, which were connected to the workshop, I moved to Molokans Street near the railway station, and Yelov, with his books, moved over there also.

Yelov was short, thick-set and dark, with eyes always burning like two live coals. He was very hairy, with shaggy eyebrows and a beard growing nearly from the nose itself and almost covering his cheeks, the ruddiness of which nevertheless always shone through.

He was born in Turkey in the region of Van, either in the town of Bitlis itself or its environs, and from there his family, four or five years before we met, had moved to Russia. When they arrived in Tiflis, he was sent to the first gymnasium, as it was called, but soon, in spite of the fact that the customs there were very simple and unceremonious, Yelov, for some prank or mischief, made himself unbearable even for this institution and was expelled by order of the teachers' council. A short time afterwards his father turned him out and from then on he began to live as the spirit moved him. In short, as he himself expressed it, he was the black sheep of his family. His mother, however, unknown to his father, often sent him money.

Yelov cherished very tender feelings for his mother, which manifested themselves even in little things; for instance, he always had a photograph of his mother hanging over his bed and never went out without kissing this photograph, and when he returned, he would always call from the doorway, 'Good day, Mother', or 'Good evening, Mother'. It now seems to me that I grew to like him all the more for this feature. His father he also loved, but in his own way, and he considered him a petty, vain and wilful man.

His father was a contractor and was considered very rich. Among the Aïsors, moreover, he was very important, apparently because he was a descendant, though only through the female line, of the family of the Marshimoun, to which formerly the Aïsor kings belonged, and from which, ever since the end of the kingdom, the patriarchs have come.

Abram also had a brother, who was then studying in America, in Philadelphia, I believe; but his brother he did not like at all, holding the firm opinion that he was a double-faced egoist and an animal without a heart.

Yelov had many peculiarities; among others, he had the habit of always hitching up his trousers, and later it cost us, his comrades, many and persistent labours to break him of this habit.

Pogossian often poked fun at him for it, saying: 'Hah!—and you wanted to be an officer! At the very first meeting with a general, off you'd go, you poor fool, to the guard-house, for instead of saluting you'd hitch up your trousers . . .' and so on. (Pogossian expressed himself still less delicately.)

Pogossian and Yelov were forever teasing each other, and even when talking amicably, Yelov would never call Pogossian anything else but 'salted Armenian' and Pogossian would call Yelov '*khachagokh*'.

The Armenians in general are called salted Armenians and

the Aïsors *khachagokhs*. *Khachagokh* means literally 'stealer of crosses'. It seems that this nickname originated as follows:

The Aïsors are known to be cunning rogues. In Transcaucasia there even exists the following definition of them: 'Boil together seven Russians, you get one Jew; boil seven Jews, you get one Armenian; but only by boiling seven Armenians can you get one Aïsor.'

Among the Aïsors, scattered everywhere, were many priests, the majority of whom, moreover, were self-ordained—which was then easily done. Living in the environs of Mount Ararat, which marked the boundary of three countries, Russia, Turkey and Persia, and having an almost free right of passage across all the frontiers, they gave themselves out in Russia as Turkish Aïsors, in Persia as Russian Aïsors and so on.

They not only performed the church ceremonies, but traded with great success among the religious and ignorant people in all kinds of so-called holy relics. In the depths of Russia, for instance, giving themselves out as Greek priests, in whom the Russians had great faith, they did a good business by selling things purporting to have been brought from Jerusalem, from Holy Athos, and from other holy places.

Among these relics were fragments of the true cross on which Christ was crucified, hair of the Virgin Mary, finger-nails of St. Nicholas of Myra, the tooth of Judas, which brings good luck, a piece of the horseshoe of the horse of St. George, and even the rib or skull of some great saint.

These things were bought with great reverence by naïve Christians, especially those of the Russian merchant class, and many were the relics of Aïsor priest-manufacture in the houses and innumerable churches of Holy Russia. Because of this, the Armenians, well knowing this brotherhood, nicknamed them and still now call them stealers of crosses.

As for the Armenians, on the other hand, they are called salted because they have the custom of salting a child at his birth.

I must add, by the way, that in my opinion this custom is not without its use. My special observations have shown me that the new-born children of other races suffer from a skin rash in the places where one usually applies some kind of powder to prevent inflammation, but with rare exceptions Armenian children, born in the same regions, do not suffer from this raṣh, although they have all the other children's diseases. This fact I ascribe to the custom of salting.

Yelov was unlike his compatriots in his complete lack of one characteristic that is very typical of the Aïsors: although he was very hot-tempered he never bore a grudge. His anger passed quickly, and if he happened to offend anyone, as soon as his temper cooled he tried his best to smooth over whatever he had said.

He was scrupulously considerate about the religion of others. Once, in the course of a conversation about the intensive propaganda which was being carried on among the Aïsors by missionaries of almost all European countries in order to convert them to their respective faiths, he said:

'It is not a question of to whom a man prays, but a question of his faith. Faith is conscience, the foundation of which is laid in childhood. If a man changes his religion, he loses his conscience, and conscience is the most valuable thing in a man. I respect his conscience, and since his conscience is sustained by his faith and his faith by his religion, therefore I respect his religion; and for me it would be a great sin if I should begin to judge his religion or to disillusion him about it, and thus destroy his conscience which can only be acquired in childhood.'

When he expressed himself in this way, Pogossian would ask him: 'And why did you wish to be an officer?' Then the cheeks of Abram would flame and he would vehemently cry: 'Go to the devil, you salted phalanga!'

Yelov was unusually devoted to his friends. He was ready, as is said, to give his soul for anyone to whom he became attached. When Yelov and Pogossian became friends they were so attached to one another as may God grant all brothers to be. But the external manifestation of the friendship of these two was quite particular and difficult to explain.

The more they loved each other, the ruder they were to each other. But under this rudeness was hidden such a tender love that anyone who saw it could not fail to be touched to the depths of his heart. Several times I, who knew what was beneath some rudeness or other, was so moved that I could not hold back the tears which involuntarily came to my eyes.

For instance, a scene such as the following would occur. Yelov would happen to be a guest in some house where he was offered candy. According to convention he would be obliged to eat it so as not to offend the person who offered it. However, even though very fond of candy, he would not eat it for anything in the world but would hide it in his pocket to take to Pogossian. And then he would not give it to him simply, but with every kind of mockery and a volley of insults.

He usually did so as follows: during conversation at dinner, he would, as if unexpectedly, find the candy in his pocket and would offer it to Pogossian saying: 'How the devil did this garbage happen to be in my pocket? Here, gobble up this muck; you're an expert in swallowing everything that's no good to anyone else.' Pogossian would take it, also scolding: 'Such a delicacy is not for a snout like yours. You can only gorge yourself on acorns like your brothers, the pigs.' And while Pogossian was eating the candy, Yelov with a disdainful expression would say: 'Look how he is gobbling the sweet stuff: how he relishes it like a Karabakh ass munching thistles! Now, after this, he'll be running after me like a little dog merely because I gave him this loathsome rubbish.' And the talk would continue in this fashion.

Besides being a phenomenon in the knowledge of books and authors, Yelov later on became a phenomenon in the knowledge of languages. I, who then spoke eighteen languages, felt a greenhorn in comparison with him. Before I knew a single word of any European language, he already spoke almost all of them so perfectly that it was hard to tell that the language he was speaking was not his own. For example, the following incident occurred:

Skridlov, the professor of archaeology (about whom we will speak later), had to take a certain Afghan holy relic across the river Amu Darya, but to do this was impossible since a close watch was kept on all persons crossing the Russian border in either direction, both by the Afghan guards and by the British soldiers who, for some reason or other, were there at that time in great numbers.

Having obtained somewhere the old uniform of a British officer, Yelov put it on, went over to the post where the British troops were stationed and passed himself off as a British officer from India who had come there to hunt Turkestan tigers. He was able to distract their attention so well with his English stories that we had time, without hurrying and without being observed by the British troops, to take what we wanted from one bank to the other.

Yelov, in addition to everything else he did, continued to study intensively. He did not, as he had intended, enter the Cadet School, but went to Moscow, where he brilliantly passed the examination for the Lazarev Institute and several years later received a degree in philology, at the Kazan University, if I remember rightly.

Just as Pogossian had a peculiar notion about physical work, so Yelov had a very original view about mental work. He once said:

'It's all the same. Our thoughts work day and night. Instead of allowing them to think about caps of invisibility or the riches of Aladdin, rather let them be occupied with something useful. In giving direction to thought, of course a certain amount of energy is spent, but no more is needed for this purpose in a whole day than for the digestion of one meal. I therefore decided to study languages—not only to prevent my thoughts from idling but also not to allow them to hinder my other functions with their idiotic dreams and childish phantasies. Besides, the knowledge of languages can in itself sometimes be useful.'

This friend of my youth is still alive and well and is now comfortably settled in one of the cities of North America.

During the war he was in Russia and lived most of the time in Moscow. He was caught by the Russian Revolution in Siberia, where he had gone to inspect one of his numerous book and stationery stores. During the revolution he endured many hardships and all his riches were swept from the face of the earth.

Only three years ago, his nephew, Dr. Yelov, came from America and persuaded him to emigrate there.

VII

PRINCE YURI LUBOVEDSKY

REMARKABLE AND OUT OF THE USUAL RUN of men was the Russian Prince Yuri Lubovedsky. He was much older than I and for almost forty years was my elder comrade and closest friend.

The remote, indirect cause which led to our meeting on life's path, and to the close bonds of many years' friendship, was the event by which his family life had been suddenly and tragically cut short. In his youth, when the prince was an officer of the guards, he had fallen violently in love with a beautiful young girl similar in character to himself, and had married her. They lived in Moscow, in the prince's house on the Sadovaïa Boulevard.

The princess died in giving birth to her first child and the prince, seeking an outlet for his grief, first became interested in spiritualism, hoping to enter into communication with the soul of his dead beloved wife; and then, without realizing it himself, he became more and more drawn to the study of occult sciences and to the search for the meaning of life. He so buried himself in these studies that he entirely changed his former mode of living. He received no one, went nowhere and, withdrawing to his library, applied himself uninterruptedly to the questions relating to occultism which preoccupied him.

One day when he was particularly absorbed in these studies, his seclusion was broken by the visit of an unknown old man. To the astonishment of all his household, the prince immediately received the old man and, shutting himself up with him in the library, conversed with him a long time.

Very soon after this visit the prince left Moscow, and spent almost all the rest of his life in Africa, India, Afghanistan and Persia. He rarely returned to Russia and then only by necessity and for a short time.

The prince was a very rich man, but he spent all his wealth on 'searches' and on organizing special expeditions to the places where he thought he might find an answer to his questions. He lived for a long time in certain monasteries and met many persons with interests similar to his own.

When I first met him, he was already middle-aged, while I was still a young man. From then on until his death we always kept in touch with each other.

Our first meeting took place in Egypt, at the pyramids, not long after my journey with Pogossian. I had just returned from Jerusalem, where I had earned my living by showing tourists, chiefly Russians, the sights of the city and giving them the customary explanations; in a word, I had been a professional guide.

Soon after my return to Egypt I decided to take up the same profession. I knew Arabic and Greek well, and also Italian, which was indispensable then for speaking to Europeans. In a few days I had learned everything that a guide needed to know and began, along with the slick young Arabs, to confuse naïve tourists.

Since I was already well versed in this kind of work, and my pockets were not overflowing at that time either, I became a guide in order to earn the money I needed to carry out what I had planned.

One day I was taken as a guide by a certain Russian, who afterwards proved to be a professor of archaeology, named Skridlov. As we were walking from the Sphinx towards the Pyramid of Cheops, my employer was hailed by a gentleman with slightly greying hair, who called him a 'grave-digger' and, obviously delighted at the meeting, inquired about his health. They talked Russian together but to me my employer spoke broken Italian, not knowing that I spoke Russian.

They sat down at the foot of the pyramid and I sat down not far away, so that I could distinctly hear all they were saying, and began to eat my *chourek*.

The gentleman who had met us, and who turned out to be a prince, asked the professor among other things:

'Are you really still disturbing the remains of people who died long ago, and collecting the utterly worthless rubbish supposedly once used in their stupid lives?'

'What would you?' answered the professor. 'This is at least something real and tangible, and not as ephemeral as that to which you have devoted your life, a life which you as a man of health and wealth could have used to the full. You are looking for truth invented once upon a time by some crazy idler; but if what I do contributes nothing to the satisfaction of curiosity, at least, if one wishes, it contributes to the pocket.'

They talked in this way for a long time, and then my employer wished to go on to other pyramids and took leave of the prince, after arranging another meeting in ancient Thebes.

It must be said that I was spending all my free time walking among these places like one possessed, hoping to find, with the help of my map of pre-sand Egypt, an explanation of the Sphinx and of certain other monuments of antiquity.

Several days after the professor's meeting with the prince, I was sitting at the foot of one of the pyramids deep in thought, with the open map in my hands. Suddenly I felt that someone was standing over me. I hastily folded my map and looked up. It was the man who had accosted my employer at the Pyramid of Cheops. Pale and in great agitation, he asked me in Italian how and where I had obtained this map.

From his appearance and the interest he manifested in the map, I at once guessed that he must be that same prince described by the Armenian priest at whose house I had secretly made a copy of it. And without answering his question, I asked him in turn, in Russian, if he were not the man who had wished to buy the map from such and such a priest. He answered, 'Yes, I am that man', and he sat down beside me.

Then I told him who I was and how this map had come into my possession and how I already knew of his existence. Gradually we entered into conversation. When the prince had become quite calm again, he proposed that we should return to his apartment in Cairo and quietly continue our conversation there.

From then on, owing to our common interests, a real bond was established between us; we met often, and our correspondence continued uninterruptedly for almost thirty-five years. During this period we travelled together many times, in India, Tibet and various parts of Central Asia.

We met the last time but one in Constantinople, where the prince had a house in Pera, which was not far from the Russian Embassy and where from time to time he stayed for rather long periods.

This meeting took place in the following circumstances:

I was returning from Mecca in the company of some Bukharian dervishes whose acquaintance I had made there, and of several Sart pilgrims who were going home. I wished to go to Tiflis via Constantinople, then to Alexandropol to see my family, and afterwards to go on with the dervishes to Bukhara. But all these plans were changed owing to my unexpected meeting with the prince.

On arriving at Constantinople I learned that our steamer would stay there for six or seven days. For me this was most annoying news. To wait for a week, hanging about without anything to do was not the most agreeable of prospects. I therefore decided to make use of this time to visit a dervish acquaintance of mine in Broussa and incidentally see the famous Green Mosque. Going ashore at Galata, I decided to go first to the prince's house and tidy myself up, and at the same time to see the prince's amiable old Armenian housekeeper, Mariam Badji.

According to his last letters, the prince should by then have been in Ceylon, but to my astonishment he turned out to be still in Constantinople and even at home. As I have already said, we frequently wrote, but it was two years since we had seen each other, and this meeting was therefore a happy surprise for both of us.

I put off my trip to Broussa and even had to give up my plan of going straight to the Caucasus, in view of the prince's request that I should accompany to Russia a young woman on whose account his trip to Ceylon had also been temporarily abandoned.

That same day I went to the bath, tidied myself up and had supper with the prince. While telling me about himself he related, with great animation and very vividly, the story of the young woman whom I had agreed to take to Russia.

As from my point of view this woman subsequently became remarkable in every respect, I wish not only to repeat her story as it was recounted by Prince Lubovedsky, but also to tell something about her later life, based on my personal meetings with her and on my own observations; the more so since the original manuscript in which I had written a more complete description of the life of this remarkable woman, under the title of 'Confessions of a Polish Woman', has remained in Russia among my many other manuscripts, the fate of which is still entirely unknown to me.

VITVITSKAIA

The prince told me the following story:

'A week ago I was leaving for Ceylon on a ship of the Volunteer Fleet. I was already on board. Among those who were seeing me off was an attaché of the Russian Embassy, who in the course of conversation drew my attention to a certain passenger, a venerable-looking old man.

' "You see that old man," he said. "Can anyone possibly believe that he is an important agent of the white slave traffic? Nevertheless it is so."

'This was said in passing. There was a great bustle on board and many people had come to see me off. Having no time to pay much attention to the old man, I quite forgot what the attaché had told me.

'The boat started. It was morning. The weather was fine. I was sitting on deck reading. Near me, romping about, was Jack.' (Jack was the prince's fox-terrier, who accompanied him everywhere.)

'A pretty girl passed and patted Jack. Then she brought him some sugar, but Jack never takes anything from anyone without my permission, so he cocked his head at me as if to ask "May I?" I nodded and said in Russian: "Yes, you may."

'It turned out that the young woman also spoke Russian and a conversation was started with the usual questions as to where each was going. She told me that she was going to Alexandria to take a place as governess in the family of the Russian consul.

'During our conversation the old man whom the attaché had pointed out to me came on deck and called the young woman. When they had gone off together, I suddenly recalled what had been said about this old man, and his acquaintance with this girl seemed to me suspicious. I began to think, searching my memory. I knew the consul in Alexandria and, as far as I could remember, he could not have needed a governess. My suspicions increased.

'Our boat had to stop at several ports, and at the first stop in the Dardanelles I sent two telegrams, one to the consul at Alexandria, asking whether he needed a governess, and the other to the consul at Salonika, where the boat was to stop next. I also confided my suspicions to the captain. In short, when we arrived at Salonika, what I had suspected was confirmed, and it became clear that this girl was being carried off under false pretences.

'I found the girl appealing, and I resolved to rescue her from the danger menacing her, to take her back to Russia and not to start off again for Ceylon until I had arranged something for her.

'We left the boat together at Salonika and the same day boarded another which was returning to Constantinople. As soon as we arrived I wished to send her back to her home, but it turned out that she had no one to whom she could go. That is why I have been delayed here.

'Her history is rather unusual. She is Polish, born in the Volyne province, and as a child lived not far from Rovno, on the estate of a certain count for whom her father was superintendent. There were two brothers and two sisters in the family. The mother died when they were all quite young and they were brought up by an old aunt. When this girl, Vitvitskaïa, was fourteen and her sister sixteen, their father died.

'At that time one brother was studying somewhere in Italy, preparing for the Catholic priesthood. The other had turned out to be a great scoundrel. He had run away from college the year before, and was in hiding, so it was rumoured, somewhere in Odessa.

'At the death of the father, the two sisters and their aunt were compelled to leave the estate since a new superintendent had been taken on. They moved to Rovno. Shortly afterwards, the old aunt also died. The situation of the sisters became difficult. On the advice of a distant relative, they sold their belongings and moved to Odessa, where they entered a vocational school to learn to be dressmakers.

'Vitvitskaïa was very beautiful and, in contrast to her elder sister, frivolous. She had a great many admirers, among them a commercial traveller who seduced her and took her off to St. Petersburg. As she had quarrelled with her sister, she took with her her share of their heritage. In St. Petersburg the commercial traveller robbed and deserted her, and she found herself penniless in a strange city.

'After many struggles and misfortunes, she finally became the mistress of an old senator; but he soon became jealous of some young student and turned her out. She then got into the "respectable" family of a certain doctor, who trained her to extend his practice by a very original method.

'The doctor's wife had met her in the garden in front of the Alexandra theatre, had sat down beside her, and had persuaded her to come and live with them. She then taught her the following manœuvre:

'She was to walk along the Nevski and when accosted by a man she was not to put him off, but allow him to accompany her home, give him diplomatic encouragement and leave him at the door. He would of course ask the porter about her and would be told that she was the companion of a certain doctor's wife. As a result of this procedure the doctor would acquire new patients, who invented some kind of ailment merely to get into his apartment in the hope of a pleasant meeting.

'In so far as I have had time to study the nature of Vitvitskaïa,' observed the prince with conviction, 'she must have been subconsciously depressed all the time by such a life, and only dire need could have constrained her to resort to it.

'One day, when she was walking on the Nevski for the purpose of picking up patients, she quite unexpectedly met her younger brother, whom she had not seen for several years. He was very well dressed and gave the impression of being rich. This meeting with her brother brought a ray of light into her cheerless life. It appeared that he had some kind of business in Odessa and abroad. When he learned that she was not particularly well off, he proposed that she should come to Odessa, where he had many connections and could arrange something good for her. She consented. On her arrival in Odessa her brother found her a very good situation with excellent prospects—governess in the family of the Russian consul in Alexandria.

'Several days later her brother introduced her to a very distinguished-looking old man, who happened to be going to Alexandria and who agreed to accompany her. And so, one fine day, accompanied by this apparently reliable gentleman, she went on board the boat and started on her way.

'What followed, you know. . . .'

The prince told me he believed that only circumstances and the unhappy conditions of her family life had brought her to the brink of ruin, that her nature was unspoiled and that she had many excellent qualities. He had therefore decided to interest himself in her life and put her on the right path. 'For this,' said the prince, 'I must first of all send the unfortunate girl to my sister on my estate in the Tambov province, so that she may have a good rest, and after that we will see. . . .'

Knowing the prince's idealism and kindness, I took a very

sceptical attitude toward his project and considered that in this case his efforts would be in vain. I even thought then: 'What falls from the wagon is lost!'

Without having even set eyes on Vitvitskaïa, there arose in me, for some reason or other, something like hatred for her; but I could not refuse the prince, and with a reluctant heart consented to accompany this, as I then thought, worthless woman.

I first saw her several days later when we boarded the boat. She was above middle height, very beautiful, with a good figure and brown hair. She had kind, honest eyes, which sometimes became diabolically cunning. It seems to me that the Thaïs of history must have been of the same type. At the first sight of her, she aroused in me a dual feeling towards her—now of hate, now of pity.

And so I went with her to the Tambov province. She stayed with the prince's sister, who became very fond of her and took her abroad where they lived for long periods, particularly in Italy. Little by little, under the influence of the prince's sister and the prince himself, she grew interested in their ideas, which soon became an integral part of her essence. She began to work on herself in earnest, and anyone who met her, even if only once, could feel the result of that work.

After I had taken her to Russia, I did not see her again for a long time. It was, it seems to me, at least four years later that I met her, quite by chance, with the sister of Prince Yuri Lubovedsky in Italy in the following peculiar circumstances:

Once I was in Rome, as always pursuing my aim, and since my money was fast running out, I followed the advice of two young Aïsors whose acquaintance I had made there, and with their help began to shine shoes on the street.

It could not be said that my business went very well at first, and so, to increase my income, I decided to run it on new and original lines. For this purpose I ordered a special armchair under which, hidden from onlookers, I placed an Edison phonograph. To this I attached a rubber tube with ear-pieces on the end, in such a way that whoever sat in the armchair could put them to his ears, and I would then unnoticeably set the machine in motion.

In this way my clients could listen to the 'Marseillaise' or an operatic air while I shined their shoes. In addition to this, I fastened to the right arm of the chair a little tray of my own make, on which I put a glass, a decanter of water, vermouth, and some illustrated magazines. Thanks to this, my business became more than successful, and lire, not centesimi, began to pour in. Rich young tourists paid particularly well.

Curious gapers would stand round me all day long, most of them waiting for their turn to sit in the armchair so that, while I shined their shoes, they could enjoy something never before seen or heard of, and incidentally show themselves off to the others who hung round all day, the same conceited fools as themselves.

In this crowd I often noticed a certain young lady. She attracted my attention because she seemed quite familiar to me, but for lack of time I did not look at her closely. One day I happened to hear her voice as she said in Russian to the elderly woman with her, 'I bet it is he', and I became so intrigued that, managing somehow to get free of my clients, I went straight up to her and asked her in Russian: 'Tell me please, who are you? It seems to me that I have seen you somewhere.'

'I am the person,' she replied, 'whom you once so hated that the flies which came into the sphere of the radiations of your hate perished. If you recall Prince Lubovedsky, then perhaps you will also recall the unfortunate girl you accompanied from Constantinople to Russia.'

I then immediately recognized her and also the elderly woman with her, the prince's sister. From that day until they left for Monte Carlo, I spent every evening with them at their hotel.

A year and a half after this meeting, accompanied by Professor Skridlov, Vitvitskaïa came to the meeting place for one of our big expeditions, and from then on was a permanent member of our itinerant band.

To illustrate the character of the inner world of Vitvitskaïa—this woman who had stood on the brink of moral ruin and who later, thanks to the aid of persons with ideas who chanced to cross the path of her life, became, I may boldly say, such as might serve as an ideal for every woman—I will confine myself here to telling about only one aspect of her many-sided inner life.

Among other interests she was particularly drawn to the science of music. The seriousness of her attitude towards this science may be shown clearly by a conversation we had during one of the expeditions of our group.

On this journey through the centre of Turkestan, thanks to special introductions, we stayed for three days in a certain monastery not accessible to everyone. The morning we left this monastery, Vitvitskaïa was as pale as death, and her arm, for some reason or other, was in a sling. For a long time she could not mount her horse by herself, and another comrade and I had to help her.

When the whole caravan was under way, I rode beside Vitvitskaïa, a little behind all the others. I very much wanted to know what had happened to her and questioned her insistently. I thought that perhaps one of our comrades had acted the brute and had dared in some way to insult her—a woman who had become sacred for us all—and I wished to find out who the scoundrel was, in order, without dismounting and without words, to shoot him down like a partridge.

To my questions Vitvitskaïa finally replied that the cause of her state was, as she expressed it, that 'damned music', and she asked me if I remembered the music of the night before last.

I did indeed remember how all of us, sitting in some corner of the monastery, had almost sobbed, listening to the monotonous music performed by the brethren during one of their ceremonies. And although we had talked about it afterwards for a long time, none of us could explain the reason for it.

After a little pause Vitvitskaïa began to talk of her own accord, and what she said about the cause of her strange state took the form of a long story. I do not know whether it was because the scenery through which we were riding that morning was indescribably glorious or whether there was some other reason, but what she then told me with such sincerity, I still remember almost word for word even after all these years. Each of her words was so strongly imprinted on my brain that it seems to me I hear her at this moment.

She began as follows:

'I do not remember whether there was anything in music that touched me inwardly when I was still quite young, but I do remember very well how I thought about it. Like everybody else I did not wish to appear ignorant and, in praising or criticizing a piece of music, I judged it only with my mind. Even when I was quite indifferent to the music I heard, if my opinion was asked about it, I expressed a view, for or against, according to the circumstances.

'Sometimes when everyone praised it I spoke against it, using all the technical words I knew, so that people should think I was not just anyone, but an educated person who could discriminate in everything. And sometimes I condemned it in unison with others, because I thought that, if they criticized it, there was doubtless something in it which I did not know about, for which it should be criticized. But if I praised a piece of music, it was because I assumed that the composer, whoever he might be, having been occupied with this matter all his life, would not let any composition see the light if it did not deserve it. In short, in either praising or blaming, I was always insincere with myself and with others, and for this I felt no remorse of conscience.

'Later, when that good old lady, the sister of Prince Lubovedsky, took me under her wing, she persuaded me to learn to play the piano. "Every well-educated, intelligent woman," she said, "should know how to play this instrument." In order to please the dear old lady, I gave myself up wholly to learning to play the piano, and in six months I did indeed play so well that I was invited to take part in a charity concert. All our acquaintances present praised me to the skies and expressed astonishment at my talent.

'One day, after I had been playing, the prince's sister came over to me and very seriously and solemnly told me that, since God had given me such a talent, it would be a great sin to neglect it and not let it develop to the full. She added that, as I had begun to work on music, I should be really educated in this field, and not just play like any Mary Smith, and she therefore thought that I should first of all study the theory of music and, if necessary, even take an examination.

'From that day on she began sending for all kinds of books on music for me, and she even went to Moscow herself to buy them. Very soon the walls of my study were lined with enormous bookcases filled to overflowing with all kinds of musical publications.

'I devoted myself very zealously to studying the theory of music, not only because I wished to please my benefactress but also because I myself had become greatly attracted to this work, and my interest in the laws of music was increasing from day to day. My books, however, were of no help to me, for nothing whatsoever was said in them either about what music is, or on what its laws are based. They merely repeated in different ways information about the history of music, such as: that our octave has seven notes, but the ancient Chinese octave had only five; that the harp of the ancient Egyptians was called *tebuni* and the flute *mem*; that the melodies of the ancient Greeks were constructed on the basis of different modes such as the Ionian, the Phrygian, the Dorian and various others; that in the ninth century polyphony appeared in music, having at first so cacophonic an effect that there was even a case of premature delivery of a pregnant woman, who suddenly heard in church the roar of the organ playing this music; that in the eleventh century a certain monk, Guido d'Arezzo, invented solfege, and so on and so forth. Above all, these books gave details about famous musicians, and how they had become famous; they even recorded what kind of neckties and spectacles were worn by such and such composers. But as to what music is, and what effect it has on the psyche of people, nothing was said anywhere.

'I spent a whole year studying this so-called theory of music. I read almost all my books and finally became definitely convinced that this literature would give me nothing; but my interest in music continued to increase. I therefore gave up all my reading and buried myself in my own thoughts.

'One day, out of boredom, I happened to take from the prince's library a book entitled *The World of Vibrations*, which gave my thoughts about music a definite direction. The author of this book was not a musician at all, and from the contents it was obvious that he was not even interested in music. He was an engineer and mathematician. In one place in his book he mentioned music merely as an example for his explanation of vibrations. He wrote that the sounds of music are made up of certain vibrations which doubtless act upon the vibrations which are also in a man, and this is why a man likes or dislikes this or that music. I at once understood this, and I fully agreed with the engineer's hypotheses.

'All my thoughts at that time were absorbed by these interests and, when I talked with the prince's sister, I always tried to turn the conversation to the subject of music and its real significance. As a result she herself became interested in this question, and we pondered over it together and also began to make experiments.

'The prince's sister even bought several cats and dogs and other animals specially for this purpose. We also began inviting some of our servants, served them tea and for hours on end played the piano for them. At first our experiments produced no result; but once, when we had as guests five of our servants and ten peasants from the village formerly owned by the prince, half of them fell asleep while I was playing a waltz of my own composition.

'We repeated this experiment several times, and each time the number of those who fell asleep increased. And although the old lady and I, making use of all kinds of principles, composed other music intended to have different effects on people, nevertheless the only result we attained was to put our guests to sleep. Finally, from constantly working on music and thinking about it, I grew so tired and thin that one day, when the old lady looked at me attentively, she became alarmed and, on the suggestion of an acquaintance, hastened to take me abroad.

'We went to Italy and there, distracted by other impressions, I gradually began to recover. It was only after five years had passed, when we went on our Pamir-Afghanistan expedition and witnessed the experiments of the Monopsyche Brotherhood, that I again began to think about the effect of music, but not with the same enthusiasm as at first.

'In later years, whenever I remembered my first experiments with music, I could not help laughing at our naïveté in giving such significance to the guests' falling asleep from our music. It never entered our heads that these people fell asleep from pleasure, simply because they had gradually come to feel at home with us, and because it was very agreeable after a long day's work to eat a good supper, drink the glass of vodka offered them by the kind old lady, and sit in soft armchairs.

'After witnessing the experiments and hearing the explanations of the Monopsyche brethren, I later, on my return to Russia, resumed my experiments on people. I found, as the brothers had advised, the absolute "la" according to the atmospheric pressure of the place where the experiment was to be carried out, and tuned the piano correspondingly, taking into consideration also the dimensions of the room. Besides this, I chose for the experiments people who already had in themselves the repeated impressions of certain chords; and I also took into consideration the character of the place and the race of each one present. Yet I could not obtain identical results, that is to say, I was not able by one and the same melody to evoke identical experiences in everyone.

'It cannot be denied that when the people present corresponded absolutely to the mentioned conditions, I could call forth at will in all of them laughter, tears, malice, kindness and so on. But when they were of mixed race, or if the psyche of one of them differed just a little from the ordinary, the results varied and, try as I might, I could not succeed in evoking with one and the same music the mood I desired in all the people without exception. Therefore I gave up my experiments once more, and as it were considered myself satisfied with the results obtained.

'But here, the day before yesterday, this music almost without melody evoked the same state in all of us—people not only of different race and nationality, but even quite unlike in character, type, habits and temperament. To explain this by the feeling of human "herdness" was out of the question, as we have recently experimentally proved that in all our comrades, thanks to corresponding work on themselves, this feeling is totally absent. In a word, there was nothing the day before yesterday that could have produced this phenomenon and by which it could somehow or other be explained. And after listening to this music, when I returned to my room, there again arose in me the intense desire to know the real cause of this phenomenon, over which I had racked my brains for so many years.

'All night long I could not sleep, but only thought what could be the real meaning of it all. And the whole day yesterday I continued to think, and even lost my appetite. I neither ate nor drank anything, and last night I grew so desperate that either from rage or exhaustion or for some other reason, I almost without knowing it bit my finger, and so hard that I nearly severed it from my hand. That is why my arm is now in a sling. It hurts so much that I can hardly sit on my horse.'

Her story touched me deeply, and with all my heart I wanted to help her in some way. In my turn I told her how a year earlier I had happened to come across a phenomenon, also connected with music, which had greatly astonished me.

I told her how thanks to a letter of introduction from a certain great man, Father Evlissi, who had been my teacher in childhood, I had been among the Essenes, most of whom are Jews, and that by means of very ancient Hebraic music and songs they had made plants grow in half an hour, and I described in detail how they had done this. She became so fascinated by my story that her cheeks even burned. The result of our conversation was that we agreed that as soon as we returned to Russia we would settle down in some town where, without being disturbed by anyone, we could really seriously carry out experiments with music.

After this conversation, for all the rest of the trip, Vitvitskaïa was her usual self again. In spite of her injured finger, she was the nimblest of all in climbing every cliff, and she could discern at a distance of almost twenty miles the monuments indicating the direction of our route.

Vitvitskaïa died in Russia from a cold she caught while on a trip on the Volga. She was buried in Samara. I was there at the time of her death, having been called from Tashkent when she fell ill.

Recalling her now, when I have already passed the half-way mark of my life and have been in almost all countries and seen thousands of women, I must confess that I never have met and probably never will meet another such woman.

And so, to continue my interrupted story of my elder comrade, my essence-friend Prince Lubovedsky, I will say that soon after my departure from Constantinople he also left, and I did not see him again for several years. But thanks to letters which I received from him periodically, I was kept more or less informed as to where he was and what was the most important interest of his life at the given time.

First he went to the island of Ceylon, and then undertook a journey up the river Indus to its source. After that he wrote to me at various times from Afghanistan, from Baluchistan, from Kafiristan, until our correspondence suddenly ceased; and from then on there was neither news nor rumour of him.

I was convinced that he had perished on one of his journeys, and little by little I had become accustomed to the thought that I had lost for ever the man nearest to me, when suddenly, quite unexpectedly, I ran across him again in exceptional circumstances in the very heart of Asia.

In order to throw more light on this last meeting of mine with a man who, according to my notions, represents in contemporary conditions of life an ideal worthy of imitation, I must again interrupt my present story to say something about a certain Soloviev, who also became my friend and comrade. Soloviev was later an authority on what is called Eastern medicine in general, and on Tibetan medicine in particular, and he was also the world's greatest specialist in the knowledge of the action of opium and hashish on the psyche and organism of man.

My last meeting with Yuri Lubovedsky took place during a journey in Central Asia on which I was accompanied by Soloviev.

SOLOVIEV

Four or five miles from the town of Bukhara, the capital of the Bukharian khanate, the Russians had built round the station of the Transcaspian Railway the big new town called New Bukhara.

I was living in this new town when I first met Soloviev. I had gone there chiefly to visit places where I could gain a more thorough knowledge of the fundamental principles of the religion of Mohammed, and to be able to meet Bukharian dervish acquaintances of various sects, among whom was my great and old friend Bogga-Eddin. He was not at that time in Bukhara and nobody knew where he had gone; but I had grounds for counting on his speedy return.

On my arrival in New Bukhara I had taken a small room in the house of a fat Jewess who sold Russian *kvass*. I lived in this room with my devoted friend, a large Kurd sheep-dog, Philos, who for nine years accompanied me on all my wanderings. This Philos, by the way, quickly became famous in any town or village where I happened to stay for a while, particularly among small boys, thanks to his talent for bringing me hot water for my tea from the *chaikhanas* and taverns to which I sent him with a kettle. He even used to go with a note from me to make purchases.

In my opinion this dog was so astonishing that I do not consider it superfluous to spend a little of my time acquainting the reader with his rare psyche. I will in any case describe a few incidents showing the associative ingenuity of his psychic manifestations.

A little before this, I had gone to the Bukharian town of P to see several dervishes of a certain sect who were then living there, and with whom Bogga-Eddin had advised me to get acquainted. The first incident took place just after these dervishes had left the town of P and I myself had decided to move to the city of Samarkand.

My financial resources were almost at an end and, after paying for my room in the caravanserai and settling my other debts in P, the very most I would have left would be sixty kopeks. It was impossible in that town to earn money in any way, because it was not the working season, and it was none too easy in such a remote place, far from European civilization, to sell any artistic or mechanical trifles. In Samarkand, on the other hand, there were many Russians and other Europeans; besides, foreseeing the possibility of my going to Samarkand, I had already given instructions to have money sent to me there from Tiflis.

Not having the wherewithal to pay for the trip, I decided to do this distance, about seventy miles, on foot, and one fine day I set out with my friend Philos. Before leaving I bought myself five kopeks' worth of bread and for another five kopeks a sheep's head for Philos. I drew on our supply of food, mine as well as Philos', very economically, so it could not be said that we were satisfied.

At a certain place on both sides of the road were *bostani*, that is, vegetable gardens. In many parts of Turkestan it is the custom to fence off one garden from another and from the road, by planting hedges of Jerusalem artichokes, which grow very high and thick and serve the purpose of wooden or wire fences. Walking along, I came to just this kind of fence.

As I was very hungry, I decided to dig up several artichokes. Looking round to see whether anyone could see me, I hastily dug up four big artichokes and, as I continued on my way, ate them with great pleasure. I also gave a piece to Philos to try, but after sniffing at it he refused to eat it.

Arriving in New Samarkand, I took a room in the house of a local inhabitant on the outskirts of the town, and went off at once to the post-office to see if my money had come from Tiflis, but it had not yet arrived. Pondering on where to get money I decided to earn some by making artificial paper flowers. For this purpose I immediately went to a shop to buy coloured paper, but, calculating that for my fifty kopeks I could get very little, I decided simply to buy some thin white paper and a little aniline dye of different colours and to colour the paper myself. In this way for a trifling sum I could produce a large quantity of flowers.

From the shop I went to the town gardens to rest on a bench in the shade of the trees. My Philos sat down beside me. Buried in my thoughts, I looked at the trees where sparrows flitted from branch to branch enjoying the stillness of the afternoon. Suddenly the thought entered my head: 'Why not try to make money with the sparrows? The inhabitants of this place, the Sarts, are very fond of canaries and other kinds of song birds; is a sparrow any worse than a canary?'

On the street which ran alongside the town gardens was a cab-stand, where a number of drivers were resting and dozing on their boxes in the afternoon heat. I went over and plucked from the horses' tails the hairs I needed, made snares of them and set them in various places, Philos watching me all the time with great attention. A sparrow soon fell into one of the snares. I carefully took it out and carried it home.

At the house I asked the landlady for scissors, clipped my sparrow to the shape of a canary, and then coloured it fantastically with the aniline dyes. I took this sparrow to Old Samarkand, where I immediately sold it, claiming that it was a special 'American canary'. I charged two roubles for it. With the money I at once bought several simple painted cages and from then on began selling my sparrows in cages. In two weeks I sold about eighty of these American canaries.

The first three or four days when I went to catch sparrows, I took Philos with me; but after this I did not take him any more because by then he had become a celebrity among the small boys of New Samarkand, and a crowd of them would come up to him in the town gardens, scare the sparrows and interfere with my catching them.

The day after I stopped taking Philos with me, he disappeared from the house early in the morning and only returned in the evening, tired and covered with dirt, and solemnly placed on my bed a sparrow—to be sure, a dead one. This was repeated each day; he would leave early in the morning and would invariably bring back and place on my bed a dead sparrow.

I did not risk a long stay in Samarkand. I was afraid that the devil would play a joke, and that my sparrows might suddenly get wet in the rain or that some American canary in its cage might take a fancy to bathing in its drinking trough, and then indeed there would be a great uproar, as my American canaries would be turned into disfigured, clipped and miserable sparrows. So I hastened to get away with my skin whole.

From Samarkand I went to New Bukhara, where I expected to find my friend, the dervish Bogga-Eddin. I felt like a rich man, for I had over a hundred and fifty roubles in my pocket, which at that time was considered a fairly large sum.

In New Bukhara, as I have already said, I took a room in the house of a fat Jewish woman who sold *kvass*. This room had no furniture, and at night I spread out a clean sheet in one corner for a bed and slept on it without a pillow. I did not do this for economy alone. No. . . . It cannot be denied that such a way of sleeping is indeed very cheap, but I did this chiefly because at that period of my life I was a pure-blooded follower of the ideas of the famous Hindu yogis. All the same I must confess that in those days, even at times of great material difficulty, I could not deny myself the luxury of lying on a clean sheet and of rubbing myself at night with eau de Cologne, which had to be of a strength not less than eighty per cent.

Five or ten minutes after I lay down, when according to the calculations of Philos I should already be asleep, he too would lie down on this improvised bed of mine, never on the side towards my face but at my back. At the head of this 'ultra-comfortable' bed there was a no less comfortable little table formed of books, tied together with a string, and dealing with the questions to which I was particularly drawn at the time. On this original library table I put all the things I might need at night such as an oil lamp, a notebook, bug-powder and so on.

One morning, several days after my arrival in New Bukhara, I found on my improvised table a large Jerusalem artichoke. I remember thinking at the time: 'Ah, that minx of a landlady! In spite of her weight, she is so perceptive that she has immediately detected my weakness for Jerusalem artichokes,' and I ate it with great pleasure.

I was quite convinced it was the landlady who had brought me this artichoke for the simple reason that so far no one besides her had entered my room. So, when I met her the same day in the corridor, I confidently thanked her and even teased her about the artichoke, but to my great surprise she made it clear to me that she knew nothing whatever about it.

The next morning I again saw a Jerusalem artichoke in the same place and, although I ate this one with no less pleasure, I began to think seriously about its mysterious appearance in my room.

What was my astonishment when on the third day the same thing was repeated! This time I firmly resolved to investigate, and find out without fail who was playing such puzzling but pleasant tricks on me; but for several days I could not discover anything, although punctually every morning I found a Jerusalem artichoke in the same place.

One morning, in order to clear up this matter, which mystified me more and more each day, I hid behind a barrel of fermenting *kvass* in the corridor. After a short time I saw Philos cautiously stealing past the barrel, carrying in his mouth a large Jerusalem artichoke. He went into my room and placed it just where I usually found them. From then on I began to keep a close watch on Philos.

The next morning when I was about to leave the house, I patted Philos on the left side of his head, which meant between us that I was going far away and was not taking him with me; but going out into the street, I walked only a short distance and then returned to the shop opposite our house and began watching my door.

Very soon out came Philos, and glancing round he set off in the direction of the market; surreptitiously, I followed. At the market, near the municipal scales, were a great many provision shops and a crowd of people. I saw Philos quietly walking through the crowd and did not let him out of my sight.

Passing in front of a shop, he looked round and, when he was sure that nobody was watching him, he quickly snatched a Jerusalem artichoke from a sack standing there and set off at a run, and when I returned home I found a Jerusalem artichoke in the usual place.

I will describe one more feature of the psyche of this astonishing dog. Usually, when I left home and did not take him with me, he lay outside my door and awaited my return. In my absence anyone who wished could enter my room, but he would not allow anyone to leave it. If anyone did wish to leave my room while I was away, this huge dog would begin growling and baring his teeth, which was quite enough to make any stranger's heart sink into his boots.

I will tell for example about an incident, connected with my late really genuine friend Philos, which also took place in New Bukhara. The day before this incident a certain Pole, who was what was then called a travelling cinematographer, came to me, on the advice of local inhabitants who knew me as the only specialist in this work, with an order to repair one of his two containers for acetylene gas, by means of which these strolling artists projected their cinematographic pictures. I had promised this Pole to call soon in my spare time and repair his container.

But it turned out that the very day after our conversation, the Polish cinematographer noticed that the gas was beginning to escape from the other container also, and, fearing that his entire next show would break down, he decided not to wait for me to come, but to bring me the container himself. When he learned that I was not at home but that my room was open, he decided not to carry back the heavy container but to leave it in my room.

That morning I had gone to Old Bukhara, where I intended to visit a certain mosque, and since it is considered a great desecration, particularly among the followers of the Mohammedan religion, for dogs to enter temples or their adjacent courts, I was obliged to leave Philos at home, and as usual he was lying outside the door waiting for my return.

And so, as was his custom, Philos allowed the travelling cinematographer to enter the room, but to leave it—not on your life! And after several vain attempts to leave, this poor Pole had to resign himself to sitting on the floor of my room, without food or drink, fretting all the time, until I returned late in the evening.

And so, I was living in New Bukhara . . . and this time I really began to work at making artificial paper flowers, to earn money and for various other advantages. In selling them I was able to enter almost all the places of interest to me in Bukhara, and, besides this, the income from this trade at that season of the year promised to be good.

It was near the end of Lent and, as is well known, the inhabitants of those places like to decorate their rooms and tables with flowers for the Easter Holidays. Moreover, that year the Jewish and Christian Easter almost coincided and, as the population of New Bukhara and part of Old Bukhara consisted mostly of people belonging to these two religions, the demand for artificial flowers was particularly great.

I buckled down to work in real earnest, day and night, leaving only rarely to go and see my dervish friends, or occasionally, on evenings when I was very tired, to play billiards at a near-by restaurant. In my youth I was very fond of this game and quite skilful at it.

One night, the evening of Holy Thursday, having finished my work, I had gone to play billiards, when suddenly during the game I heard noise and shouting in the next room. Throwing down my cue, I ran in and saw four men beating up another one.

Although I did not know these people at all or what the trouble was about, I ran to the rescue of the one who was being attacked. In my youth I used to be enthusiastic about Japanese ju-jutsu and Hivintzian *fiz-les-loo* and was always glad of an opportunity to apply my knowledge of these methods. So now also, just for the sport of it, I joined hotly in the fight, with the result that the two of us, the stranger and I, gave our opponents a good licking and soon forced them to retire.

At that time New Bukhara was still quite a new town. The population was made up of haphazard elements, including many exiles from Russia living under the surveillance of the police on what were called 'wolf tickets'.

They were a motley crowd of people of all nationalities, some with a past, some perhaps with a future. Among them were criminals who had already served their terms, and also many political exiles either sent there by the courts or by the administrative orders widely used at that time in Russia.

The surroundings and conditions of life of these exiles were so wretched that all of them without exception gradually became drunkards; even those who formerly never drank and had no hereditary predisposition to drink fell quite naturally and easily into this common tendency.

The company in whose fight I had got mixed up belonged to this category. After the fight I wished to take my companion-in-arms to his home, fearing that if he went alone something unpleasant might happen to him on the way, but it turned out that he lived in the same place as the other four, in repair cars on the railroad tracks. As it was already night, there was nothing to be done but suggest that he come home with me, to which he agreed.

My new acquaintance—and this was Soloviev—turned out to be still a young man, but it was clear that he had already taken to drink. He had come out of the fight rather damaged; his face was all bruised and one eye badly blackened. The next morning his eye was swollen almost shut, and I persuaded him not to leave but to stay with me until it was better, the more so since the Easter Holidays had begun and he had finished work the day before. On Good Friday he went off somewhere, but came back to spend the night with me.

The next day I had to run about almost all day long. I had to deliver the flowers ordered for Easter. I was not free until evening, and as I had no Christian acquaintances and nowhere to go to celebrate, I bought a *khoulitch*, *paskha*, some painted eggs and everything else customary for this feast, as well as a small bottle of vodka, and brought them home.

I did not find Soloviev in, and so, after washing and making myself tidy—I had no other clothes to change into—I went off alone to the evening service at the church. When I returned, I found Soloviev already asleep. As there was no table in my room, I quietly, so as not to disturb him, brought in from the court outside a large empty case, covered it with a clean sheet and placed on it all the things I had bought for the feast, and only then woke Soloviev.

He was very surprised at everything he saw, and gladly consented to participate in this solemn repast. He got up and we sat down together at the 'table', he on my books and I on a pail turned upside down.

First of all I poured out a glass of vodka for each of us, but to my astonishment he thanked me and refused to drink. I drank alone, and Soloviev began to eat. Philos, who was present at this celebration, received a double portion, two sheep's heads. We sat in silence and ate. It was not a happy Easter either for me or for Soloviev. Picturing to myself the familiar scene of the family feast, I began to think of my family far away. Soloviev also was thinking about something, and we sat a rather long time without speaking.

All of a sudden, as if to himself, Soloviev exclaimed: 'Help me, O Lord, in memory of this night, to be able never again to drink this poison which has brought me to such a life!' He fell silent, and then with a disconsolate gesture murmured, 'Ah . . . me!' and began telling me about his life.

I do not know what had affected him. Was it because Easter recalled to him distant and dear memories of the time when he had been a man, or was it the sight of the carefully arranged table and the unexpected feast, or both together? Whatever it was, he poured his heart out to me.

It seemed that Soloviev had once been a post-office employee, but had become so quite by chance. He came from a merchant family of Samara, where his father owned big flour mills. His mother came of an impoverished noble family. She had been educated at a finishing school for the aristocracy, and her upbringing of her children consisted exclusively in teaching them good manners and how to behave; this was all they had been stuffed with.

His father was hardly ever at home, spending his time at his mills and grain shops. Moreover, he was addicted to drink, and regularly several times a year he would drink steadily for several weeks. Even when sober he was, in the words of his son, an 'overbearing fool'.

The parents of Soloviev, each living their own separate lives and with their own interests, merely endured one another. Soloviev had one younger brother, and both boys went to the public school. The parents had even, as it were, divided up the children. The elder son was the mother's favourite, the younger the father's, and on this account there were frequent scenes. The father never addressed his elder son without a sneer, so that a kind of hostility gradually grew up between them. The mother, who received money from her husband for expenses, gave Soloviev a certain amount monthly. But with the years his appetites increased, and his allowance was not sufficient for paying court to girls. Once he stole a bracelet from his mother and sold it to make some gift or other.

When she discovered this theft, she concealed it from his father; but the thefts began to be repeated and one day his father, learning of them, made a great scene and turned Soloviev out of the house, although later, through the intervention of relatives and the mother, he pardoned him.

Soloviev was in the fifth—or next to the highest—class of the school when a travelling circus stopped in Samara and he lost his head completely over a bare-back rider named Verka. When the circus moved to Tsaritsyn, Soloviev followed her there, having got hold of money in some fraudulent way from his mother.

At this time he had already begun to drink. In Tsaritsyn he learned that his Verka had taken up with a captain of the mounted police and, out of bitterness, he took to drinking heavily. He began to frequent the port taverns and found a great many companions like himself.

It ended one fine day in everything being stolen from him while drunk, and he found himself in a strange town without a kopek and not daring to send word of himself to his family.

Having gradually sold his personal belongings and clothing, he was finally compelled to exchange even the clothes he was wearing for mere rags, and thus became an outcast in the full sense of the word.

Hunger forced him to work in a fishery, and, passing from one job to another, he finally came, in the company of other outcasts, to the town of Baku. Here fate smiled on him a little; someone gave him clothes and he succeeded in becoming a telephone operator in the district of Balakhna.

The adversities of his recent past made him think and he began to work steadily. One day he met someone from Samara who, having learned who he was, that is, of what family he came, decided to help him get a better position.

As Soloviev had a fifth-class education, he was taken on in Baku as an assistant in the postal-telegraph service, but for the first few months he had to work without a salary. After this, he received a post in Kushka and worked there as a clerk. Thanks to his abstinence, he was able to dress decently and even saved a small sum of money.

When he was twenty-one he received a notice from the military authorities that he was about to be called up for military service. This obliged him to return to his native town, and on arriving in Samara he put up at a hotel and wrote to his mother. His mother, who had been receiving letters from him before this, was glad that her son had apparently turned over a new leaf, and succeeded in obtaining his father's pardon for him.

Soloviev was again received into the house and his father, seeing that his son had come to his senses, was glad that things had turned out no worse and began to treat him well.

On reporting to the military authorities Soloviev drew a lot to serve, but being a telegraphist in the postal service he had to wait several months for his appointment, since recruits of this category were appointed to vacancies by the central administration of the army. So he lived with his parents another three or four months before being ordered to a post with the railway battalion in charge of the Transcaspian Railway, which at that time was still militarized.

When he arrived at his post and had done several weeks of compulsory service as a private soldier in the second company, he was assigned to what was called the Kushka Line, but soon afterwards he fell ill with jaundice and was sent to the hospital at Merv, where his company was stationed. When he recovered he was sent to the battalion headquarters at Samarkand, and then to the military hospital there, to be examined for his fitness for further military service.

In the main building of the hospital, in which Soloviev was placed, there was also a ward for prisoners. Walking along the corridor, and occasionally talking with the prisoners through a little window, he made the acquaintance of one of them, a Pole, who had been accused of counterfeiting.

When Soloviev was given leave from service on account of poor health and discharged from the hospital, this prisoner asked him to take a letter to a friend of his who lived near the station in Samarkand. As thanks for delivering the letter, he stealthily handed him a phial of blue liquid, explaining that this liquid could be used to counterfeit the green three-rouble notes—but not any other kind—and that this was done in the following way:

Special paper, moistened with this liquid, was applied to both sides of the note and then everything was pressed together in a book. The negatives obtained in this way from both sides of the note gave three or four good copies.

In Central Asia, where people were not well acquainted with Russian money, these notes were very easy to pass. Soloviev, who first tried this process out of curiosity, found himself in need of money just before his departure for home and with no particular risk passed a small quantity of his counterfeits.

At home he was warmly welcomed, and his father urged him to stay and help him as the younger brother was doing. Soloviev consented and was given the direction of one of the mills somewhere outside Samara. But after working there several months he began to get bored and, longing for his vagabond life, went to his father and told him frankly that he could not go on any longer. His father let him go and even gave him a good deal of money.

After this, Soloviev went to Moscow and to St. Petersburg, again took to drink, and finally arrived, drunk, in Warsaw. It was about a year after he had been given leave from military service. In Warsaw he was stopped on the street by a man who turned out to be the prisoner he had known in the Samarkand hospital. It seemed he had been acquitted by the court and had come to Warsaw chiefly for paper and for a note-printing machine which he was expecting from Germany. He invited Soloviev to enter into partnership with him and help him in his 'work' in Bukhara.

Soloviev was tempted by this criminal but easy profit. He went to Bukhara to wait for his companion, but the Polish counterfeiter was delayed in Warsaw waiting for his machine. Soloviev continued to drink and, having squandered what was left of his money, got some job with the railway, where he had been working for three months before I met him—drinking incessantly all the while.

Soloviev's frank story touched me deeply. At that time I already knew a great deal about hypnotism and, after bringing a man into a certain state, could influence him by suggestion to forget any undesirable habit. I therefore proposed to Soloviev that I should help him, if he really wished to get rid of this pernicious habit of drinking vodka, and explained to him how I would do it. He agreed, and the next day and each day thereafter I brought him into the hypnotic state and made the necessary suggestions. He gradually came to feel such an aversion to vodka that he could not even bear to look at this 'poison', as he called it.

By this time Soloviev, having given up his railway work, had moved over to stay with me. He began to help me make the flowers, and sometimes took them to the market to sell.

When he had thus become my assistant and we had grown accustomed to living together like two good brothers, my friend, the dervish Bogga-Eddin, of whom I had had no news for two or three months, finally returned to Old Bukhara. Learning that I was in New Bukhara, he came to see me the next day.

When I asked him why he had been away so long, Bogga-Eddin answered as follows: 'I was away all this time because in one of the towns of Upper Bukhara I chanced to meet an extremely interesting man, and in order to see him more often and converse with him as much as possible about questions which profoundly disturbed me, I arranged to serve as his guide for a journey through Upper Bukhara and along the banks of the Amu Darya, and it is with him that I have come here now.'

'This old man,' continued Bogga-Eddin, 'is a member of a brotherhood, known among the dervishes by the name of Sarmoung, of which the chief monastery is somewhere in the heart of Asia.'

Bogga-Eddin further told me: 'During one of my conversations with this extraordinary being, it turned out that he somehow knew a great deal about you. I therefore asked him whether he would have anything against it if you should wish to see him.

'To this question he answered that he would be glad to see you, a man who—though by origin a *kaphir*—has succeeded, thanks to his impartial attitude towards all people, in acquiring a soul similar to ours.'

Kaphir is the name given to all foreigners of other faiths—and this includes all Europeans in general—who, according to the notions there, live like animals, without principles and without anything holy in them.

Everything that Bogga-Eddin told me about this man set my brain in a whirl, and I begged him to arrange a meeting for me as soon as possible. He readily agreed to do so, as at that moment the old man was not far away, staying with some acquaintances in Kishlak, near New Bukhara. We arranged to go there the next day.

I had several very long conversations with this old man. In the last one he advised me to go to his monastery and stay there for a time.

'Perhaps,' he explained, 'you will succeed in talking with someone or other there about the questions which interest you, and maybe in this way you will make clear to yourself what it is you seek.' He added that if I wished to go there, he would be willing to help me, and would find the necessary guides, on condition that I would take a solemn oath never to tell anyone where the monastery was situated.

I, of course, instantly agreed to everything. My only regret was to part from Soloviev, to whom I had become greatly attached; so, just on the chance, I asked the old man whether I could take a good friend of mine with me on this journey. After thinking a little, he replied: 'I think you may, if, of course, you can vouch for his honour and for his keeping the oath, which will be required of him also.'

I could fully vouch for Soloviev, as during our friendship he had already proved his ability to keep his word.

When we had talked everything over, it was agreed that a month later, to the day, we would be met near the ruins of Yeni-Hissar on the banks of the Amu Darya, by people whom we would recognize by a password, and who would serve as our guides to the monastery.

On the appointed date, Soloviev and I arrived at the ancient ruins of the fortress of Yeni-Hissar, and that same day met the four Kara-Kirghiz who had been sent for us. After the customary ceremony, we all ate together, and when it began to grow dark we repeated the oath they required of us, and after they had pulled *bashliks*[1] over our eyes, we mounted our horses and rode off.

Throughout the whole of our journey, we strictly and conscientiously kept our oath not to look and not to try to find out where we were going and through what places we were passing. When we halted for the night, and occasionally by day when we ate in some secluded place, our *bashliks* were removed. But while on the way we were only twice permitted to uncover our eyes. The first time was on the eighth day, when we were about to cross a swinging bridge which one could neither cross on horseback nor walk over two abreast, but only in single file, and this it was impossible to do with eyes covered.

From the character of the surroundings then revealed to us we deduced that we were either in the valley of the Pyandzh River or of the Zeravshan, as there was a broad stream flowing

[1] A *bashlik* is a hood which may be put on in such a way as to cover the face completely.

beneath us, and the bridge itself with the mountains surrounding it was very similar to the bridges in the gorges of these two rivers.

It must be said that, had it been possible to cross this bridge blindfold, it would have been much better for us. Whether it was because we had gone for a long time before that with our eyes covered or for some other reason, I shall never forget the nervousness and terror we experienced in crossing this bridge. For a long time we could not bring ourselves even to set foot on it.

Such bridges are very often met with in Turkestan, wherever there is no other possible route, or in places where to advance one mile would otherwise require a twenty-day detour.

The sensation one has when one stands on one of these bridges and looks down to the bottom of the gorge, where there is usually a river flowing, can be compared to that of looking down from the top of the Eiffel Tower, only many times more intense; and when one looks up, the tops of the mountains are out of sight —they can only be seen from a distance of several miles.

Moreover, these bridges hardly ever have a handrail, and they are so narrow that only one mountain pack-horse can cross at a time; furthermore, they rock up and down as if one were walking on a good spring mattress—and I will not even speak about the feeling of uncertainty as to their strength.

For the most part they are held in place by ropes, made from the fibre of the bark of a certain tree, one end attached to the bridge and the other fastened to some near-by tree on the mountain side or to a projection of rock. In any case, these bridges are not to be recommended even to those who in Europe are called thrill-chasers. The heart of any European crossing these bridges would sink, not into his boots, but somewhere still lower.

The second time our eyes were uncovered was when we were about to pass a caravan. Evidently not wishing the peculiar cowls over our eyes to attract attention or excite suspicion, our guides considered it advisable that we remove them for this encounter. We did so just as we were going by a monument typical of Turkestan, standing right at the top of a mountain pass. In Turkestan there are many of these monuments, which are very cleverly placed; without them, we travellers would have no possibility of orienting ourselves in this chaotic, roadless region. They are usually erected on some elevated spot so that, if one knows the general plan of their placement, they can be seen a long way off, sometimes even from a score of miles. They are nothing more than single high blocks of stone or simply long poles driven into the ground.

Among the mountain folk there exist various beliefs concerning these monuments, such as the following: that at this spot some saint was either buried or was taken up alive to heaven, that he killed the 'seven-headed dragon' there, or that something else extraordinary happened to him at that place. Usually the saint in whose name the monument was erected is considered the protector of the entire surrounding countryside, and when a traveller has successfully overcome any difficulty natural to the region— that is, has escaped an attack by brigands or wild beasts, or has safely crossed a mountain or river, or surmounted any other danger—it is all attributed to the protection of this saint. And so any merchant, pilgrim or other traveller who has passed through these dangers brings to the monument some kind of offering in gratitude.

It became an established custom to bring as an offering something which, as is believed there, would mechanically remind the saint of the prayers of the person who brought the offering. Accordingly, they bring gifts such as a piece of cloth, the tail of an animal or something else of the kind, so that, with one end tied or fastened to the monument, the other end can flutter freely in the wind.

These things, moving in the wind, make the spot where the monument is placed visible to us travellers from a great distance. Whoever knows approximately the arrangement of these monuments can locate one of them from some elevated spot and make his way in its direction, and from it to the next, and so on. Without knowing the general pattern of their arrangement it is almost impossible to travel through these regions. There are no well-defined roads or footpaths and, if some paths do form of themselves, then, owing to the sudden changes of weather and the ensuing snowstorms, they very quickly change or are totally effaced. So if these landmarks were not there, a traveller trying to find suitable paths would become so confused that even the most delicate compass would be of no help to him. It is possible to pass through these regions only by establishing the direction from monument to monument.

On the way we changed horses and asses several times, and sometimes went on foot. More than once we had to swim rivers and cross mountains, and by our sensations of heat and cold it was evident that we sometimes descended into deep valleys or climbed very high. At last, when at the end of the twelfth day our eyes were uncovered, we found ourselves in a narrow gorge through which flowed a small stream whose banks were covered with a rich vegetation.

As it turned out, this was our last halt. After eating, we set off again, but this time not blindfold. We rode on asses up the stream, and after we had ridden half an hour through the gorge, a small valley opened up in front of us surrounded by high mountains. On our right, and in front of us, but a little to the left, we could see snow-capped peaks. While crossing the valley, after a bend in the road, we saw some buildings in the distance on the slope to our left. As we came nearer we were able to make out something like a fortress such as one finds on a smaller scale on the banks of the Amu Darya or the Pyandzh. The buildings were encircled by a high unbroken wall.

Finally we rode in at the first gate, where we were met by an old woman to whom our guides said something; they then immediately rode out again through the same gate. We were left alone with the old woman and, without haste, she led us to one of a number of small rooms, like cells, which were built round a small court, and, pointing to two beds that stood there, went away.

Soon a very venerable old man came and without questioning us about anything began conversing with us very amiably in Turkoman, as though we were old acquaintances of his. He showed us where everything was, and said that for the first few days our meals would be brought to us there. He advised us to rest after our journey, but added that if we were not tired we could go out and walk around. In short, he gave us to understand that we could live as we pleased.

As we were indeed very tired from our journey, we decided to rest a little and lay down. I slept like a log and was only awakened by a boy bringing tea-things and a samovar with green tea and our morning meal of hot maize-cakes, goat's cheese and honey. I wanted to question the boy as to where we could bathe, but unfortunately it turned out that he spoke no language but *Pshenzis*, and I knew nothing of that peculiar language except a few swear words.

Soloviev was already up and out; he returned about ten minutes later. He too had fallen sound asleep in the evening, but had waked late at night and, fearing to disturb someone, had at first lain quietly in bed memorizing Tibetan words. At sunrise he went out to look around but, as he was about to go out through the gate, an old woman had called to him and beckoned him to a small house in the corner of the court. He followed her, thinking that it was doubtless forbidden to go out, but when he entered her house it turned out that the good woman had simply wanted to give him some fresh, warm milk to drink, after which she even helped him herself to open the gate.

As no one else came to us, we decided, after drinking tea, to go for a walk and explore the neighbourhood. First of all we walked all round the high wall enclosing the buildings. Besides the gate through which we had entered, there was one other, smaller, on the north-west side.

Everywhere reigned an almost awesome quiet, broken only by the monotonous sound of a distant waterfall and the occasional twitter of birds. It was a hot summer day, the air was heavy; we were listless and not at all interested in the grandeur of the scenery round us; only the sound of the waterfall, as if bewitching us, drew us towards it. Without exchanging a word, Soloviev and I automatically went to this waterfall, which later became our favourite place.

Neither on that day nor on the following did anyone come to see us, but regularly three times a day we were brought food, consisting of milk products, dried fruit, and fish—black-spotted trout—and almost every hour our samovar was refilled. We either lay on our beds or went to the waterfall, where, to its monotonous sound, we memorized Tibetan words.

During all this time, neither at the waterfall nor on our way to it, did we meet a single person; except once, while we were sitting there, four young girls came by, but when they saw us they quickly turned aside and, passing through a little grove, entered the gate we had noticed on the north-west side.

On the morning of the third day, I was sitting in a shady spot by the waterfall and Soloviev, out of boredom, was wiseacring, in some way known only to himself, to determine by means of little sticks the altitude of the snow-capped peaks which rose before us, when suddenly we saw the boy who had brought us our first meal come running towards us. He gave Soloviev a note —a folded sheet of paper without an envelope.

Soloviev took the note and seeing the name 'Aga Georgi' written on it in Sart, he handed it to me in perplexity. When I opened the note and recognized the handwriting, everything went black before my eyes, so unexpected was it. It was the handwriting which I knew so well, of the man dearest to me in life, Prince Lubovedsky.

The note was written in Russian, and its contents were as follows:

'My dear child: I thought that I would have a stroke when I learned that you were here! I am distressed that I cannot rush at once to embrace you, and that I must wait till you yourself come to me. I am in bed; all these days I have not been out and have spoken to no one, and only just this moment have I learned that you are here. Ah, how glad I am that I shall soon see you! I am doubly glad of it, glad that you got here yourself, without my help or the help of our mutual friends (in which case I should have known), for it proves to me that during this time you have not been asleep. Come to me soon, and we will talk about everything! I also hear that you are with a comrade. Though I do not know him, I shall be happy to greet him as your friend.'

Without having read half the note, I had already begun to run, finishing the note as I ran, and waving to Soloviev to come quickly. Where I was running to I did not know. After me ran Soloviev and the boy. When we reached the first court, where we had been living, the boy took us to a second court and showed us the cell where the prince lay.

After a joyful greeting and embraces I asked the prince how he had fallen ill.

'Before this,' he said, 'I had been feeling very well. Two weeks ago, after bathing, I was cutting my toe-nails, and without noticing it I probably cut one too short, as afterwards, walking barefoot as usual, I must have got a splinter in this toe and it began to hurt. At first I paid no attention to it, thinking it would pass; but it became worse and finally began to fester. A week ago fever set in which continued to rise, and I was compelled to take to my bed. I even became delirious. The brethren tell me that I had blood-poisoning, but now the danger is over and I feel well. But enough about me. It is nothing. . . . I shall soon recover. But tell me quickly, how did you get here, by what miracle?'

I told him briefly of my life during the two years in which we had not seen each other; of chance meetings during that time, of my friendship with the dervish Bogga-Eddin, the incidents which resulted from it, and how I finally found myself there. I then asked him why he had disappeared from sight so suddenly, why I had had no news from him all this time, and why he had let me worry over the uncertainty about him until finally, with grief in my heart, I had resigned myself to the thought of having lost him for ever. And I told him how, in case by any chance they might be useful to him, I had had requiems held for him, regardless of expense and even though I did not fully believe in their efficacy.

Then I asked how he himself had got there and the prince answered as follows:

'When we last met in Constantinople, there had already begun in me a kind of inner lassitude, something like apathy. On the way to Ceylon and for the next year and a half, this apathy gradually took the form of what one might call a dreary disillusionment, and consequently there grew in me a sort of inner emptiness and all interests connected with life faded.

'When I arrived in Ceylon, I made the acquaintance of the famous Buddhist monk A. We spoke together often with great sincerity and as a result of our conversations we organized an expedition up the river Ganges, with a programme planned in advance and a route mapped out in detail, in the hope of finally clearing up the questions which evidently had been perturbing him just as they had me.

'This venture was for me personally as the last remaining straw at which I clutched and therefore when this journey turned out to have been just another chase after a mirage, everything finally died in me and I had no wish to undertake anything further.

'After this expedition I happened to go to Kabul again, where I gave myself up entirely to oriental idleness, living without any aims or interests whatsoever, automatically meeting old acquaintances and new. I often went to the house of my old friend, the Aga Khan. In the company of a host so rich in adventures as he, one could somehow pass one's time in the boring life of Kabul.

'One day I saw there among his guests, sitting in the place of honour, an old Tamil in a costume not at all suitable for the house of the Aga Khan. After greeting me, the Khan, seeing my perplexity, hurriedly whispered to me that this venerable old man was a great friend of his, a queer fellow to whom he was under great obligations, even for having once saved his life. The old man lived somewhere in the north, but occasionally came to Kabul either to see relatives or on some other business, and whenever he was there he came to see him, which always made the Aga Khan inexpressibly glad, as he had never in his life met a better man. He advised me to talk with him and added that, if I did, I should speak loudly as he was hard of hearing.

'The conversation interrupted by my entrance was resumed. It was about horses. The old man also took part in the discussion, and it was evident that he was a connoisseur of horses and had once been a great lover of them. Then the conversation changed to politics. They talked of the neighbouring countries, of Russia, and England, and when they were speaking of Russia, the Aga Khan, indicating me, jokingly said, "Please, do not say anything bad about Russia. You might offend our Russian guest."

'Although this was said in jest, it was clear to me that the Khan desired to prevent the inevitable denunciation of the Russians. There was at that time a widespread hatred there of the Russians and the English.

'Then the general conversation died down, and we began talking among ourselves in separate groups. I talked with the old man, to whom I felt more and more drawn. He spoke with me in the local language, asked where I came from and how long I had been in Kabul. Suddenly he started to speak Russian, very correctly, though with a pronounced accent, explaining that he had been in Russia, even in Moscow and St. Petersburg, and had also lived a long time in Bukhara, where he had met many Russians and had thus learned to speak Russian. He added that he was very glad of an opportunity to speak this language again, as for lack of practice he had already begun to forget it.

'A little later he said, among other things, that if it were agreeable to me and if I wished to speak in my native language and honour an old man, we could leave together and go to a *chaikhana* to sit for a while and talk. He explained that sitting in cafés and *chaikhanas* had been a weakness and habit of his from his youth, and that now, whenever he came to the city, he could not deny himself the pleasure of spending his free time that way, because, in spite of the noise and bustle, nowhere else could he think so well, and he added, "Doubtless that very noise and bustle is just the reason why one can think so well there."

'I consented to go with him, with the greatest pleasure, not of course in order to speak Russian, but for some reason I myself could not explain. Though already old myself, I was beginning to feel towards this old man as a grandson feels towards his beloved grandfather.

'Soon all the guests began to leave. The old man and I left together, talking on the way of one thing and another. When we reached the *chaikhana* we sat down on the open terrace where we were served green Bukharian tea. From the attention and deference paid to the old man it was evident that he was known and respected there.

'He had been speaking of the Tadzhiks, but after the first cup of tea he suddenly broke off the conversation, saying: "But these are trifles we are speaking about; this is not the point," and, after looking at me steadily, he glanced aside and became silent.

'The way he had so unexpectedly cut short the conversation, how he had ended it and that piercing look, all seemed to me strange and I said to myself, "Poor fellow, doubtless his thinking faculty has already begun to weaken with age and his mind has begun to wander," and I became painfully sorry for this dear old man.

'The feeling of pity began little by little to pass to myself. I reflected that my mind also would soon begin to wander and that the day was not far off when I too would not be able to direct my thoughts, and so on. I was so lost in these heavy but fleeting thoughts that I even forgot the old man. Suddenly I again heard his voice. The words he spoke instantly dispelled my gloomy thoughts, and shook me out of my state. My pity changed to such an astonishment as I think I had never experienced in my life before.

' "Eh, Gogo, Gogo! Forty-five years you have worked, suffered and laboured incessantly, and not once did you decide for yourself or know how to work so that, if only for a few months, the desire of your mind should become the desire of your heart. If you had been able to attain this, you would not now in your old age be in such solitude as you are!"

'The name "Gogo" which he had used made me start with amazement. How could this Hindu, who saw me for the first time somewhere in Central Asia, know the nickname by which I had been called in my childhood sixty years before, and then only by my mother and nurse, and which no one had ever repeated since then?

'Can you imagine my astonishment? I instantly recalled an old man who had come to see me once in Moscow after the death of my wife, when I was still a young man. I wondered, could this be the same mysterious man? But no. Firstly, the other was tall and did not resemble this one, and secondly, the other had surely died long before, as more than forty years had passed since that time and he had then been quite old. I could not find any explanation of this old man's obvious knowledge not only of me but also of my inner state, known to myself alone.

'While various similar thoughts flowed within me, the old man sat deeply absorbed in thought, and he gave a start when I finally mustered the strength to exclaim: "But who are you, who know me so well?"

' "Is it not all the same to you, just now, who I am and what I am?" he replied. "Is there really still alive in you that curiosity which is one of the chief reasons why the labours of your whole life have been without result? And is it really still so strong in you that even at this moment you are ready to give yourself up with your whole being to an analysis of my knowledge of your personality—only in order to explain to yourself who I am and how I know you?"

'The old man's reproach hit me in my weakest spot. "Yes, father, you are right," I said. "Is it not indeed all the same to me what is done and how it is done outside of me? Have I not witnessed many genuine miracles before this, and what understanding have I gained from them all? I only know that now I am empty within and I well know that I need not have been so empty if it had not been, as you say, for my inner enemy, and if, instead of wasting my time in being curious about what went on outside of me, I had struggled with this enemy.

' "Yes . . . now it is already too late! I ought to be indifferent to everything that goes on outside me, and therefore I do not wish to know what I just asked you nor do I wish to trouble you any further. I sincerely ask your pardon for the distress you have experienced on my account during these last few minutes."

'After this we sat for a long time, each occupied with his own thoughts. At last he broke the silence by saying:

' "No, perhaps it is not yet too late. If you feel with all your being that you really are empty, then I advise you to try once more. If you quite clearly feel and recognize without any doubt that everything for which you have striven until now has been a mirage, and if you agree to one condition, I will try to help you. And this condition is that you consciously die to the life you have led until now, that is to say, break away at once from all the automatically established practices of your external life and go where I shall indicate."

'To tell the truth there was no longer anything for me to break away from. It was not even a condition for me, because, apart from my ties with a few people, no interests existed for me any longer and, as for these ties, for various reasons I had recently had to force myself to stop thinking of them.

'I told him then and there that I was ready that very moment to go wherever necessary. He stood up, told me to liquidate all my affairs, and without another word disappeared in the crowd. The next day I settled all my affairs, gave certain instructions, wrote home several letters of a business character, and began to wait.

'Three days later a young Tadzhik came to me and said simply and laconically: "I have been hired as a guide for you. The journey will last about a month. I have prepared for it such and such . . ." and he enumerated what he had prepared. "Will you please tell me what else to order and when and where you wish the caravan to assemble?"

'I had no need of anything else, as everything for the journey had been provided, and I replied that I was ready to start out the next morning if necessary; as for the place of departure I asked him to fix it himself. He then added, laconically as before, that I should meet him at six o'clock the following morning at the caravanserai Kalmatas, just outside the city in the direction of Ousun-Kerpi. The next day we set out with a caravan, which brought me here in two weeks. And what I found here you will see for yourself.

'But now maybe you will tell me what you know about our mutual friends.'

Seeing that his story had fatigued my dear old friend, I proposed that we postpone any further conversation, saying that later I would tell him with pleasure about everything, but that meanwhile he should rest and so recover sooner.

As long as Prince Lubovedsky had to keep to his bed, we went to see him in the second court, but when he was better and could leave his cell, he used to come to us, and we talked every day for two or three hours.

So it continued for about two weeks, until one day we were

called into the third court, to the sheikh of the monastery, who spoke to us through an interpreter. He appointed as our guide one of the oldest monks, an aged man who looked like an icon and was said by the other brethren to be two hundred and seventy-five years old.

After this we, so to say, entered into the life of the monastery, were allowed access almost everywhere, and began gradually to find out about everything.

In the centre of the third court was a large building like a temple, where twice a day all those who lived in the second and third courts assembled to watch the sacred dances of the priestesses or to hear the sacred music.

When Prince Lubovedsky completely recovered, he went everywhere with us and explained everything, and was thus, as it were, a second guide for us.

The details of everything in this monastery, what it represented, and what was done there and how, I shall perhaps recount at some time in a special book. But meanwhile I find it necessary to describe in as much detail as possible one peculiar apparatus I saw there, the construction of which, when I had more or less grasped its significance, made a tremendous impression on me.

When Prince Lubovedsky had become our second guide, one day on his own initiative he obtained permission to take us to a fourth court, at one side, called the Women's Court, to the class of pupils directed by the priestess-dancers who, as I have said, daily performed sacred dances in the temple.

The prince, well knowing my great and absorbing interest in the laws of movement of the human body and psyche, advised me to pay special attention, while watching this class, to the apparatuses with the aid of which the young candidates for priestess-dancers were taught their art.

The external appearance of these peculiar apparatuses gave the impression, even at the first glance, that they were of very ancient workmanship. They were made of ebony inlaid with ivory and mother-of-pearl. When they were not in use and stood grouped together, they reminded one of 'Vesanelnian' trees, with branches all alike. On close examination, we saw that each apparatus consisted of a smooth column, higher than a man, which was fixed on a tripod. From this column, in seven places, there projected specially designed branches, which in their turn were divided into seven parts of different dimensions, each successive part decreasing in length and width in proportion to its distance from the main column.

Each part or segment of a branch was connected to the adjacent segment by means of two hollow ivory balls, one inside the other. The outer ball did not wholly cover the inner, so that one end of any segment of a branch could be fastened to the inner ball, and the end of the adjacent segment to the outer ball. In this way, these junctures were of the same type as the shoulder-joint of a man and allowed the seven segments of each branch to be moved in any desired direction. On the inner balls certain signs were inscribed.

There were three of these apparatuses in the room and beside each of them stood a little cupboard, filled with square plates of some metal, on which were also certain inscriptions. Prince Lubovedsky explained to us that these plates were copies and that the originals, made of pure gold, were kept by the sheikh. Experts had determined that the plates and the apparatuses themselves were at least four thousand five hundred years old. The prince further explained that, by making the signs on the inner balls correspond to those on the plates, these balls and the segments fastened to them could be placed in certain positions.

When all the balls are placed as designated, the form and extent of the given posture are fully defined, and the young pupils stand for hours before the apparatuses, regulated in this way, and learn to sense and remember this posture.

Many years pass before these young future priestesses are allowed to dance in the temple, where only elderly and experienced priestesses may dance.

Everyone in the monastery knows the alphabet of these postures and when, in the evening in the main hall of the temple, the priestesses perform the dances indicated for the ritual of that day, the brethren may read in these dances one or another truth which men have placed there thousands of years before.

These dances correspond precisely to our books. Just as is now done on paper, so, once, certain information about long past events was recorded in dances and transmitted from century to century to people of subsequent generations. And these dances are called sacred.

Those who are to become priestesses are mostly young girls who by the vow of their parents or for some other reason are consecrated from an early age to the service of God, or of this or that saint. They are given to the temple in childhood, where they are taught and prepared for everything necessary, as for example, for the sacred dances.

When several days after I first saw this class I went to see the performance of the genuine priestesses, I was astounded, not by the sense and meaning contained in their dances, which I did not as yet understand, but by the external precision and exactitude with which they performed them. Neither in Europe, nor in any other place where I have lived and have watched with conscious interest this sort of automatized human manifestation, have I seen anything to compare with this purity of execution.

We had been living in this monastery about three months and were beginning to get used to the conditions existing there, when one day the prince came to me with a sorrowful face. He said that that morning he had been called to the sheikh, with whom were several of the older brethren.

'The sheikh told me,' continued the prince, 'that I have only three years to live, and he advises me to spend this time in the Olman monastery, which is on the northern slopes of the Himalayas, in order to make a better use of these three years for what I have dreamed about all my life. The sheikh said that if I should consent to go he would give me the appropriate guiding instructions and would arrange everything so that my stay there would be productive. Without hesitating, I immediately consented and it was decided that in three days I should set out for the monastery with certain qualified persons.

'I therefore wish to pass these last few days entirely with you, who happen to be the man nearest to me in this life.'

The unexpectedness of it all dumbfounded me; and for a long time I was unable to say a word. When I had recovered a little, I could only ask him, 'Is it really true?'

'Yes,' replied the prince. 'There is no better way to make use of this time; perhaps I shall be able to make up for the time which I uselessly and senselessly lost when I had at my disposal so many years of possibilities. We had better not speak of this any more, but let us spend these last days on something more essential to the present moment. And you, continue to think of me as if I had died along ago. Did not you yourself say recently that you had held requiems for me, and had gradually resigned yourself to the thought of having lost me? And now, as by chance we have met again, so by chance, and without grief, let us part.'

Perhaps it was not difficult for the prince to speak of this so calmly, but for me it was very hard to realize the loss—this time for ever—of this man, dearest to me of all men.

We spent almost the whole of those last three days together and talked of everything and anything. But all the time my heart was heavy, especially whenever the prince smiled. Seeing his smile, my heart was torn, because for me his smile was the sign of his goodness, love and patience.

Finally, the three days were over and, on a morning sorrowful for me, I myself helped to load the caravan which was to take away this good prince from me for ever. He asked me not to accompany him. The caravan began to move, and as it passed behind the mountain, the prince turned, looked at me, and three times blessed me.

Peace be to thy soul, saintly man, Prince Yuri Lubovedsky!

As a conclusion to this chapter devoted to Prince Lubovedsky, I will describe in detail the tragic death of Soloviev, which occurred in exceedingly peculiar circumstances.

THE DEATH OF SOLOVIEV

Soon after our sojourn at the chief monastery of the Sarmoung Brotherhood, Soloviev joined the group of persons I have already mentioned, the Seekers of Truth, the required guarantees being furnished by me. He became a full member of this group and from then on, thanks to his persistent and conscientious efforts, he not only worked for the attainment of his individual perfection but at the same time took a serious part in all our general activities and in the various expeditions for special purposes.

During one of these expeditions, in the year 1898, he died from the bite of a wild camel in the Gobi Desert. I will describe the occurrence in as much detail as possible, because not only was the death of Soloviev very strange, but our method of crossing the desert was unprecedented and in itself highly instructive.

I shall begin the description from the time when, having travelled with great difficulty from Tashkent up the course of the river Sharakshan and over several mountain passes, we arrived at F, a very small place on the edge of the Gobi Desert.

We decided before beginning our proposed crossing of the desert to rest at this village for several weeks. And while staying there we, sometimes as a group, sometimes individually, met various local inhabitants, who in answer to our questions told us all sorts of beliefs connected with the Gobi Desert.

What we chiefly heard in these conversations was that, under the sands of the present-day desert, villages and even entire cities lay buried, and that these sands also covered many treasures and other riches of the ancient peoples who had inhabited this once flourishing region. It was said that information about the location of these riches was known to certain men living in the neighbouring villages and was handed down from father to son under vows of secrecy. The violation of these vows, as many had already learned, entailed a punishment whose severity depended upon the importance of the secret betrayed.

Repeated mention was made of a certain region of the Gobi Desert where, it seemed, it was definitely known to many that a great city lay buried; and in this connection there were a number of suspicious indications, not contradictory to each other, which seriously interested many of us, particularly Professor Skridlov, the archaeologist, who was among the members of our expedition.

After long discussions among ourselves we decided to plan our crossing of the Gobi Desert so as to pass through that region where, according to the many indications just mentioned, the city buried beneath the sands should be. There we intended to carry out some exploratory excavations under the direction of old Professor Skridlov, who was a great specialist in this field. And in accordance with this plan we mapped out our route.

Although this region was not near any of the more or less known routes across the Gobi Desert, not only did we all, holding to our already long-established principle never to follow the beaten track, treat lightly all the difficulties before us, but there even arose in each of us a feeling somewhat like elation. When this feeling subsided, we set ourselves to work out the details of our plan, and then all the extreme difficulties of our project became apparent, and to such an extent that the question actually arose whether it were possible to carry it out at all.

The trouble was that this journey, by the route we had planned, would be very long and impossible to accomplish by ordinary means. The greatest difficulty lay in providing ourselves with sufficient water and provisions, as even by the most modest calculations the quantity would have to be so great that to carry such a burden ourselves was in no way feasible. At the same time, it was out of the question to use pack-animals for this purpose, as we could not count on a single blade of grass or drop of water on the way. We could not even be sure of passing a small oasis on our route.

In spite of all this we did not give up our plan, but, having pondered over the question, we decided by common agreement that we should not undertake anything for the time being but that for one month each of us should concentrate all his thought on finding some way out of this hopeless situation; and each was to be provided with the means of doing whatever he pleased and going wherever he wished.

Professor Skridlov, as our senior member and the most respected among us, was entrusted with the direction of this affair, and, among other things, he was in charge of our common treasury. When everyone had received from him a certain sum of money, some left the village, while others settled down there, each according to his plan.

The meeting place which had been fixed was a small village lying on the edge of the sands from where we intended to begin our crossing. A month later we assembled at this appointed place and under the direction of Professor Skridlov set up a camp; and then each made his report on what he had found out. The order of the reports was decided by lot.

The first three to report were, first, Karpenko, the mining engineer, then Dr. Sari-Ogli, and thirdly, Yelov, the philologist. These reports were of such an intense interest on account of their new and original thoughts, and even for the way in which they were expressed, that they deeply engraved themselves on my memory, and I can even now reproduce them almost word for word.

Karpenko began his report as follows:

'Although I well know that none of you like the ways of the European scientists, who, instead of coming straight to the point, usually spin out a long rigmarole going back almost to Adam, nevertheless, in the present case, in view of the seriousness of the question, I consider it necessary before telling you my conclusions to put before you the reflections and deductions which led me to what I shall propose today.'

He continued:

'The Gobi is a desert whose sands, according to the assertions of science, are of very recent formation. Concerning their origin there exist two suppositions: either they are the sands of a former sea-bed, or they drifted down, blown by winds from the rocky heights in the Tian-Shan, Hindu Kush and Himalayan ranges, and from mountains which once lay to the north of this desert but which no longer exist, having been worn away by winds for centuries.

'And so, bearing in mind that we must first of all make sure of providing enough food for the entire length of our journey across the desert, both for ourselves and any animals we may find necessary to have with us, I took into consideration both of these suppositions and tried to think whether the sand itself might in some way be made use of for this purpose.

'I deliberated thus:

'If this desert is a former sea-bed, then the sands must surely contain strata or zones consisting of various shells, and, as shells are formed by organisms, consequently they must be organic matter. Therefore, we have only to find some means of converting this matter so that it can be digested and in this way provide the energy required for life.

'But if the sands of this desert are drift sands, that is to say, if they are of rocky origin, then again, it has been proved beyond any doubt that the soil of most of the great oases of Turkestan and also of the regions adjacent to this desert is of purely vegetable origin and consists of organic substances deposited there from higher altitudes. So we can conclude that, in the course of centuries, such organic substances must have drifted into the general mass of sands of this desert and become mixed with it. I further reflected that according to the law of gravity all substances or elements always group themselves according to their weight; therefore, here in the desert, the organic substances deposited, being much lighter than sand of rocky origin, must also have gradually grouped themselves in special layers or zones.

'Having come to this theoretical conclusion, I organized a small expedition into the desert to verify it in practice, and after travelling three days began to carry out my investigations. I soon found in certain places layers which, although barely distinguishable from the general mass of the sands, were nevertheless even on superficial examination clearly of a different origin. By microscopic examination and chemical analysis of the separate parts of this mixture of substances, I found out that it consisted of the dead bodies of small organisms and various tissues of the vegetable world. Having loaded all the seven camels I had at my disposal with this peculiar sand, I returned here, and with Professor Skridlov's permission purchased a number of different animals and set to work experimenting on them.

'I bought two camels, two yaks, two horses, two mules, two asses, ten sheep, ten goats, ten dogs and ten Keriskis cats, and keeping them hungry, that is to say, giving them a very limited quantity of food, only just enough to sustain life, I began little by little introducing into their food this sand which I had prepared in various ways. For the first few days of my experiments, none of the animals would eat any of these mixtures. But when I began to prepare this sand in an entirely new way, after only a week's trial the sheep and goats suddenly began to eat it with great pleasure.

'I then concentrated all my attention on these animals. In two days I completely convinced myself that the sheep and goats had already begun to prefer this mixture to all other kinds of food. It was composed of seven and a half parts of sand, two parts of ground mutton and one-half part of ordinary salt. At the beginning, all the animals undergoing my experiments, including the sheep and goats, had daily lost from a half to two and a half per cent of their total weight, but, from the day when the sheep and goats began to eat this mixture, they not only stopped losing weight but began gaining from one to three ounces daily. Thanks to these experiments, I personally have no doubt whatever that this sand could be used for feeding goats and sheep, provided it be mixed with the necessary quantity of their own meat. I can therefore propose to you today the following:

'To overcome the chief difficulty of our trip across the desert, we must buy several hundred sheep and goats, and gradually, as the need arises, kill them and use their meat both for food for ourselves and for preparing the aforesaid mixture as food for the remaining animals. We need not fear any lack of the required sand, as all the data in my possession convince me that in certain places it can always be found.

'Now, as regards water, in order to provide ourselves with a sufficient supply, we must obtain a large quantity of sheep's or goats' bladders or stomachs—twice as many as there are animals —and making them into *khourdjeens* fill them with water and load each sheep or goat with two *khourdjeens*.

'I have already verified that a sheep can carry this quantity of water with ease and without any harm to itself. In addition, experiment and calculation have shown me that this quantity of water will suffice for our own needs and also for the animals, provided we exercise a little economy in the use of it during the first two or three days. After this we will be able, with the water carried by the sheep we have killed, to satisfy ourselves and the remaining sheep in full.'

When Karpenko had finished, the second report was made by Dr. Sari-Ogli. I had met and made friends with Dr. Sari-Ogli five years before. Although by origin a Persian, from Eastern Persia, he had been educated in France. Perhaps I shall at some time write a detailed account of him, as he was a most distinguished and highly remarkable man.

Dr. Sari-Ogli spoke approximately as follows:

'After hearing the report of the mining engineer, Karpenko, I shall say "Pass" as regards the first part of my report, because I consider that nothing better than his proposals can be found. However, coming to the second part of my report, which concerns the task I set myself of finding a means of overcoming the difficulties of movement in the desert during sand-storms, I wish to tell you my thoughts and the results of my experiments. The conclusions I arrived at and the experimental data I obtained complement very well, in my opinion, the proposals of Karpenko, and I shall therefore submit them to you.

'In these deserts, one has very often to pass through winds and storms, during which movement sometimes becomes quite impossible both for man and beast, since the wind lifts quantities of sand up into the air and, whirling it along, deposits mountains of it where only a moment before there were hollows.

'And so I reflected that any progress would be impeded by the whirlwinds of sand. My next thought was that sand, because of its weight, cannot rise very high and that probably there was a limit beyond which not a single grain could rise. Deliberating in this way, I decided to find out about this hypothetical limit.

'For this purpose, I ordered here in the village a specially high, folding step-ladder, and with two camels and a driver set off into the desert. After one day's journey I was preparing to camp for the night, when a wind suddenly rose, and within an hour the storm had become so violent that it was impossible to remain stationary and even to breathe owing to the sand in the air.

'With great difficulty we began to set up the ladder I had brought, and somehow, even making use of the camels, we steadied it as best we could and I climbed up. Can you imagine my astonishment when, at a height of no more than twenty-five feet, I found not a grain of sand in the air?

'My ladder was some sixty feet in length; I had not climbed up a third of its height before I emerged from that hell. There above was a beautiful starry and moonlit sky, silence and a stillness such as is rarely found even at home in Eastern Persia. Below, there still reigned something unimaginable; I had the impression of standing on some high cliff on a sea-coast overlooking the most terrible storm and upheaval.

'While I stood up there on the ladder admiring the beautiful night, the storm began to abate and after half an hour I descended. But below a calamity awaited me. Although now the wind was only half as strong, the man who had accompanied me was still walking, as is customary in these storms, along the crests of the dunes away from the wind, leading after him only one camel; the other, he told me, had broken loose soon after I had mounted the ladder, and had gone off he knew not where.

'When it began to grow light, we set out to search for the second camel and very soon saw its hoofs sticking out of a dune not far from the place where the ladder had stood. We did not try to dig the camel out, as it was obviously dead and buried quite deep in the sand. We immediately set off on the return journey, eating our food as we went so as not to lose time, and by evening we reached our village.

'The next day I ordered several pairs of stilts of different sizes, getting them in different places to avoid suspicion, and, taking with me one camel loaded with provisions and a few necessities, I again set out into the desert, where I began practising walking on stilts—first on low ones, and then gradually on higher and higher ones. To walk over the sands on stilts was not so difficult once I had fastened to them the iron soles I had devised, and which I had ordered, again out of caution, in different places from the stilts.

'During the time I spent in the desert to practise walking on stilts, I went through two more storms. One of them, to be sure, was mild, but, even so, it would have been unthinkable to move and orient oneself in it by ordinary means; but with the aid of my stilts I walked around over the sands during both of these storms, in any desired direction, as though I were in my own room. At first it was somewhat difficult not to stumble, because very often and particularly, as I have already said, during storms, there are ups and downs in the dunes. But fortunately, as I soon discovered, the upper surface of the sand-filled atmosphere has irregularities of contour exactly corresponding to the irregularities of the sands, so that walking on stilts is considerably facilitated by the fact that one can clearly see by the contours of the sand-filled atmosphere where one dune ends and another begins.

'In any case,' concluded Dr. Sari-Ogli, 'it has been shown that the sand-filled atmosphere has a definite and not very high limit, and that the contours of its upper surface always correspond to the contours of the desert itself; and one must admit that it is absolutely necessary to make use of this discovery in the journey we have ahead of us.'

The third to report was Yelov, the philologist, who, with the peculiar, expressive manner of speech characteristic of him, addressed us as follows:

'If you will allow me, gentlemen, I will say the same thing as our esteemed Aesculapius concerning the first half of his report, namely, "I pass", but I pass also concerning everything in general which I had thought out and wiseacred about during the past month.

'What I had wished to communicate to you today is simply child's play in comparison with the ideas presented by the mining engineer, Karpenko, and my friend the doctor—as irreplaceable in respect of his origin as of his possession of a diploma.

'However, just now while the two previous speakers were making their proposals some new ideas arose in me, which you may perhaps find admissible and effective for our journey. They are as follows:

'According to the proposal of the doctor, we are all going to practise walking on stilts of different heights, but the stilts to be used on the journey itself, one pair of which each of us must take with him, will be not less than twenty feet long. Further, if we

follow the proposal of Karpenko, we shall probably have a great
many sheep and goats. Now I think that when our stilts are not in
use, instead of carrying them ourselves, we can very easily arrange
for them to be carried by the sheep and goats. As you all know, a
flock of sheep is in the habit of following the first sheep, or as it is
called, the leader, and therefore it will only be necessary to direct
and guide those sheep harnessed to the first pair of stilts, and the
rest are bound to follow in a long line, one after the other.

'In this way, apart from the advantage of not having to carry
our own stilts, we can also arrange that our sheep should carry
us as well. Between stilts twenty feet long placed parallel, we can
easily put seven rows of sheep, three in a row, that is, twenty-one
sheep in all, and for this number of sheep, the weight of one man
is a trifle. We need only harness the sheep to the stilts in such a
way as to leave an empty place in the centre about five and a half
feet long and three feet wide, which can be used to fix up a very
comfortable couch. Then each of us, instead of toiling and
sweating under the weight of his own stilts, can loll about like
Moukhtar Pasha in his harem or ride like a rich parasite in his
private carriage through the *allées* of the Bois de Boulogne
Crossing the desert in such conditions, we can even, during this
time, learn almost all the languages we shall need in our future
expeditions.'

After the first two reports and this finale from Yelov, there was
obviously no further need for other proposals. We were all so
astounded at what we had heard that all of a sudden it seemed to
us that the difficulties of crossing the Gobi had been intentionally
exaggerated, and even the impossibility of it suggested expressly
for the traveller.

And so, accepting these proposals, we all of us agreed, without
any discussion, to conceal from the local inhabitants, for the time
being, our impending departure into the desert—that world of
hunger, death and uncertainty. Accordingly, we planned to pass
off Professor Skridlov as a daring Russian merchant, who had
come to this region on some wild commercial venture. He had
come, supposedly, to buy up sheep to send to Russia, sheep being
very dear there, whereas here they could be bought much more

cheaply; and he intended at the same time to export strong, long, thin poles to the factories in Russia, where they would be made into frames for stretching calico. In Russia, such hard wood is unobtainable and the frames made of the wood there soon wear out, owing to the constant movement in the machines, so that poles of this quality would bring a high price. For these reasons, the daring merchant wished to embark on this risky commercial enterprise.

Having decided this, we all became high-spirited and spoke of the journey ahead of us as though it were no more than crossing the Place de la Concorde in Paris.

The next day we moved to the bank of the river, near the place where it disappears into the fathomless depths of the sand, and there we pitched the tents brought from Russia, which we still had with us. Although the site of our new camp was not at all far from the village, nevertheless no one lived in that place, and it was not probable that it would enter anyone's head to come there, to the very gates of that arid hell. Some of us, passing ourselves off as clerks and other servants of the eccentric Russian merchant, Ivanov, made the rounds of the bazaars in the vicinity and began buying up thin poles of various lengths, and also sheep and goats—and soon we had a whole flock in our camp.

We then began intensive practice at walking on stilts, first on low ones, and then gradually on higher ones.

One fine morning twelve days later, our extraordinary cortège moved off into the wastes of the sands, amid the bleating of sheep and goats, the barking of dogs, and the whinnies and brays of the horses and asses we had purchased in case of need.

The cortège soon spread out into a long procession of litters, like the grandiose processions of ancient kings. Long rang out our jovial songs and the shouting back and forth to each other from our improvised litters, which followed each other some distance apart. Of course, as always, the remarks coming from Yelov produced roars of laughter.

Although we went through two terrible sand-storms, we arrived several days later almost at the heart of the desert, without any fatigue and fully satisfied with everything—even with having learned the language we needed. We were approaching the spot which was the principal goal of our expedition.

Everything would probably have ended as we had planned, if it had not been for the accident to Soloviev.

We had been travelling mostly at night, making use of the abilities of our comrade, the experienced astronomer Dashtamirov, to orient ourselves by the stars.

One day we made a halt at dawn to eat and also to feed our sheep.

It was still very early. The sun had only just begun to grow hot. We were just sitting down to our freshly prepared mutton and rice, when on the horizon there suddenly appeared a herd of camels. We at once guessed that they must be wild ones.

Soloviev, a passionate hunter and a dead shot, immediately seized his rifle and ran in the direction where the silhouettes of the camels could be seen; and we, laughing at Soloviev's passion for hunting, settled down to the hot food, excellently prepared in these unprecedented conditions. I say unprecedented because, in the midst of these sands, and so deep in the interior, it is usually considered impossible to build a fire, as there is sometimes not even *saksaul*[1] to be found for hundreds of miles. But we built fires at least twice a day to cook our meals and prepare coffee or tea, and not only ordinary tea, but also Tibetan tea, brewed in the stock from the bones of the slaughtered sheep. For this luxury we were indebted to the device of Pogossian, who had the idea of making saddles of special wooden sticks for loading the sheep with the bladders of water; so now, as we killed the sheep, there was quite enough wood left over every day for the fires.

An hour and a half had passed since Soloviev had gone after the camels. We were already preparing to continue our journey, and there was still no sign of him. We waited a further half-hour. Well knowing the punctiliousness of Soloviev, who never kept anyone waiting, and fearing some mishap, all but two of us took our guns and set off to search for him. Soon we again perceived the silhouettes of the camels in the distance and went towards

---

[1] A tree or tree-like shrub that grows in the sands.

them. As we came near, the camels, evidently sensing our approach, fled to the south, but we kept on going.

Four hours had passed since Soloviev had gone. Suddenly one of us noticed a man lying several hundred paces away, and when we came up we recognized Soloviev, who was already dead. His neck had been bitten half through. All of us were overwhelmed with heart-rending grief, for we had all loved this exceptionally good man.

Making a litter of our guns, we carried Soloviev's body back to the camp. The same day, headed by Skridlov, who performed the duty of priest, we buried Soloviev with great solemnity in the heart of the desert, and immediately left that for us accursed place.

Although we had already done much towards the discovery of the legendary city which we had expected to find on our journey, we nevertheless changed all our plans and decided to leave the desert as soon as possible. So we struck out more to the west and in four days arrived at the Keriyan oasis, where normal country begins. From Keriya we continued further, but now without Soloviev, dear to us all.

Peace to thy soul, honest and ever loyal friend of all friends!

VIII

EKIM BEY

I WISH TO DEVOTE THIS CHAPTER to my reminiscences of another man whom I consider remarkable, and whose manner of life in his later years, either by the will of fate or thanks to the laws operating in a 'self-developed individuality', was arranged down to the smallest detail like my own. At the present time this man is in good health from the ordinary point of view, but according to my view, and speaking between ourselves, only his physical body is in good health.

It is interesting to note that, contrary to the generally accepted opinion that people belonging to two different nationalities which have been engaged in centuries of racial struggle ought to feel towards each other instinctive hostility and even hate, and in spite of the difference of upbringing in family traditions and religious convictions, nevertheless, between Ekim Bey and myself, after our first meeting in early youth in quite unusual circumstances, there gradually arose a close friendship; and later, when through all kinds of trivial incidents our inner worlds had been drawn together like two 'arisings from the same source', our feeling for each other was like that of brothers.

In this chapter I shall describe my first chance meeting with Dr. Ekim Bey, who is respected by all serious persons that know him, as well as by the common run of people, who regard him as a great magician and wizard. I will also recount briefly several significant events which took place during our wanderings in the depths of Asia and Africa.

At the present time, rewarded for his past merits by many decorations which have proved to be 'not ephemeral', he somehow lives out his remaining years in a small and insignificant place in Egypt, with the title of the Great Turkish Pasha. It must be said that he chose such a solitary spot as his dwelling-place for his old age, in spite of having the means to live wherever he pleased and to enjoy all the comforts of present-day life, chiefly because he wished to avoid the importunities of idle people and their curiosity—a property unworthy of man which has become inherent in most of our contemporaries.

The first time I met Ekim Bey was when he was still quite young. He was a student in a military school in Germany and had come, as he always did, to spend the summer with his father in Constantinople. We were of the same age.

Before describing the circumstances in which I met him, I must say that, in the period before my first visit to Echmiadzin and my meeting with Pogossian, related in a previous chapter, when I was still being chased about everywhere like a harassed dog, seeking answers to the questions arising in my brain—which according to the notions of most contemporary people had become sick with psychopathy—I also happened to go to Constantinople, drawn by rumours of numerous marvels supposed to be performed by the dervishes there.

On my arrival at Constantinople I arranged to stay in the district called Pera and went from there to visit the monasteries of various dervish orders. Living at that time in the company of these 'dervish zealots', and of course not being occupied with anything practical and thinking about nothing except all kinds of dervish nonsense, one gloomy day, I clearly recognized without any illusions that very soon I would have absolutely no what-is-called 'dough'.

After realizing this fact, I went about for a couple of days far from care-free, while all the time thoughts swarmed beneath my cranium, like the favourite flies of Spanish mules, about how to get hold of that contemptible something which for contemporary man is almost the sole stimulus of his life.

With these worries, I was standing one day on the large bridge between Pera and Stamboul. Leaning on the parapet, I began to ponder on the sense and significance of the continuous movement of the whirling dervishes, which at first glance seems automatic and without any participation of the consciousness. Under the bridge and near it, steamers were constantly passing and small boats plied unceasingly in every direction.

On the Galata shore next to the bridge, there was a landing stage for the steamers crossing between Constantinople and the opposite shore of the Bosphorus. Near this landing stage, around the arriving and departing steamers, I saw boys swimming about and diving for coins thrown by people from the steamers. This interested me a great deal. I went nearer and looked on. Without any hurry the boys very skilfully retrieved the coins thrown by the passengers in different places, without missing a single one.

I watched for a long time, admiring the ease and dexterity of these boys, who were of various ages, from eight to about eighteen. Suddenly the thought entered my head: 'Why should not I also take up this profession? Am I any worse than these boys?' And on the following day I went to the shore of the Golden Horn, to a place just below the Admiralty, to learn how to dive.

While practising my diving I even chanced to come across a teacher, a certain Greek, an expert, who used to go there to bathe. He taught me of his own accord some of the details of this 'great wisdom' and the rest I drew out of him by cunning—then already proper to me—over a cup of coffee which we took after bathing, in a Greek café near by. Of course, I will not go into details as to who paid for the coffee.

At first it was very difficult. One had to dive down with open eyes and the sea-water irritated the membranes of my eyes, causing sharp pain, especially at night. But soon they grew accustomed to it and I began to see as freely in the water as in the air.

Two weeks later I began to 'earn' a living around the steamers, with the local boys of all ages, by fishing for coins. Of course, I was not too successful at first, but very soon I never missed a single one.

It must be said that when a coin is thrown into the water it begins to sink very quickly, but the further from the surface the more slowly it sinks, so if the water is very deep it takes a long time before it finally reaches the bottom. In such a case, before diving, one has only to note well the place where the coin fell, and then it is not difficult to see it in the water and go after it.

One day, a passenger, occupied with his thoughts, was leaning over the side of a ship watching the coin-catchers, when he inadvertently let fall from his hands what is called a chaplet, an appurtenance indispensable for every serious Asiatic for those intervals when he is not fulfilling his life obligations.

He immediately called to the diving-boys to get the chaplet, but in spite of their attempts they could not find it, since, being far from the ship, they had not noticed where it fell. Evidently the chaplet was very valuable, as the passenger promised to pay the finder twenty-five Turkish pounds.

After the steamer had left, all the coin-catchers searched for a long time, but their efforts were fruitless. The water was deep and, as they expressed it, to grope all over the bottom was impossible. In general it is very difficult to reach the bottom of deep water. Just as water easily supports the living body on the surface, so it offers a strong resistance to its descent.

Several days later, while I was diving for coins at that spot, a passenger happened to throw one so far away that, before I could swim up to where it had fallen, it had already sunk out of sight. As there had not been a good 'catch' that day, I was determined at any cost to get that coin.

Just as I reached it I caught a glimpse of something that looked like a chaplet. Swimming back to the surface, I remembered the chaplet for which twenty-five pounds had been offered.

Having noted the spot, I dived down again without telling anyone, and when I realized that it was impossible to reach the bottom in the ordinary way, I brought with me the next day some heavy sledge-hammers which I had hired from a blacksmith, and, tying them round my body, dived down with this weight. I soon found the chaplet, which turned out to be of amber, set with small diamonds and garnets.

The same day I discovered that the passenger who had lost the chaplet was Pasha N, the former governor of a small district near Constantinople, and that he was then living on the opposite shore of the Bosphorus not far from Scutari.

As I had recently been not too well and was feeling worse each day, I decided not to dive for coins the next day, but to deliver the chaplet to its owner, and at the same time to visit the cemetery at Scutari.

I went the following morning and soon found the pasha's house. He happened to be at home, and when he was told that one of the coin-catchers had come, who insisted on seeing him personally, he evidently understood at once what it was about and came out to me himself. When I handed him the chaplet he was so sincerely overjoyed and so simple in his manner towards me that I was deeply moved, and did not wish for anything in the world to accept the promised reward.

He begged me at least to lunch at his house, and this I did not decline. After lunch I left immediately in order to catch the last but one returning steamer. But on the way to the steamer I felt so ill that I had to sit down on the steps of a house, where I lost consciousness.

Passers-by noticed my condition and, as I was not far from the pasha's house, the news soon reached him that a boy had suddenly been taken ill. Hearing that the boy was the one who had brought him the chaplet, the pasha himself came quickly with his servants and gave orders for me to be carried to his house, and for a military physician to be called.

Although I soon recovered consciousness, my condition was such that I could not move and was compelled to remain for the time being in the pasha's house.

That night all my skin began to crack and burn unbearably; evidently, being unaccustomed to long immersion in sea-water, it could not tolerate the action of the salt.

I was put in a wing of the house and an old woman named Fatma Badji was appointed to take care of me. The pasha's son, a student in a German military school, also came and helped the old woman look after me. This was Ekim Bey, who later became my bosom friend.

While I was getting better we conversed and chatted about all kinds of things, but gradually our talks began to take a philosophical turn, and when I had recovered we parted as friends, and from then on kept up an uninterrupted correspondence.

That year he left the military school in Germany to enter medical school, as his inner convictions had changed during this time and impelled him to give up his military career in order to become an army physician.

Four years passed.

One day, in the Caucasus, I received a letter from him in which he wrote that he was already a physician and would like to see me, and at the same time to visit the Caucasus which had interested him for a long time, and he asked when and where he could meet me.

I was living that summer in the town of Suram, where I was at work making objects in plaster-of-Paris. I sent him a telegram that I was impatiently awaiting his arrival. A few days later he came.

That year Pogossian, Yelov and Karpenko, who had been a friend of my boyhood, had also come to Suram to spend the summer. Ekim Bey soon became intimate with these comrades of mine and felt like an old friend of theirs.

We spent the entire summer in Suram, from where we frequently made short excursions, usually on foot. We climbed the Suram mountain pass, and explored the environs of Borzhom and Mikhaïlov in order to come in contact with the people in these places who had not yet been exposed to the effects of contemporary civilization, and once we even visited the famous Khevsurs, who have driven all the learned ethnographers mad.

Ekim Bey, living several months in such conditions with us—young men of his own age who were already thoroughly stuffed with all kinds of Don Quixotic aspirations—and taking part in all our exchanges of opinion, was willy-nilly drawn into our 'psychopathy' and, like us, burned with eagerness to jump over his own knees.

Ekim Bey

The four of us, Pogossian, Yelov, Karpenko and I, were at that time having many discussions about a proposal made to us a short time before by Prince Yuri Lubovedsky, to join him and his friends in a big expedition on foot, starting from the frontier town of Nakhichevan and crossing Persia to the Persian Gulf.

These discussions of ours, and all the perspectives opened up by this kind of travel, interested Ekim Bey so much that he asked us to put in a word with the prince for him to be allowed to join this expedition, and he began to think out how to obtain his father's permission and a year's leave of absence from his superiors.

The upshot of it all was that, after making the necessary arrangements, partly by telegram, and partly in person on his return home to prepare for this long journey, he began his first big expedition in our company on the day we set out from Nakhichevan, the first of January of the following year.

We started at midnight from Nakhichevan and by morning were already exposed to a demonstration of the 'wisdom' of those biped inhabitants of our dear planet who are called frontier guards, and who are everywhere equally highly developed in the art of expressing their perspicacity and omniscience.

There were twenty-three of us, including all those friends and comrades of mine to whom I have decided to devote separate chapters in this series of my writings. Three of them, Pogossian, Yelov, and Prince Lubovedsky, I have already written about; with Dr. Ekim Bey I will acquaint the reader in this chapter; and to the two others, Karpenko the engineer, and the archaeology professor Skridlov, I will devote the subsequent chapters of this book.

Our journey to the town of Tabriz, which we reached ten days later, passed without any special incident. But not long after leaving Tabriz an event occurred which I will describe in as much detail as possible, not merely because Ekim Bey took an active part and manifested a deep interest in it, but also because it turned my own outlook on life completely upside down.

While in Tabriz we had heard a great deal about a certain Persian dervish, supposedly a performer of extraordinary miracles, and our interest was aroused. A little later in our journey we again heard about him from a certain Armenian priest, and we then decided, although he lived in a place a good deal out of our way, to change the route we had planned in order to see him and find out for ourselves who and what he was.

It was on the thirteenth day of a tiring journey, during which we spent the nights in the huts of Persian or Kurd shepherds or in small settlements, that we finally reached the village where this dervish lived.

We were directed to his house, which was some distance beyond the village. We immediately made our way there and found him near his house in the shade of some trees, where he usually spoke with the people who came to him.

We saw a man of fairly advanced age, dressed in rags, barefoot and seated cross-legged on the ground. Near him sat a number of young Persians who, as we discovered later, were his pupils. We approached, asked his benediction, and also seated ourselves on the ground, forming a half-circle round him. Our conversation began.

We put questions and he answered us, and in his turn he asked us questions.

At first he received us rather coldly and showed little inclination to talk, but later, when he found that we had come a considerable distance especially to talk with him, he became more cordial. He expressed himself very simply, in unpolished language, and at the beginning gave the impression, at least to me personally, of being an ignorant man, that is to say, uneducated in the European sense of the word.

The conversation with the dervish was conducted in Persian, but in a particular dialect which none of our company knew except myself, Dr. Sari-Ogli and one other who was not very fluent in it. Consequently Sari-Ogli and I asked the questions, immediately translating all that was said for the benefit of the others.

It was dinner-time. A pupil came bringing the dervish his food—rice in a bowl made out of a gourd. Continuing the conversation, the dervish began to eat. As we had eaten nothing since we had risen and started on our way early in the morning, we opened our knapsacks and began to eat also.

I must remind you that at that time I was an ardent follower of the famous Indian yogis and carried out very exactly all the indications of what is called Hatha Yoga, and when eating I tried to masticate my food as thoroughly as possible. So, long after everyone, including the old man, had finished their simple meal, I continued slowly eating, trying not to swallow a single morsel without masticating it according to all the rules.

Seeing this, the dervish asked me: 'Tell me, young stranger, why are you eating like that?'

I was so sincerely astonished by this question—which seemed to me very strange and to say not very much for his knowledge—that I even had no desire to reply to him, and thought that we had made such a long detour in vain, to meet a man who was not worth talking with seriously. Looking into his eyes, I felt not only pity but also ashamed for him, and replied with self-assurance that I chewed my food carefully so that it might be better assimilated in the intestines, and, referring to the well-known fact that properly digested food gives the organism a larger quantity of calories necessary for all our functions, I repeated all that I had extracted from various books on the subject.

Shaking his head, the old man slowly and with conviction uttered the following saying which is known throughout Persia:

Let God kill him who himself does not know and yet presumes to show others the way to the doors of His Kingdom.

After that Sari-Ogli put a question to the dervish which he answered briefly. He then turned again to me and asked:

'Tell me, young stranger, you probably also do gymnastics?'

I was in fact working very hard at gymnastics at that time and although I knew all the methods recommended by the Indian Yogis, I kept to the system of the Swede, Mueller. I told the dervish that I did work at gymnastics and considered it necessary to practise twice a day, morning and evening, and I explained briefly the kind of exercises I was doing.

'This is only for the development of arms, legs and in general the external muscles,' said the old man, 'but you have also inner muscles which are not affected at all by your mechanical movements.'

'Yes, certainly,' said I.

'Good. Let us now return to your way of chewing your food,' the old man continued. 'If you chew in this way as a means to health or for the sake of other attainments, then I shall have to say, if you would like to know my sincere opinion, that you have chosen the worst possible way. By chewing your food so carefully you reduce the work of your stomach. Now you are young and everything is all right, but you are accustoming your stomach to do nothing; and when you are older, owing to the lack of normal work, your muscles will be to a certain extent atrophied. And that is bound to occur if you continue this system of chewing. You know that our muscles and body get weaker in old age. Now, in addition to the natural weaknesses of old age, you will have another brought on by yourself, because you are accustoming your stomach not to work. Can you imagine how it will be then?

'On the contrary, it is not at all necessary to masticate carefully. At your age it is better not to chew at all, but to swallow whole pieces, even bones if possible, to give work to your stomach. I can see that those who have advised you to practise this mastication, and also those who write books about it, have, as is said, "heard a bell without knowing where the sound came from".'

These simple, obvious and consistent words of the old man made me completely change my first opinion of him. Until then I had put questions to him out of curiosity, but from that moment I felt a serious interest in him, and began to listen with the greatest attention to everything he said.

Suddenly I understood with the whole of my being that ideas I had hitherto accepted as indisputable truths were incorrect. I realized that up till then I had seen things only from one side. Now many things appeared in quite a new light. Hundreds of new questions arose in my mind concerning this subject.

Carried away by our conversation with the dervish, the doctor and I quite forgot about the rest of our comrades and stopped translating what was said. Seeing how deeply we were interested, they kept interrupting us with the questions: 'What did he say?' 'What is he talking about?' and each time we had to put them off, promising to tell them everything in detail later.

When the dervish had finished speaking about artificial mastication, and the different means of assimilating food and its automatic transformation in us according to law, I said:

'Be so kind, Father, and also explain to me what you think of what is called artificial breathing. Believing it useful, I practise it according to the instructions of the yogis, namely, after breathing in the air, I hold it a certain time, and then slowly exhale it. Perhaps this also should not be done?'

The dervish, seeing that my attitude towards his words had completely changed, began to be more in sympathy with me and explained the following:

'If you harm yourself with your way of chewing food, you harm yourself a thousand times more by the practice of this breathing. All the exercises in breathing which are given in books and taught in contemporary esoteric schools can do nothing but harm. Breathing, as every sane thinking man should understand, is also a process of feeding, but on another sort of food. Air, just like our ordinary food, entering the body and being digested there, disintegrates into its component parts, which form new combinations with each other as well as with the corresponding elements of certain substances which are already present. In this way those indispensable new substances are produced which are continuously being consumed in the various unceasing life processes in the organism of man.

'You must know that, to obtain any definite new substance, its constituent parts must be combined in exact quantitative proportions.

'Let us take the most simple example. You have to bake bread. For this you must first of all prepare the dough. But to make dough you must take definite proportions of flour and water. If there is too little water, you will get, instead of dough, something that will crumble at the first touch. If you take too much water, you will simply get a mash, such as is used for feeding cattle. It is the same in either case. You will not get the dough necessary for baking bread.

'The same thing occurs in the formation of every substance necessary for the organism. The parts composing these substances must be combined in strict proportions, both qualitatively and quantitatively.

'When you breathe in the ordinary way, you breathe mechanically. The organism, without you, takes from the air the quantity of substances that it needs. The lungs are so constructed that they are accustomed to work with a definite amount of air. But if you increase the amount of air, the composition of what passes through the lungs is changed, and the further inner processes of mixing and balancing must also inevitably be changed.

'Without the knowledge of the fundamental laws of breathing in all particulars, the practice of artificial breathing must inevitably lead, very slowly but none the less surely, to self-destruction.

'You should bear in mind that besides substances necessary for the organism, the air contains others which are unnecessary and even harmful.

'Well then, artificial breathing, that is to say, a forced modification of natural breathing, facilitates the penetration into the organism of these numerous substances in the air which are harmful to life, and at the same time upsets the quantitative and qualitative balance of the useful substances.

'Artificial breathing also disturbs the proportion between the amount of food obtained from the air and the amount obtained from all our other foods. Hence, on increasing or diminishing the intake of air, you must correspondingly increase or diminish the amount of other kinds of food; and to maintain the correct proportion you must have a full understanding of your organism.

'But do you know yourself so well? Do you know, for example, that the stomach needs food not only for nourishment but also because it is accustomed to taking in a certain quantity of food? We eat chiefly to gratify our taste and to obtain the accustomed sensation of pressure which the stomach experiences when it contains this particular quantity of food. In the walls of the stomach there branch out what-are-called wandering nerves which, beginning to function when there is not a certain pressure, give rise to the sensation we call hunger. Thus, we have different hungers: a so-called bodily or physical hunger, and, if it may be so expressed, a nervous or psychic hunger.

'All our organs work mechanically and in each, owing to its nature and habits, there is created a special tempo of functioning, and the tempos of the functioning of different organs are in a definite relation to each other. So there is established in the organism a certain equilibrium: one organ depending on another —all are connected.

'By artificially changing our breathing, we change first of all the tempo of the functioning of our lungs, and, as the activity of the lungs is connected, among other things, with the activity of the stomach, the tempo of the functioning of the stomach is also changed, at first slightly, then more and more. For the digestion of food, the stomach needs a certain time; let us say that food must remain there an hour. But if the tempo of the stomach's functioning is changed, then the time for the passing of food through the stomach is also changed: the food may pass through so quickly that the stomach has only time to do a part of what it has to do. It is the same with the other organs. That is why it is a thousand times better to do nothing with our organism. Better leave it damaged than try to repair it without knowing how.

'I repeat, our organism is a very complicated apparatus. It has many organs with processes of different tempos and with different needs. You must either change everything or nothing. Otherwise, instead of good you might do harm.

'Numerous illnesses arise just from this artificial breathing. In many cases it leads to enlargement of the heart, constriction of the windpipe, or damage to the stomach, liver, kidneys or nerves.

'It very rarely happens that anyone who practises artificial breathing does not harm himself irreparably, and this rare case occurs only if he stops in time. Whoever does it for a long time invariably has deplorable results.

'If you know every small screw, every little pin of your machine, only then can you know what you must do. But if you just know a little and experiment, you risk a great deal, because the machine is very complicated. There are many tiny screws which might easily be broken by a strong shock and which cannot afterwards be bought in any shop.

'Therefore—since you have asked me for it—my advice to you is: stop your breathing exercises.'

Our conversation with the dervish continued for quite a long time. Before we left I had managed to talk over with the prince what we should do next, and so, after thanking the dervish, I told him that we proposed staying another day or two in the neighbourhood, and asked whether he would allow us to converse with him once more. He consented and even said that if we wished we could come to see him the following evening after dinner.

We stayed not two days, as we intended, but a whole week, and every evening we all went to this dervish and conversed with him, and afterwards, until late each night, Sari-Ogli and I repeated to our comrades everything that had been said.

The last time we went to the dervish, to thank him and take our leave, Ekim Bey, to our great surprise, suddenly turned to him and, in a humble voice unusual for him, said in Persian:

'Good Father! During these days I have become convinced with the whole of my being that you . . .'

Interrupting himself at this point, he hurriedly asked Sari-Ogli and me not to hinder him from speaking for himself and to correct him only when the expressions he used had a special meaning in the local dialect which might change the sense of what he was saying. Then he continued: '. . . that you are the very man I have instinctively been searching for, a man to whom I could wholly entrust the guidance of my inner world, in order to regulate and neutralize the struggle which has recently arisen in me between two totally opposite strivings. On the other hand, numerous life circumstances over which I have no control do not permit me to live here, somewhere near you, so that whenever necessary I could come and reverently hear your directions and counsels as to how I should live, in order to put an end to this tormenting inner struggle and to prepare myself to acquire the being worthy of man.

'That is why I beg you, if it is possible, not to refuse to give me now a few brief indications and guiding principles of life, appropriate to a man of my age.'

To this unexpected and high-sounding request of Ekim Bey, this venerable man, the Persian dervish, replied with precision and in great detail.

I will not record here, in this second series of my writings, what he then explained, considering it premature for serious readers and, as regards the correct sequential perception of all my writings, even harmful to the aim of genuine understanding. I have therefore decided, with a clear conscience, to expound the quintessence of these explanations only later, in a corresponding chapter of the third series of my writings, entitled 'The physical body of man, its needs according to law, and possibilities of manifestation'.

Early in the morning following this last visit to the dervish, we resumed our journey. Instead of going, as previously mapped out, in the direction of the Persian Gulf, we went west towards Bagdad, since two of our company, Karpenko and Prince Nijeradze, had fallen sick with fever and were becoming worse from day to day.

We reached Bagdad, and after staying there about a month we separated and went off in different directions. Prince Lubovedsky, Yelov and Ekim Bey left for Constantinople; Karpenko, Nijeradze and Pogossian decided to follow the Euphrates upstream as far as its source, then to go over the mountains and cross the Russian frontier. But Dr. Sari-Ogli and I, with the others, agreed to turn back and go in the direction of Khorasan, and only when there to decide on the final stage of our journey.

In setting down my memories of Dr. Ekim Bey, I must not fail to mention his ardent interest in hypnotism and everything relating to it. He was particularly interested in those phenomena which in their totality are called the 'power of human thought' and the study of which is a distinct branch of the contemporary science of hypnotism.

And indeed he obtained, especially in the said branch, unprecedented practical results. Thanks chiefly to the experiments he performed on people in order to elucidate from every aspect the various manifestations of the power of human thought, he was reputed by those round him to be a redoubtable magician and wizard.

The experiments which he performed on his friends and acquaintances with the mentioned aim led, among other things, to the result that some of the people who had met or even only heard about him began to be afraid of him, while others, on the contrary, became exaggeratedly respectful, and even, as is said, began to lick his boots.

I think that the main cause of this false conception which people formed of him was not his deep knowledge and the extraordinary development of inner forces he had achieved, but simply his understanding of one property of the functioning of man's organism, which might be connected to a certain degree with the servility of human nature.

This property, which is inherent in every ordinary man, to whichever class he may belong and whatever his age, is that, whenever he thinks about something concrete outside himself, then his muscles instantly strain, that is to say vibrate, in the direction taken by his thoughts.

For example, if he thinks about America and his thoughts are turned in the direction where, according to his notions, America lies, certain of his muscles, particularly, so to say, the fine ones, vibrate towards the same place; in other words, their entire tension strains in that direction.

In the same way, if the thoughts of a man are turned towards the second floor of a house when he himself is on the first floor, certain of his muscles are strained and, as it were, raised upwards; in short, a movement of the thoughts in a definite direction is always accompanied by a tension of the muscles in the same direction.

This phenomenon proceeds even among those who are aware of its existence and who try by all the means known to them to avoid it.

Ekim Bey

Everyone has probably happened to see, in some theatre or circus or other public place, how various so-called Indian fakirs, conjurors, wonder-workers and other remarkable exponents of the secrets of supernatural knowledge, astonish people with their magical phenomena, finding hidden objects or performing some other action previously decided upon by the audience.

In accomplishing these miraculous feats these magicians hold the hand of one of the spectators, who of course is thinking about the action decided on, and, simply by means of the unconscious indications or shocks received from the person's hand, they 'guess' the action and carry it out.

They can do this not because they possess some special knowledge, but merely because they know the secret of this property of man. Knowing this secret, anyone could do the same with a little practice.

One has only to be able to concentrate one's attention on the other person's hand and catch its slight almost imperceptible movements. With practice and perseverance one can always succeed, like a magician, in guessing what has been thought of.

For instance, if the idea is that the magician should pick up a hat lying on the table, then, even if the person knows the trick and tries hard to think about the shoes lying under the couch, he will still unconsciously be thinking about the hat, and the muscles which guide the magician will tense in that direction, as they are subject more to the sub-consciousness than to the consciousness.

As I have said, Ekim Bey performed experiments of this sort on his friends in order to learn more about the human psyche and thus determine the causes of hypnotic influences.

Among the experiments he made to accomplish this task he had set himself was a highly original one which astounded the uninitiated more than any of the fakirs' tricks.

He proceeded as follows:

On a sheet of paper divided into squares he wrote the entire alphabet in order, and on the bottom line all the numbers from one to nine followed by nought. He prepared several such sheets and on each sheet he wrote the alphabet of a different language.

Sitting at a table, he put one of the alphabet sheets in front of him, a little to the left; and with his right hand he took a pencil. On his left, just opposite the alphabet, he seated the subject of the experiment, for example, somebody who had asked him to tell his fortune. Then with his left hand Ekim Bey took the right hand of this person, and began to speak more or less as follows:

'First of all I must know your name . . .' and then, as if talking to himself, he continued slowly—'the first letter of your name . . .' and he placed on the alphabet the hand of the person wishing to know his fate.

Thanks to the mentioned human property, when the hand passed over the letter with which the name began it gave an involuntary start.

Ekim Bey, knowing the significance of this movement, perceived it and continued: 'The first letter of your name is . . .' and he pronounced the letter over which the hand had trembled and wrote it down.

Continuing in this way, he found out the next few letters of the name and, having done so, guessed the whole name; for example, having obtained the letters S, T, and E, he could tell that the name was Stephen.

Then he said, 'Your name is Stephen. Now I must find out how old you are,' and he began to move the hand over the numbers.

He then discovered whether the man was married or not, how many children there were, the name of each child, the name of his wife, the name of his greatest enemy, greatest friend and so on and so forth.

After several of these miraculous guesses, his clients were so astonished that they forgot everything on earth and proceeded to tell Ekim Bey all he wanted to know, and, letting go their hand, he had only to repeat what they themselves had said. Then, whatever fantastic stuff he might tell them about their future, they believed it all and hung with awe on every word.

Later, everyone on whom Ekim Bey had made this experiment went around talking about it on all possible occasions and, of course, made such extravagant additions about his powers that the listeners' hair stood on end.

And so, among those who knew and heard about him, an image was built up which gradually acquired the aura of a magician, and even his name was uttered in a whisper and with trepidation.

Many people, not only Turks but also people from other countries, chiefly from Europe, began to write to him and pester him with all kinds of requests. Some begged him to foretell their future from their handwriting; others, to remedy their unrequited love; yet others to cure them from a distance of their chronic ailments. He received letters from pashas, generals, officers, mullahs, teachers, priests, merchants, and from women of every age, but especially from young women of all nationalities.

In short, there were such heaps of these letters with different kinds of requests that, if Ekim Bey had wished to send even empty replies to each of the writers, he would have had to have no less than fifty secretaries.

One day when I visited him in Scutari at his father's estate on the shores of the Bosphorus, he showed me many of these letters and I remember how we almost split our sides with laughter at the naïveté and stupidity of people.

He ultimately grew so weary of it all that he even gave up his well-loved work as a physician and left the places where he was known.

Ekim Bey's thorough knowledge of hypnotism and of all the automatic properties of the psyche of the ordinary man turned out to be very useful during one of our journeys, when he succeeded in getting us out of a very difficult situation into which we had fallen.

Once, when Ekim Bey and I with several of our comrades were in the town of Yangishar in Kashgar, having one of our usual long rests, intending to go next into the valleys of the Hindu Kush Mountains, Ekim Bey received news from his uncle in Turkey that his father was failing rapidly and would probably not live long.

This news disturbed Ekim Bey so much that he decided to interrupt his journey and return to Turkey as quickly as possible.

in order to spend what little time remained with his beloved father.

As these incessant wanderings from place to place under constant nervous strain had begun to weary me, and as I also wished to go and see my parents, I decided to break off my journey and travel as far as Russia with Ekim Bey.

Taking leave of our comrades, we went through Irkeshtam towards Russia. After many adventures and a host of great difficulties, without following the usual roads from Kashgar, all of which went to Osh, we managed to reach the town of Andijan in the Ferghana region.

We had decided to go through this once great region, because we wished to take advantage of the opportunity to inspect the ruins of several ancient towns, about which we had heard a great deal and which we expected to find chiefly by means of logical deductions from certain historical data.

We had thus greatly lengthened our journey before we came out on to the main road near Andijan. In Margelan we bought our railway tickets to Krasnovodsk and were already seated in the train when we found, to our great distress, that we had not enough money for the rest of our trip nor even for the next day's food. Moreover, during our travels through Kashgar our clothes had become so shabby that we were not fit to be seen in public, so money was also needed for buying clothes.

We therefore decided not to go as far as Krasnovodsk, but to change trains at Chernyaevo and go to Taskhent, a large centre where we could send for money by telegraph and manage to live as best we could until it arrived.

We did so. Having arrived at Tashkent and taken a room in a cheap hotel not far from the station, we first of all went to send off the telegrams and then, as this took almost all the money we had left, we went to the bazaar to sell our remaining possessions: rifles, watches, pedometer, compass, maps, in short, everything on which we could hope to raise any money at all.

In the evening, while we were walking along the street and pondering on our situation, and wondering where the people to whom we had telegraphed might be and whether they would have the sense to remit the money immediately, without noticing it we reached Old Tashkent. We sat down in a Sart *chaikhana*, continuing to ponder on what we would do if the money were delayed; and after long deliberation and examination of the various possibilities, we finally decided that, there in Tashkent, Ekim Bey should give himself out to be an Indian fakir and I a sword-swallower and a man who could consume any quantity of poisonous substances. And we made all kinds of jokes about it.

The next morning the first thing we did was to go to the offices of a Tashkent newspaper, to the department which accepted advertisements and also took orders for all sorts of posters.

The clerk there was a very friendly Jew who had recently arrived from Russia. After chatting with him a little, we arranged for advertisements to be inserted in all three of the Tashkent newspapers, and also ordered large posters announcing that a certain Indian fakir had arrived—I do not at the moment remember what Ekim Bey called himself, but I think it was Ganez or Ganzin—and that, with his assistant Salakan, on the following evening in the hall of a certain club, he would give a demonstration of hypnotic experiments and many other supernatural phenomena.

The clerk also undertook to obtain the permission of the police for putting up the posters throughout the town, and by the next day posters about unprecedented miracles were already eyesores to the inhabitants of both New and Old Tashkent.

By that time we had found two unemployed men who had come from the interior of Russia and, after sending them to the baths for a good scrub, we took them to our hotel and prepared them for hypnotic seances. We finally brought them into such a state of hypnosis that one could stick a large pin into their chests, sew up their mouths, and, placing them between two chairs with the head on one and the feet on another, put enormous weights on their stomachs; after which anyone in the audience who wished could come and pull a hair out of their heads, and so on and so forth.

But what particularly astonished all the learned doctors, lawyers and others, was when Ekim Bey, by the means I have described, found out their names or their ages. In short, at the end of the first seance, besides a full cash-box, we received hundreds of invitations to dinner; and how the women of all classes of society made eyes at us—of this there is no need to speak.

On three evenings in succession we gave seances, and, as we had earned more money than we needed, we left without delay to escape from our burdensome admirers.

In writing this chapter, which has revived in my memory our various expeditions and wanderings through Asia, I have recalled by association the curious notion about this continent which is held by most Europeans.

Having lived fifteen years uninterruptedly in the West, and being constantly in contact with people of all nationalities, I have come to the conclusion that no one in Europe knows or has any idea about Asia.

Most people in Europe and America have the notion that Asia is a kind of indefinite, great continent adjoining Europe, and inhabited by savage or, at best, semi-savage groups of peoples who just happened to be there and go wild.

Their ideas about its size are very vague; they are always ready to compare it with European countries and do not suspect that Asia is such a vast continent that several Europes could be put into it, and that it contains whole races of people about whom not only Europeans but even Asiatics themselves have never heard. Furthermore, among these 'savage groups' certain sciences, as, for example, medicine, astrology, natural science and so on, without any wiseacring or hypothetical explanations, have long since attained a degree of perfection which European civilization may perhaps reach only after several hundred years.

IX

PIOTR KARPENKO

THIS CHAPTER WILL BE DEVOTED to Piotr Karpenko, friend of my childhood, who later became, by his own real achievements and not merely by diploma, a prominent mining engineer, and who is now deceased. . . .

May he attain the Kingdom of Heaven!

It will be sufficient, I think, for portraying all the aspects of the individuality of Piotr Karpenko, and also for fulfilling my aim in this series of my writings, namely, that the reader should obtain instructive and really useful material, if I begin this chapter by describing the circumstances in which our first inner intimacy arose, and then relate several incidents which occurred on one of our expeditions, during which there befell, by the will of fate, the misfortune which led to his premature death.

This close friendship of ours began when we were still boys. I will describe what happened in as much detail as possible, the more so as this may very well throw light on certain aspects of the psyche of young scamps in general, some of whom may later grow up to be unusual men.

We were living in the town of Kars and at that time I was one of the choir-boys of the fortress cathedral.

I must say first of all that, after my teacher Bogachevsky had left Kars and my first tutor, Dean Borsh, had gone away on leave of absence owing to illness, I was deprived of both of these men who were real authorities for me; and as there was also talk in my family about the possibility of returning to Alexandropol in the near future, I no longer wished to remain in Kars and began to think about going to Tiflis, where I had dreamed for a long time of joining what was called the Archdeacon's Choir—a proposal which had often been made to me and which was very flattering to my youthful self-love.

It was at this period of my life, while such dreams were still the centre of gravity of my as yet undeveloped thinking faculty, that early one morning there came running up to me one of the choristers of the fortress cathedral, an army clerk, who had become my friend chiefly because I sometimes brought him good cigarettes, which I must confess I filched surreptitiously from my uncle's cigarette case. Panting for breath, he told me that he had accidentally overheard a discussion between the commandant of the fortress, General Fadeef, and the chief of the mounted police about the arrest and cross-examination of several persons in connection with an affair relating to the artillery range, and my name had been mentioned as having possibly been mixed up in it.

This news greatly alarmed me because I had, as is said, something on my conscience in connection with the artillery range, so, wishing to avoid any awkward possibilities, I decided not to delay my departure but to leave Kars the very next day.

This incident of the artillery range, through which a factor was formed in my psyche for engendering remorse of conscience, and on account of which I hurriedly made my departure, was the cause of my intimate friendship with Piotr Karpenko.

At that particular time I had a number of friends of my own age as well as others many years older. Among the former was one very agreeable boy, the son of a vodka manufacturer. His name was Riaouzov or Riaïzov, I do not remember which. He often used to invite me to his house and occasionally I would drop in without invitation.

His parents spoiled him a great deal. He had his own separate room where we could prepare our lessons in comfort. On his writing-table there was almost always a plateful of freshly baked pies of flaky pastry, of which I was then very fond. But what was perhaps most important was that he had a sister about twelve or

thirteen years old, who often came to his room when I happened
to be there.

A friendship sprang up between us and, without noticing it, I
fell in love with her. It seemed that she also was not indifferent to
me. In short, a silent romance began between us.

Another friend of mine, the son of an artillery officer, also used
to come there. And he, like us, was studying at home in order to
enter some school, as he had not been admitted to the cadet corps,
having been found a little deaf in one ear.

This was Piotr Karpenko. He too was in love with the Riaouzov
girl and she obviously liked him also. She was nice to him, it
seems, because he often brought her sweets and flowers, and to
me because I played the guitar well and was skilful at making
designs on handkerchiefs, which she loved to embroider and say
afterwards that she had designed herself.

So here we were, both in love with this girl, and little by little,
so to say, the jealousy of rivals began to flame in us.

Once after evening service in the cathedral, where this breaker
of hearts was also present, I thought out some plausible excuse
and asked the choir-master's permission to leave a little early,
as I wished to meet her as she went out and accompany her
home.

At the doors of the cathedral I found myself face to face with
my rival. Although hate for one another raged in both of us, we
escorted our 'lady' home like chivalrous knights. But after we had
left her I could no longer restrain myself and, picking a quarrel
over something or other, I gave him a sound thrashing.

The evening after the fight I went as usual with some of my
comrades to the cathedral bell-tower. At that time there was no
real bell-tower in the grounds of the fortress cathedral. It was just
then being built and the bells were hung in a temporary wooden
structure with a high roof, rather like an octagonal sentry-box.
The space between the roof and the beams on which the bells hung
was our 'club' where we met almost every day, and, sitting astride
the beams or on the narrow ledge around the walls under the roof,
we smoked, told anecdotes and even prepared our lessons. Later,
when the permanent stone bell-tower was completed and the bells

put in, this temporary one was presented by the Russian government to the new Greek church being built at that time, and there, it seems, it continues to serve as a bell-tower.

Besides the regular members of the club, I found there my friend Petia from Alexandropol, who had come to Kars on a visit. He was the son of Kerensky, a postal-telegraph inspector who was later one of the officers killed in the Russo-Japanese war. There was also a boy from the Greek quarter of Kars nicknamed Fekhi, whose real name was Korkhanidi, and who later became the author of many school-books. He had brought home-made Greek halva as a present from his aunt to us choir-boys, whose singing had often affected her to the depths of her soul.

We sat, ate the halva, smoked and chatted. Soon after, Piotr Karpenko arrived with his eyes bandaged, accompanied by two other Russian boys, not members of the club. He came up to me demanding an explanation for my having insulted him the day before. Being one of those youths who read a good deal of poetry and love to express themselves in high-faluting language, he delivered a lengthy harangue which he brought to an abrupt close with the following categorical declaration: 'The earth is too small for both of us; hence one of us must die.'

On hearing his bombastic tirade I wanted to knock this nonsense right out of his head. But when my friends began to reason with me, saying that only people who have not yet been touched at all by contemporary culture, as, for instance, Kurds, square accounts in this manner, and that respectable people have recourse to more civilized methods, my pride began to assert itself; and in order not to be called uneducated or cowardly, I entered into a serious discussion of this incident.

After a lengthy dispute, called by us a debate, during which it turned out that several of the boys present were on my side and several on the side of my rival—and which debate at times developed into a deafening din and brought us perilously near to throwing each other down from the top of the bell-tower—it was decided that we must fight a duel.

Then the question arose, where to obtain weapons? Neither pistols nor swords were to be had anywhere and the situation became very perplexing. All our emotions, which a moment before had reached the limits of excitement, were suddenly concentrated on how to find a way out of the difficulty which had arisen.

Among the company was a friend of mine, a boy named Tourchaninov, who had a very squeaky voice and whom we all considered a very comical fellow. While we were sitting pondering on what was to be done, he suddenly chirped up and exclaimed: 'If it's difficult to get pistols, it's easy to get cannon.'

Everybody laughed, as they always did at everything he said.

'What are you laughing at, you silly devils!' he retorted. 'It's quite possible to use cannon for your purpose. There's only one drawback. You've decided that one of you must die, but in a duel with cannon both of you might die. If you consent to take such a risk, then to carry out my proposal is the easiest thing in the world.'

What he proposed was that we should both go to the artillery range where firing practice was held, lie down and hide somewhere between the guns and the targets and await our doom. Whichever of us should be hit by a random shell would be the one fated to die.

We all knew the artillery range very well. It was not far away in the mountains encircling the town. It was a fairly large tract of land, from six to nine miles square, which it was absolutely forbidden to enter at certain times of the year, during firing practice, and which was strictly guarded on all sides.

We often went there, chiefly at night, at the instigation of two big boys named Aivazov and Denisenko, who had a certain authority over us, to collect, or more truly to steal, the copper parts of the used shells and the scraps of lead which lay scattered about after the shells had burst, and which we later sold by weight for a good price.

Although it was strictly forbidden to collect, let alone sell, the remnants of the shells, we nevertheless contrived to do so by taking advantage of moonlight nights and of those times when the guards were less vigilant.

As a result of the fresh debate held on Tourchaninov's

proposal, it was categorically decided by all present to carry out this project the very next day.

According to the stipulations of the 'seconds', who were Kerensky and Korkhanidi on my side, and on the side of my rival the two strange boys whom he had brought along with him, we were to go to the artillery range early in the morning before the firing began, and at approximately one hundred yards from the targets lie down at a certain distance from each other in some large shell-hole where no one could see us, and remain there until dusk; whichever one was still alive by then could leave and go where he wished.

The seconds also decided to remain all day near the range, by the banks oft he river Kars Chai, and in the evening to look for us in our holes to find out the result of the duel. If it should turn out that one or both of us were merely wounded, then they would do the necessary; and if it should turn out that we had been killed, they would then spread the tale that we had gone to collect copper and lead, not knowing that there would be firing that day, and so had been 'wiped out'.

The next morning at break of day the whole party of us, supplied with provisions, made our way to the Kars Chai. Arriving there, we two rivals were given our share of the provisions and were conducted by two of the seconds to the range, where we lay down in separate hollows. The seconds returned to the others at the river and passed the time fishing.

So far everything had seemed rather a joke, but when the firing began it was anything but a joke. I do not know either the form or the sequence in which the subjective experiencings and mental associations of my rival flowed, but I do know what proceeded in me as soon as the firing started. What I experienced and felt when the shells began to fly and burst over my head, I remember now as if it were only yesterday.

At the beginning I was completely stupefied, but soon the intensity of feeling which flooded through me, and the force of logical confrontation of my thought increased to such an extent that, at each moment, I thought and experienced more than during an entire twelvemonth.

Simultaneously, there arose in me for the first time the 'whole sensation of myself', which grew stronger and stronger, and a clear realization that through my thoughtlessness I had put myself in a situation of almost certain annihilation, because at that moment my death seemed inevitable.

Instinctive fear in face of this inevitability so took possession of my entire being that surrounding realities seemed to disappear, leaving only an unconquerable living terror.

I remember I tried to make myself as small as possible and to take shelter behind a ridge in the ground, so as to hear nothing and think about nothing.

The trembling which began in the whole of my body reached such a frightful intensity that it was as if each tissue vibrated independently, and, in spite of the roaring of the guns, I very distinctly heard the beating of my heart, and my teeth chattered so hard that it seemed as if at any moment they would break.

I will remark here, by the way, that in my opinion it was owing to this incident in my youth that there first arose in my individuality certain data—which later took definite form, thanks to various conscious actions upon me on the part of certain normally educated people—data which have always prevented me from being perturbed by life questions in which exclusively my own egoistic interests were at stake, and from acknowledging or experiencing any but authentic fears, while on the other hand, they have enabled me, without being carried away or deluded, to understand the fear of another and to enter into his position.

I do not remember how long I lay there in this state; I can only say that in this case, as always and in everything, our most supreme, inexorable Sovereign, Time, did not fail to assert his rights, and I began to grow accustomed to my ordeal as well as to the roar of the cannon and the bursting of the shells round me.

Little by little the tormenting thoughts of the possibility of my sad end began to disappear. Although as usual the firing was broken up into several periods, it was impossible to escape during the intervals, chiefly because of the danger of falling into the hands of the guards.

There was nothing to be done but to keep lying there quietly.

After eating some lunch I even, without knowing it, fell asleep. Evidently the nervous system, after such intensive activity, urgently demanded rest. I do not know how long I slept, but when I woke up it was already evening and everything was quiet.

When I was fully awake and realized clearly the reasons for my being in that place, I first assured myself with great joy that I was safe and sound, and it was only when this egoistic gladness of mine had subsided that I suddenly remembered and began to feel concerned about my comrade in misfortune. So creeping quietly out of my hole and taking a good look round, I went over to the place where he should have been.

Seeing him lying there motionless, I was very frightened, though I thought and was even quite sure that he was asleep; but when I suddenly noticed blood on his leg, I completely lost my head, and all the hatred of the day before turned into pity. With a fear as great as I had experienced only a few hours earlier for my own life, I crouched down as though still instinctively trying not to be seen.

I was still in this position when the seconds crawled up to me on all fours. Seeing me looking so strangely at the outstretched Karpenko and then noticing the blood on his leg, they felt that something terrible had happened, and crouching there, glued to the spot, they also began to stare at him. As they later told me, they too were quite certain that he was dead.

The whole group of us remained as though self-hypnotized, until accidentally we were aroused out of our stupor by Kerensky. As he later explained, having been for some time in a cramped position while staring at Karpenko, he suddenly felt his corn hurting him, and leaning forward a little to change his position, he noticed that the edge of Karpenko's coat was moving at regular intervals. Creeping nearer, he became convinced that he was breathing, and informed us of this almost with a shout.

Instantly brought back to our senses, we also crept forward, and right there in the ditch round the motionless Karpenko, we began, constantly interrupting each other, to deliberate on what was to be done. Suddenly by some kind of tacit agreement, we made a chair of our arms and carried Karpenko to the river.

We stopped at the ruins of an old brick factory and there, having hurriedly made an improvised bed out of some of our clothes and laid Karpenko on it, we began to examine the wound. It appeared that only one leg had been grazed by shrapnel and not in a dangerous place.

As Karpenko was still unconscious and no one knew what to do, one of us ran off to find a friend of ours in the town, an assistant surgeon, who was also a member of the cathedral choir, while the others washed the wound and somehow or other bandaged it.

The assistant surgeon soon arrived in his buggy and we explained to him that the accident had occurred while we were collecting copper, not knowing that the firing would take place. Having examined the wound, he said that it was not dangerous and that the fainting was due to loss of blood. In fact, when he administered a whiff of smelling salts, the patient immediately came to himself.

We of course begged the assistant surgeon not to tell anyone how the accident had happened, since it would certainly get us into great trouble because of the strict orders against trespassing on the firing-range.

As soon as Karpenko came to, he looked round at everyone present; and when, resting his gaze on me longer than on the others, he smiled, something moved within me and I was overcome with remorse and pity. From that moment I began to feel towards him as towards a brother.

We carried the patient home, and explained to his family that, in crossing a ravine to go fishing, a boulder had become dislodged and had fallen and injured his leg.

His parents believed our tale, and I obtained their permission to spend every night at his bedside until his recovery. During those days while he was still weak and lay in bed, I took care of him like a kind-hearted brother and, talking about one thing and another, our close friendship began.

As for the love of our 'lady' on whose account all this had occurred—in Karpenko as well as in me, this feeling had suddenly evaporated.

Soon after his recovery his parents took him to Russia, where later he passed his examinations and was admitted to some technical institute.

For several years after this incident I did not see Karpenko, but regularly on each of my Saint's-days and birthdays I received a long letter from him, in which he usually began by describing his inner and outer life in detail and went on to ask my opinion on a long list of questions which interested him, chiefly on religious subjects. His first serious enthusiasm for our common ideas arose seven years after the duel I have described.

One summer, while travelling to Kars for the holidays by mail-coach—at that time there was no railway there—he passed through Alexandropol, and learning that I was there at the time, he stopped off to see me. I had gone to Alexandropol that summer in order to carry out, in solitude and without being disturbed, certain practical experiments relating to questions which particularly interested me then, concerning the influence of the vibrations of sound on various types of human beings as well as on other forms of life.

The day he arrived I had lunch with him, and suggested that he should accompany me to the large stable which I had converted into an original kind of laboratory, where I used to spend every afternoon. He examined everything that I had there and became so interested in what I was doing that, when he left that day for Kars to visit his family, he decided to return in three days. On his return he stayed with me almost the entire summer, going only for a day or two, from time to time, to see his family in Kars.

At the end of the summer several members of our recently formed group, the Seekers of Truth, joined me in Alexandropol with the object of going to make some excavations among the ruins of Ani, the ancient capital of Armenia. On this expedition Karpenko joined us for the first time, and, being in contact for several weeks with various members of our group, he was gradually drawn into the sphere of the questions which interested us.

When the expedition was over he returned to Russia, and soon afterwards obtained his diploma as a mining engineer. I did not see him again for three years, but thanks to our uninterrupted correspondence we did not lose touch with each other. Karpenko also corresponded during this period with other members of the Seekers of Truth with whom he had become friends.

At the end of these three years he became a full member of our original society, and from then on took part in several serious expeditions of ours in Asia and Africa.

It was during one of these big expeditions, when we were intending to cross the Himalayas from the Pamir region to India, that the incident occurred which was the cause of his premature death. From the start we had encountered great difficulties. In our journey up the north-western slopes of the Himalayas, while crossing a steep mountain-pass, a large avalanche buried us all in snow and ice. With much effort all but two of us extricated ourselves from beneath the snow. Although we dug out the two others as fast as we could, they were already dead. One of them was Baron X, an ardent occultist; the other, our guide, Karakir Khaïnu.

By this misfortune we lost not only one of our good friends, but also a guide who knew the locality very well.

By the way, it must be said that the entire region between the Hindu Kush mountains and the great Himalayan range, where this accident took place, is a maze of narrow, intersecting gorges, the most bewildering of all the formations of similar cataclysmic origin on the surface of our planet over which we ever had to wander. These regions seem to have been intentionally made so confusing and complicated by the Higher Powers in order that not a single human being should ever dare to try to find his way through them.

After this accident, which deprived us of our guide, who was considered even among his own people as the one who knew best all the corners and windings of these regions, we wandered for several days, searching for a way out of this inhospitable place.

'Did they not have map or compass?' every reader will doubt-less ask.

How not? We had them and even more than necessary, but in fact, it would be fortunate for travellers if these so-called maps of uninhabited regions did not exist.

A map, as my friend Yelov used to say, is called in a certain language by the word *khormanoupka*, which means 'wisdom', and 'wisdom' in that language is characterized as follows: 'Mental proof that twice two makes seven and a half, minus three and a little bit of something'.

In my opinion in employing contemporary maps it would be ideally useful to put into practice the sense of a judicious saying which declares: 'If you wish to succeed in anything then ask a woman for advice and do the opposite'.

It is the same in this case: if you wish to find the right road, consult the map and take one in the opposite direction, and you can always be sure of reaching just where you want to go. These maps may perhaps be all right for those contemporary people who, sitting in their studies with neither the time nor the possi-bility to go anywhere, nevertheless have to write books on all kinds of travel and adventures. Indeed, these maps are excellent for such people, because thanks to them they have more leisure for concocting their fantastic stories.

Good maps may perhaps exist for some localities, but with all I have had to do with them in my life, from ancient Chinese maps to special military topographic maps of many countries, I was never able to find one that was of practical use when it was really needed. Certain maps may, at times, more or less help travellers to find their way in thickly populated areas, but in uninhabited regions, that is to say, where they are the most necessary, as, for instance, in Central Asia, then, as I have already said, it would be better if they did not exist at all. Reality is distorted in them to the point of absurdity.

Such maps have many undesirable and distressing consequences for genuine travellers. For example, let us say that, according to the indications of the map, you will have to cross the next day over a high elevation where of course you expect to find it cold.

At night while packing your baggage, you take out your warm clothes and other things for protection against the cold and put them aside. Tying up all the remaining things into packs and loading them on your animals—horses, yaks or whatever they are—you put the warm things on top of the packs in order to have them ready as soon as they should be needed.

Well then, it almost always turns out that the next day, in spite of the indications of the map, you have to go down through valleys and lowlands, and that instead of the cold you expected, there is such a heat that you want to take off literally all your clothes. And as the warm things are neither packed up nor fastened tightly on the backs of the animals, they slip and shift at every step, disturbing the balance and bothering not only the animals but also the travellers themselves. And what it means to have to repack on the way, he alone can understand who has had to do it, even if only once, on a long day's journey over the mountains.

Of course, for journeys undertaken on behalf of some government or other for a certain political aim and for which large sums are allocated, or on a journey for which the funds are disbursed by a banker's widow, an ardent Theosophist, one might hire as many porters as one wishes to pack and unpack everything. But a genuine traveller has to do all this himself, and even if he should have servants he would be bound to help them, as in the midst of the hardships of travel it is difficult for a normal man to look on idly at the exertions of others.

These contemporary maps are what they are, evidently because they are prepared by methods such as I myself once witnessed. It was when I was travelling with several members of the group, Seekers of Truth, through the Pamirs, past the Alexander III Peak. At that time the headquarters of the surveyors from the Turkestan Military Topographic Department was located in one of the valleys near this peak. The chief surveyor was a certain colonel, a good friend of one of our travelling companions, and because of this we made a special visit to their camp.

The colonel had several young staff officers with him as assistants. They welcomed us with great joy as they had been living for several months in places where, for hundreds of miles, there was scarcely a single living soul. We stayed with them three days, intending to have a good rest in their tents.

When we were getting ready to leave one of the young officers begged permission to come with us, as he had to make a map of a locality two days distant in the direction we were going. He brought along two private soldiers to assist him.

In a certain valley we came across a camp of nomad Kara-Kirghiz and entered into conversation with them. The officer who was with us also spoke their language. One of the Kara-Kirghiz was elderly, and obviously an experienced man. The officer, one of my friends and I asked this Kara-Kirghiz to share a meal with us, hoping that we might profit by his knowledge of these places to extract from him such information as we needed.

We ate and spoke. We had brought bags made of sheep's stomachs which had been stuffed with excellent *kovurma*, and the officer also had vodka, which he had brought from Tashkent and which these nomads greatly relish, particularly when none of their own people see what they are drinking. While pouring down the vodka, the Kara-Kirghiz gave us various hints about these regions and indicated where certain points of interest were to be found. Pointing to a perpetually snow-capped mountain which was already familiar to us, he said: 'You see that summit yonder? Well, just behind it there is this . . . and that . . . and there is also the famous cave of Iskander.' The officer sketched all this down on paper. He was, by the way, rather a good artist.

When we had finished eating and the Kara-Kirghiz had gone back to his camp, I looked at the drawing which the officer had made and saw that he had put everything that the old man had described not behind the mountain as the latter had indicated, but in front of it. I pointed out this discrepancy to him and it appeared that the officer had confused 'in front of' with 'behind' as in that language the words 'behind' and 'in front of', *bou-ti* and *pou-ti*, are almost the same, and to someone who does not know this language well they sound almost alike, especially when they are pronounced quickly with other words.

When I explained all this to the officer, he merely said: 'Oh, well, devil take it!' and he slammed his sketch-book shut. He had been drawing for almost two hours and of course did not wish to do it all over again, the more so as we were all ready to proceed on our way.

I am sure that this sketch was afterwards embodied in a map exactly as the officer had made it. Later, the printer of the maps, having never been to these regions, would place those details not on the side of the mountain where they belong but on the other side, and of course that is where our brother traveller will expect to find them. With few exceptions everything connected with the making of these maps proceeds in this way. Therefore, when a map indicates that you are approaching a river, you should not be surprised to come across one of the 'gorgeous daughters of Mr. Himalaya'.

And so we continued for several days at random, without a guide, observing great caution to avoid meeting any of those bands of brigands who, particularly at that time, were not great lovers of the Europeans who fell into their hands, and transformed them with solemn ceremony into captives and later, with no less ceremony, exchanged them with some other tribe inhabiting this part of the surface of our dear planet for a good horse, or a rifle of the latest model, or simply for a young girl, also, of course, a captive.

Moving from place to place, we reached a small stream and decided to follow its course, reckoning that it must ultimately lead us somewhere. We did not even know whether it would lead us north or south, as the area we were in was a watershed.

We followed the banks of this stream as long as we could, but soon, when they became very steep and almost impassable, we decided to go along the bed of the stream itself.

We had not gone more than a few miles in this way when it was apparent that the stream, swollen by the water from numerous small tributaries, was rising to such a height that it was becoming impossible to continue our journey along its bed, and we were obliged to stop and deliberate seriously how to proceed.

After long discussions, we decided to slaughter all the goats, which we had brought with us for transporting our things and for our subsistence, in order to make *bourdiouks* out of their skins which we could inflate and attach to a raft, and thus float further down the river.

To carry out this decision of ours, we chose a convenient place not far from the stream, where we could easily defend ourselves against any danger, and set up our camp. Finding that it was too late to do anything more that day, we pitched our tents and, lighting fires in our customary way, we ate and lay down to sleep, having of course arranged watchmen to take turns during the night.

The first thing next day, with the consent of our consciences, degenerated like those of all contemporary people and corresponding exactly to the requirements of Hell, we killed all the goats, which only the day before we had regarded as our sincere friends and associates in overcoming the difficulties of the journey.

After this admirable Christian-Mohammedan manifestation, one of us began to cut their meat into small pieces in order to roast it and fill some of the skins; some began to prepare the *bourdiouks* and inflate them; others twisted the goats' intestines to make cords for tying the raft together and attaching the *bourdiouks*; and still others, including myself, took axes and went to look for hard wood suitable for the raft.

In our search we wandered rather a long distance from our camp. We were looking for a kind of plane tree called there *karagatch* and for a fibrous birch. Of all the wood to be found in that neighbourhood, only these two kinds were, in our opinion, strong enough to withstand collisions with boulders and rocks in the narrow passages and over the rapids.

Near our camp we came across chiefly fig-trees and other varieties not hard enough for our purpose. As we were going along examining trees, we suddenly saw, sitting on the ground, a man belonging to one of the local tribes. Having talked it over amongst ourselves, we decided to go up to him and ask him where the trees we needed were to be found. Approaching nearer, we saw that he was clothed in rags, and we could tell by his face that he was a kind of *ez-ezounavouran*, that is, a man who was working on himself for the salvation of his soul, or as Europeans would say, a fakir.

As I have happened to use the word 'fakir', I do not consider it superfluous to digress a little in order to throw some light on this famous word. It is, indeed, one of the many empty words which, on account of the incorrect meaning given them, particularly in recent times, has an automatic action upon all contemporary Europeans and has become one of the chief causes of the progressive dwindling of their thinking capacity.

Although the word 'fakir' in the meaning given it by Europeans is unknown to the peoples of Asia, nevertheless, this same word is in use there almost everywhere. Fakir, or more correctly *fakhr*, has as its root the Turkoman word meaning 'beggar', and among almost all the peoples of the continent of Asia whose speech is derived from ancient Turkoman, this word has come down to our day with the meaning of 'swindler' or 'cheat'.

As a matter of fact, to express this meaning of 'swindler' or 'cheat' two different words are used among these peoples, both derived from ancient Turkoman. One is this word 'fakir' and the other is *lourie*. The former is the word used for a cheat or swindler who uses his guile to take advantage of others by way of their religiousness, while the latter is applied to someone who simply takes advantage of their stupidity. The name *lourie*, by the way, is given to all gypsies, both as a people and as individuals.

Generally speaking, gypsies are found among all other peoples and everywhere lead a nomadic life. They are chiefly engaged in dealing in horses, tinkering, in singing at feasts, fortune-telling and kindred occupations. They usually make their camps near populated places and deceive naïve townspeople and villagers by every kind of cunning. Consequently the word *lourie*, denoting the gypsy people, has from long ago come to be used in Asia for every person, regardless of race, who is a swindler or a cheat.

For conveying the meaning which Europeans wrongly ascribe to the word 'fakir', several words are employed among Asiatic peoples, the most widely used being *ez-ezounavouran*, which comes from the Turkoman spoken language and means 'he who beats himself'.

I have myself read and heard many statements by Europeans about these so-called fakirs, asserting that their tricks are supernatural and miraculous, whereas actually, in the judgement of all more or less normal people in Asia, such tricks are performed by unconscionable swindlers and cheats of the highest order.

To show what confusion the wrong use of this word has caused among Europeans, I think it will be sufficient to say that, although I have travelled in almost all the countries where these fakirs, as imagined by Europeans, are supposed to live, I have never seen a single one of them; but I did have the good fortune recently to see a genuine *fakhr*, in the sense used by people of the continent of Asia, only not in India or any of those countries where Europeans think they live, but in the very heart of Europe, in the city of Berlin.

I was strolling one day along Kurfurstendamm in the direction of the main entrance to the Zoological Gardens, when I saw on the pavement, on a little hand-wagon, a cripple who had lost both legs, turning an antediluvian musical-box.

In Berlin, the capital city of Germany, as in other large centres representing, as it were, the epitome of contemporary civilization, it is forbidden to ask for charity directly, but anyone who wishes may beg and will not be bothered by the police, if he grinds an old barrel-organ, or sells empty match-boxes or indecent postcards and various kindred literature.

This beggar, dressed like a German soldier, was turning his musical-box, which had half its notes missing. As I passed by I threw him a few small coins and, happening to glance at him, his face seemed familiar to me. I did not question him, as in general I did not then, any more than now, risk speaking alone with strangers in my broken German, but I began to think where I could have seen him before.

When I had finished my business, I returned along the same street. The cripple was still there. I approached very slowly and looked at him closely, trying to recall why his face was so familiar, but at that moment I could not. It was only on arriving at the Romanische Café, that it suddenly came to me that the man was no other than the husband of a lady who, several years before in

Constantinople, was sent to me by a close friend of mine, with a letter of introduction appealing to me to give her medical treatment. The lady's husband was a former Russian officer who, it seems, had been evacuated from Russia to Constantinople with Wrangel's Army.

I then remembered how the young lady had come to me with a dislocated shoulder and her body covered with bruises. While I was busy with her arm, she told me that her husband had beaten her because she had refused to sell herself for a good sum to a certain Spanish Jew. Somehow or other with the help of Drs. Victorov and Maximovitch I put her shoulder right, after which she left.

Two or three weeks after that I was sitting in a Russian restaurant in Constantinople called the 'Black Rose', when this lady approached me. Nodding in the direction of a man with whom she had been sitting, she said: 'There he is—my husband,' and added, 'I have made it up with him again. He is really quite a good man although he does lose his temper at times.' Having told me this, she quickly left. It was only then that I understood what kind of woman she was. Afterwards, I sat there and scrutinized the face of this officer for a long time, as I was interested in such a rare type.

And now here was this same officer, a legless cripple, in the uniform of a German soldier, turning a musical-box and collecting small German coins. In the course of a day a great many small coins were thrown by kind-hearted passers-by to this unfortunate victim of the war!

This man in my opinion was a genuine *fakhr* in the sense understood by all Asiatic peoples; as for his legs, would to God that mine were as sound and strong as his!

Well, enough about this; let us return to the story we had begun. . . .

And so we approached that *ez-ezounavouran*, and after appropriate greetings sat down beside him. Before asking him what we wanted to know, we began to speak with him, observing the various conventional courtesies habitual among these people.

It is interesting to remark that the psyche of the people

inhabiting these regions is totally different from that of Europeans. Among the latter, almost always what is in the thoughts is on the tongue. Among Asiatics this is not the case—the duality of the psyche is highly developed. Any person of these regions, however polite and friendly he may be outwardly, may none the less inwardly hate you and be thinking out all kinds of harm for you.

Many Europeans who have lived among Asiatics for decades without understanding this particularity of theirs, and who judge them according to themselves, always lose a great deal as a result of this and create many misunderstandings which might have been avoided. These people of Asia are full of pride and self-love. Each of them, irrespective of his position, demands from everyone a certain attitude towards himself as a person.

Among them the main thing is kept in the background, and one must lead up to it as if it were just by the way; if not, at the best, they will for instance direct you to the right when your road lies to the left. On the other hand, if you do everything as it should be done, then not only will they give you accurate directions, but will even be eager to help you, if possible themselves, to reach your intended destination.

Therefore, when we approached this man, we did not begin by asking him what we wanted to know. God forbid that we should do so before observing the necessary conventions.

After sitting down beside him, we spoke of the beauty of the scenery and told him that we were there for the first time, asked how the surrounding conditions suited him, and so on. And only much later I remarked as if in passing: 'We need such and such wood for a certain purpose, but we are not able to find it anywhere around here.'

He replied that he greatly regretted that he did not know where it could be found, as he had only been in the neighbourhood a short time, but that a certain respected old man, who was his teacher, might know. He lived behind the hill in a cave, and had been there a long time and knew the locality very well.

He thereupon got up to go to him, but Dr. Sari-Ogli stopped him and asked whether we could see his respected teacher and

ask him ourselves about the wood we needed. He replied: 'Of
course; let us go together. He is a man who is almost a saint and
is always ready to help anyone.'

As we went, we saw from a long way off a man sitting in a
meadow under a tree, and our guide, without waiting for us,
ran to him and, after telling him something, beckoned to us to
approach.

We exchanged the customary greetings and sat down beside
him. At that moment another of the local inhabitants came and
sat down beside us. As it turned out later he also was a pupil of
this venerable *ez-ezounavouran*.

The face of this old man appeared to us so benevolent and not
of ordinary humankind that, without any of the usual preliminary
manipulations and without concealing anything, we told him
what had happened to us and how we thought of making our
way out of that region. We also told him why we had come to
him.

He listened to us with great attention and, after thinking a
little, said that the stream by whose banks we had stopped was a
tributary of the river Chitral, which flows into the river Kabul,
which in its turn flows into the Indus. There were many roads,
he told us, leading out of that region, but they were all long and
arduous. If we were able to travel as we had planned, and if we
were fortunate enough to avoid the banks inhabited by people
who were not at all friendly to strangers, then our plan would be
the best that could be devised. As for the kind of wood we were
seeking, he thought it was not at all suitable, and that the best
wood for the purpose would be Cornelian cherry, and added that
there was a dell to the left of the path by which we had come
where thick clumps of these trees grew.

All of a sudden there was a sound from near by—the kind
that makes a man shiver from head to foot. The old man calmly
turned his head, and with his old voice called out in a special way.
Then, out of the bushes, in all its beauty and strength, emerged a
huge grey bear, carrying something in its mouth. As it came
nearer to us, the old man called out again, and the bear, looking
at us with glittering eyes, moved slowly towards him and laid

the thing it was carrying at his feet—then turned round and lumbered back into the bushes.

We were, in the full sense of the word, stupefied, and the trembling which took possession of our bodies was so strong that our teeth were chattering.

The old man explained to us in a kindly voice that the bear was a good friend of his who sometimes brought him *djungari*.[1] And it was this that the bear had laid at his feet.

Even after these reassuring words we were unable to fully recover our composure and looked at each other in deep silence, our faces revealing utter bewilderment. The old man, rising heavily from his seat, aroused us out of our stupor and said that it was the hour for his customary walk and if we wished he could accompany us to the dell where the cherry-trees grew.

Then he uttered a prayer and went on ahead, all of us with his pupils following behind. At the dell we did indeed see many clumps of this cherry, and then and there everyone, even including the old man himself, began cutting down the trees we needed, choosing the biggest.

When we had cut two good loads, considering this to be enough, we asked the old man whether he would consent to come with us to our camp, which was not far off, and permit one of our friends to make an exact portrait of him there, which could be done quickly by means of a special small machine he had. At first the old man refused, but his pupils helped us to persuade him, so, taking our loads, we went back to the banks of the stream where we had left the rest of our company at work. On reaching them we quickly explained everything, and Professor Skridlov took the old man's picture with his camera and immediately began developing it.

While he was doing this we all gathered round the old man, under the shade of a fig-tree. Among us was Vitvitskaïa, who had her neck bound up, as she had been suffering for some months from a painful affection of the throat, fairly common in the mountains, which had the appearance of a goitre.

---

[1] *Djungari* is a kind of maize which grows in these regions and is used there as a substitute for wheat.

Seeing her bandage, the old man asked what the trouble was. We explained and, calling her to him, the old man closely examined the swelling. He told Vitvitskaïa to lie on her back, and he then began to massage the swelling in various ways, at the same time whispering certain words.

We were all indescribably amazed when, after twenty minutes of massage, Vitvitskaïa's enormous swelling began to disappear before everyone's eyes, and after a further twenty minutes absolutely nothing remained of it.

Just then Professor Skridlov came back, having finished developing and printing the old man's photograph. He too was greatly astonished and, bowing deeply before the old man, humbly entreated him to relieve him of an attack, from which he had been suffering acutely the last few days, of his long established kidney trouble.

The *ez-ezounavouran* asked him for various details of his illness, and immediately sent off one of his pupils, who soon returned with the root of a certain small shrub. Giving this root to the professor, the old man said: 'You must take one part of this root with two parts of the bark of the fig-tree, which you can find almost everywhere; boil them well together and, every other day for two months, drink a glassful of this liquid before going to sleep.'

Then he and his pupils looked at his photograph which the professor had brought and which astounded them all, particularly the pupils. We invited the old man to share our meal of fresh goat *kovurma* with *pokhand*[1] cakes, which he did not refuse.

In the course of the conversation we learned that he had formerly been a top-bashi, or chief of artillery, of the Emir of Afghanistan, the grandfather of the then reigning Emir, and that, when he was sixty years old, he was wounded in a rebellion of Afghans and Baluchis against some European power, after which he returned to his native Khorasan. When he had completely recovered from his wounds, he no longer wished to return to his post as he was getting on in years, but decided to devote the rest of his life to the salvation of his soul.

[1] *Pokhand* is a flour, prepared from roasted barley, which makes the tastiest of breads.

First he got into touch with Persian dervishes; later, although not for long, he was a Baptist; and still later, returning to Afghanistan, he entered a monastery in the environs of Kabul. When he had understood everything he needed and was convinced that people were no longer necessary to him, he began to look for an isolated spot far from human habitation. Having found this place, he had settled here in the company of a few persons who wished to live according to his indications, and was awaiting his death—as he was already ninety-eight years old, and it is rare nowadays for anyone to pass a hundred.

As the old man prepared to leave, Yelov also addressed him, asking whether he would be good enough to advise him what to do about his eyes. Several years before in the Transcaspian region, he had contracted trachoma and, in spite of all kinds of treatments, the malady had not been cured but had become chronic. 'Although my eyes,' he said, 'do not bother me all the time, nevertheless in the mornings they are always closed up with excretions, and a change of climate or a sand-storm makes them rather painful.'

The old *ez-ezounavouran* advised him to grind some copper sulphate very fine and, every evening before going to sleep, to moisten a needle with his own saliva, dip it into the ground sulphate and draw it between the eyelids; and to continue this treatment for a certain period of time.

After he had given Yelov this advice, the venerable man rose and, making to each of us the gesture which in those regions signifies what we call a blessing, went towards his dwelling-place; and all of us, even our dogs, accompanied him.

On the way we resumed our conversation with the old man. Suddenly, Karpenko, without consulting any of us, addressed him in the Uzbek language and said:

'Holy Father! As by the will of fate we have met you in such unusual surroundings, a man great in knowledge and rich in experience of ordinary life as well as on the level of self-preparation for the being after death, we are all convinced beyond doubt that you will not refuse to give us your advice, of course so far as this is possible, on the life we should live and the ideals that we should hold before us, in order that we may ultimately be able to live as designed from Above and as is worthy of man.'

Before replying to this strange question of Karpenko's, the old man began to look round as if he were searching for something, and then went towards the trunk of a fallen tree.

He sat down on it, and when we had seated ourselves, some on the tree and others simply on the ground, he turned to all of us and slowly began to speak. His reply to Karpenko's question developed into a kind of lengthy sermon, of profound interest and significance.

The words then spoken by this old *eʒ-eʒounavouran* I will also record, but only in the third series of my writings, in a chapter entitled 'The astral body of man, its needs and possibilities of manifestation according to law'. Here, I will merely touch upon the results of the healing by this venerable man, which I verified by inquiries over many years.

From that time on Vitvitskaïa never had a recurrence or even any of the symptoms of the malady from which she had been suffering. Professor Skridlov did not know how to express his gratitude towards the old man who had cured him, probably for ever, of the sufferings which had tortured him for twelve years. And as for Yelov, a month later his trachoma was gone.

After this event, significant for all of us, we stayed there another three days, during which we split the wood, made the raft and prepared everything we had planned. Early in the morning of the fourth day the improvised raft was launched into the river and, boarding it, we began to move downstream.

At first our peculiar craft could not always move with the current alone, and at some places we had to push it, and at others even carry it, but the deeper the river became, the easier it was for the raft to move by itself, and at times, in spite of its load, it would fly along like one possessed.

We could not say that we felt completely secure, particularly when the raft passed through narrow places and collided against rocks, but later, when we were convinced of its sturdiness and of the efficacy of the device thought out by the engineer Samsanov, we were quite at ease and even began to crack jokes. This ingenious device of the engineer Samsanov was to attach two *bourdiouks* to the front and also to each side of the raft, to serve as buffers whenever it should strike boulders.

The second day of our trip down the river, we exchanged shots with a band of natives, who evidently belonged to one of the tribes living on the banks.

During the firing Piotr Karpenko was seriously wounded, and died two years later, while still quite young, in one of the towns of Central Russia.

Rest in peace, rare and sincere friend!

X

PROFESSOR SKRIDLOV

FROM THE EARLY YEARS OF MY RESPONSIBLE LIFE,
another essence-friend of mine, many years older than I, was
Skridlov, professor of archaeology, who disappeared, leaving no
trace, at the time of the great agitation of minds in Russia.

I first met Professor Skridlov, as I have written in the chapter
on Prince Yuri Lubovedsky, when he engaged me as his guide
for the environs of Cairo.

Soon after this I met him again in ancient Thebes, where I
ended my first trip with Prince Yuri Lubovedsky and where the
professor joined us to make some excavations.

We lived there together for three weeks in one of the tombs,
and during pauses in our work talked on all kinds of abstract
themes. And in spite of the difference in our ages, we gradually
became such intimate and good friends that when Prince Yuri left
for Russia we did not part, but decided to undertake a long
journey together.

From Thebes we travelled up the Nile to its source, and went
on into Abyssinia, where we stayed about three months; and then
coming out to the Red Sea we passed through Syria, and finally
reached the ruins of Babylon. We were there together for four
months, after which Professor Skridlov stayed behind to continue
his excavations, and I went off through Meshed to Ispahan in
the company of two Persians, traders in rugs, whom I chanced
to meet in a little village near Babylon and with whom I

became great friends owing to our common interest in antique rugs.

I next met Professor Skridlov two years later when he arrived with Prince Lubovedsky in the town of Orenburg, which was to be the starting-point of our big expedition across Siberia for a certain purpose connected with the programme drawn up by that same group of Seekers of Truth which I have already mentioned several times.

After the Siberian trip we often met again for long and short journeys through various remote places, chiefly in Asia and Africa, as well as for brief exchanges of personal opinions when necessary, and we also met by chance.

I will describe, in as much detail as possible, one meeting of ours and the ensuing long journey together, during which Professor Skridlov reached a turning-point in his general inner psyche in the sense that, from then on, it began to be activated not only by his thoughts but also by his feelings and his instinct. These latter even began to predominate or, as is said, to take the initiative.

On this occasion I met him quite by chance, in Russia, very soon after the meeting I had had with Prince Lubovedsky in Constantinople. I was on my way to Transcaucasia, and in the buffet of one of the railway stations I was hurrying to finish one of the famous 'beef' cutlets made of horse-flesh, which the Kazanian Tartars supply to the Russian railway buffets, when all of a sudden someone standing behind me put his arms around me. I turned round and saw my old friend Skridlov.

It turned out that he was going, on the same train as I, to see his daughter, who was then living at the health resort of Piatigorsk.

The meeting was a happy one for us both. We decided to sit together for the rest of the journey, and the professor gladly changed from second class to third, in which of course I was travelling. We talked all the way.

He told me how, after leaving the ruins of Babylon, he had returned to Thebes and had made some further excavations in the environs. During these two years he had made numerous interesting and valuable discoveries, but finally, becoming very homesick for Russia and his children, he had decided to take a vacation. On his return to Russia he had gone straight to St. Petersburg, and then to Yaroslavl to see his elder daughter, and he was now on his way to see the younger, who during his absence had 'prepared' two grandchildren for him. How long he would stay in Russia and what he would do next, he did not yet know.

In my turn I told him how I had spent these last two years: how, soon after we had parted, I had become very interested in Islam, and after great difficulties and by much cunning had managed to get into Mecca and Medina, inaccessible to Christians, in the hope of penetrating into the secret heart of this religion and of perhaps finding answers there to certain questions I considered essential.

But my labours had been in vain; I found nothing. I only made clear to myself that if there were anything in this religion it must be sought not there, as everyone says and believes, but in Bukhara, where from the beginning the secret knowledge of Islam has been concentrated, this place having become its very centre and source. And as I had not lost either my interest or hope, I had decided to go to Bukhara with a group of Sarts who, having come to Mecca and Medina as pilgrims, were returning home, and with whom I had intentionally established friendly relations.

I further told him of the circumstances which had then prevented me from going straight to Bukhara, namely, that on arriving in Constantinople I had met Prince Lubovedsky, who had asked me to escort a certain person to his sister in the Tambov province, from which I was just returning; and I was now thinking of going for the time being to Transcaucasia to see my family and of then retracing my steps in the direction of Bukhara and going there . . . 'with your old friend Skridlov,' he said, finishing my sentence.

He then told me that often during the last three years he had dreamed of going to Bukhara and to the Samarkand region near by, for the purpose of verifying certain data connected with Tamerlane, which he needed in order to elucidate an archaeological question that greatly interested him. Only very recently he had again been thinking about this but had hesitated to undertake the journey alone; and now, hearing that I was going there, he would gladly join me if I had no objection.

Two months later, as we had agreed, we met in Tiflis, and went from there to the Transcaspian region intending to go to Bukhara; but on reaching the ruins of Old Merv, we stayed there for about a year.

First of all, to explain why this happened, it must be said that long before our decision to go to Bukhara together, the professor and I had had many talks and made many plans for somehow getting into Kafiristan, the very country which it was then quite impossible for a European to enter at will.

We wished to go there chiefly because, according to all the information we obtained from conversations with various people, we had come to the conclusion that in that country we might find answers to a great many questions which interested us, both psychological and archaeological.

In Tiflis, we had begun to supply ourselves with everything necessary for our journey to Bukhara, including letters of introduction, and we happened to meet and have conversations with various people who knew those regions. As a result of these conversations and our own discussions afterwards, our desire to enter Kafiristan, inaccessible as it was to Europeans, became so intense that we decided to do everything possible to go there immediately after Bukhara.

All our previous interests seemed to disappear, and the whole way to Turkestan we thought and talked only about what measures we would have to take to carry out this daring project of ours. But a definite plan for getting into Kafiristan happened to take shape in the following circumstances:

When our train stopped at the station of New Merv on the Central Asiatic Railway, I went to the buffet to get some hot water for tea, and as I was returning to our carriage I was suddenly embraced by a man in Tekinian clothes.

This man turned out to be my good old Greek friend Vasiliaki, a tailor by profession, who had been living in the town of Merv for a long time. On hearing that I was passing through on my way to Bukhara, he implored me to wait until the next day's train and come to the big family festivities which were to take place that very evening on the occasion of the christening of his first child.

His request was so sincere and touching that I could not flatly refuse him and I asked him to wait a moment. Certain that there was very little time left before the departure of the train, I ran off at full speed, spilling hot water all around me, to consult the professor.

While I was squeezing my way with difficulty through the crowd of passengers getting in and out of the carriage, the professor, seeing me coming, waved his hand and shouted: 'I'm already collecting our things; go back quickly and take them through the window.'

He had evidently seen my chance meeting and had guessed the suggestion that had been made to me. When I went back no less hurriedly to the platform and began to take the things he handed me through the window, it turned out that our haste was quite unnecessary, as the train was to stay there for more than two hours, waiting for a connection from the Kushka branch which was late.

At supper that evening, after the religious ceremony of the christening, there sat next to me an old Turkoman nomad, a friend of the host and owner of a large flock of caracul sheep. In the course of my conversation with him about the life of nomads in general and about the different tribes of Central Asia, we began talking about the various independent tribes inhabiting the region of Kafiristan.

Continuing our conversation after supper, during which of course Russian vodka had not been economized, the old man, by the way and as though to himself, expressed an opinion which Professor Skridlov and I took as advice; and in accordance with it we drew up a definite plan for carrying out our intention.

He said that, notwithstanding the almost organic distaste of the inhabitants of this region for having anything to do with people not belonging to their own tribes, there was nevertheless developed in nearly every one of them, to whatever tribe he belonged, a certain something which naturally arouses in him a feeling of respect and even love towards all persons, whatever their race, who devote themselves to the service of God.

After this thought had been expressed by a nomad whom we had met by chance, and who had spoken perhaps thanks only to Russian vodka, all our deliberations, that night and the next day, were based on the idea that we might get into this country, not as ordinary mortals, but by assuming the appearance of persons who are shown special respect there and who have the possibility of going freely everywhere without arousing suspicion.

The following evening, still in the midst of our deliberations, we were sitting in one of the Tekinian *chaikanas* of New Merv, where two parties of Turkoman libertines were indulging in *kaif* with *batchi*, that is with boy dancers, whose chief occupation— authorized by local laws, and also encouraged by the laws of the great Empire of Russia which then had a protectorate over this country—is the same as that carried on in Europe, also legally, by women with yellow tickets; and here in this atmosphere, we categorically decided that Professor Skridlov should disguise himself as a venerable Persian dervish and I should pass for a direct descendant of Mohammed, that is to say, for a Seïd.

To prepare ourselves for this masquerade, a long time was necessary, as well as a quiet, isolated spot. And that is why we decided to settle down in the ruins of Old Merv, which met these requirements and where, moreover, we could at times, for a rest, make some excavations

Our preparation consisted n earning a great many sacred Persian chants and instructive sayings of former times, as well as in letting our hair grow long enough for us to look like the people for whom we intended to pass; make-up in this case was quite out of the question.

After we had lived in this way for about a year and were finally satisfied both with our appearance and our knowledge of religious verses and psalms, one day, very early in the morning, we left the ruins of Old Merv, which had come to be like home for us, and going on foot as far as the station of Baïram Ali on the Central Asiatic Railway, we took a train to Chardzhou, and from there set off by boat up the river Amu Darya.

It was on the banks of this river Amu Darya, in ancient times called the Oxus and deified by certain peoples of Central Asia, that the germ of contemporary culture first appeared on earth. And during my journey up this river with Professor Skridlov an incident occurred—extraordinary for Europeans but very characteristic of the local patriarchal morality, as yet unaffected by contemporary civilization—the victim of which was an exceedingly good old Sart. The memory of this incident has often evoked in me the feeling of remorse of conscience, since it was because of us that this good old man lost his money, perhaps forever. I therefore wish to describe this part of our journey to that country, then inaccessible to Europeans, in as much detail as possible and to describe it more or less in the style of a literary school which I happened to study in my youth and which arose and flourished, so it seems, just here on the shores of this great river—a style called the 'creation of images without words'.

The Amu Darya, which higher up in its course is called the river Pyandzh, has its main sources in the Hindu Kush mountains and flows at the present time into the Aral Sea, though formerly, according to certain historical data, it emptied into the Caspian Sea.

At the period to which the present story relates, this river washed the boundaries of many countries—the former Russia, the Khivan khanate, the Bukharian khanate, Afghanistan, Kafiristan, British India and so on.

It was formerly navigated by rafts of a special kind, but, when the region was conquered by Russia, a river fleet of flat-bottomed steamboats was launched which, besides fulfilling certain military needs, provided passenger and cargo service between the Aral Sea and the upper reaches of the river.

And so I begin, also of course for the purpose of resting, to wiseacre a little in the style of the aforementioned ancient literary school.

Amu Darya . . . clear early morning. The mountain peaks are gilded by the rays of the still hidden sun. Gradually the nocturnal silence and the monotonous murmur of the river give place to the cries of awakened birds and animals, to the voices of people, and to the clatter of the steamboat's wheels.

On both banks the fires which had burned out during the night are being rekindled, spirals begin to rise from the funnel of the boat's kitchen, mingling with the suffocating smoke of damp *saksaul* spreading everywhere.

Overnight the banks have noticeably changed in appearance, although the boat has not moved. It is the ninth day since it left Chardzhou for Kerki.

Although on the first two days the boat moved forward very slowly, it was not held up, but on the third day it ran aground and stopped for a whole day and night, until the Amu Darya, by the force of its current, washed away the sandbank and made it possible to move on.

Thirty-six hours later the same thing occurred, and now it is already the third day that the steamer has been stationary, unable to move further.

The passengers and crew are patiently waiting until this wayward river takes pity and lets them proceed.

Here this is quite usual. The river Amu Darya runs through sands for almost its entire course. Having a very strong current and an irregular volume of water, it is always either washing away its unstable banks or depositing sand on them; and its bed is thus constantly changing, with sandbanks forming where before there were whirlpool depths.

Boats going upstream go very slowly, particularly at certain seasons of the year, but downstream they fly like mad, almost without the engine.

One can never determine beforehand, even approximately, the time it will take to travel from one point to another.

Knowing this, people who travel upstream provide themselves for any emergency with enough food for several months.

The time of year in which this journey of ours up the Amu Darya takes place is the least favourable, owing to the low water. Winter is approaching, the rainy season is over, and, in the mountains where the river chiefly takes its source, the thawing of snow has ceased.

Travel is also not particularly agreeable because just at this season the cargo and passenger traffic on these boats is at its height. The cotton has been picked everywhere; the fruit and vegetables of the fertile oases have been gathered and dried; the caracul sheep have been sorted; and the inhabitants of the regions through which the Amu Darya flows are all travelling on it. Some are returning to their villages; others are taking their cheeses to market to exchange them for articles needed for the short winter; still others are going on pilgrimages or to their relatives.

That is why, when we came on board, the boat was so crammed with passengers. Among them are Bukharians, Khivans, Tekkis, Persians, Afghans and representatives of many other Asiatic peoples.

In this picturesque and motley crowd, merchants predominate; some are transporting goods, others going upstream for supplies of cheese.

Here is a Persian, a merchant of dried fruits; here an Armenian going to buy Kirghiz rugs on the spot, and a Polish agent, a cotton-buyer for the firm of Posnansky; here is a Russian Jew, a buyer of caracul skins, and a Lithuanian commercial traveller with samples of picture frames in papier-maché and all kinds of ornaments of gilt-metal set with artificial coloured stones.

Many officials and officers of the frontier guard, and fusiliers and sappers of the Transcaspian Regiment are returning from leaves or from their posts. Here is a soldier's wife with a nursing baby, going to her husband who has stayed for an extra term of service and has sent for her. Here is a travelling Catholic priest on his official rounds, going to confess Catholic soldiers.

There are also ladies on board. Here is the wife of a colonel, with her lanky daughter, returning home from Tashkent where she has taken her son, a cadet, to see him off to Orenburg to study in the cadet corps. Here is the wife of a cavalry captain of the frontier guard who has been to Merv to order some dresses at the dressmakers there; and here is a military doctor's wife escorted by his orderly, travelling from Ashkhabad to visit her husband, who is serving in solitude because his mother-in-law cannot live without 'society', which is lacking where he is stationed.

Here is a stout woman with an enormous coiffure undoubtedly of artificial hair, with many rings on her fingers and two enormous brooches on her chest; she is accompanied by two very good-looking girls who call her 'aunt', but you can see by everything that they are not at all her nieces.

Here are also many Russian former and future somebodies, going God knows where and God knows why. Also a troupe of travelling musicians with their violins and double-basses.

From the very first day out of Chardzhou, all these people, as it were, sorted themselves out; the so-called intelligentsia, the bourgeoisie and the peasants formed separate groups, where, making acquaintances among themselves, they soon began to feel as though among old friends.

The members of each of these groups began to regard and to act towards the passengers belonging to the other groups either haughtily and disdainfully or timidly and ingratiatingly, but at the same time they did not hinder one another from arranging things each according to his own wishes and habits, and little by little they became so accustomed to their surroundings that it was as though none of them had ever lived in any other way.

Neither the delays in the steamer's progress nor its crowdedness disturbed anyone; on the contrary, they all accommodated themselves so well that the whole journey was like a series of picnics.

As soon as it became clear that this time the steamer was thoroughly grounded, almost all the passengers gradually went ashore. By the end of the day there appeared on both banks clusters of tents, made from whatever came to hand. Smoke arose from many fires, and, after an evening gaily spent with music and song, most of the passengers stayed on shore overnight.

In the morning the life of the passengers resumes its rhythm of the day before. Some build fires and make coffee, others boil water for green tea, still others go in search of *saksaul* poles, get ready to go fishing, go out to the steamer and back in small boats, call back and forth between the steamer and shore or from one bank to the other; and all is done calmly and unhurriedly, as everyone knows that, as soon as it is possible to move on, the big bell

of the steamer will ring an hour before departure and there will be
plenty of time to return on board.

In that part of the boat where we had settled ourselves an old
Sart made his place beside us. It was evident that he was a rich
man because among his things were many bags of money.

I do not know how it is now, but at that time, in Bukhara and
the neighbouring countries, there were no coins of high value.

In Bukhara, for instance, the only coin worth anything was
called a *tianga*—an irregularly cut piece of silver equivalent to
approximately half a French franc. Any sum larger than fifty
francs had therefore to be carried in special bags, which was very
inconvenient, especially for travellers.

If one had thousands in this coinage and had to travel with this
money, it was necessary to have literally a score of camels or
horses to carry it from place to place. On very rare occasions the
following method was used: the quantity of *tiangi* one wished to
transport was given to some Bukharian Jew who gave in exchange
a note to some acquaintance of his, also a Jew, who lived at the
place to which one was going, and there the latter, deducting
something for his trouble, returned the same amount of *tiangi*.

And so, on arriving at the town of Kerki, which was as far as
the boat went, we left our steamer, changed to a hired *kobᶾir*[1] and
continued further.

When we were already quite a long way from Kerki and were
making a stop at Termez, where Professor Skridlov had gone
ashore with some Sart workmen to get provisions in a near-by
village, our *kobᶾir* was approached by another one carrying five
Sarts, who without saying a word began to unload from their
kobᶾir on to ours, twenty-five large sacks filled with *tiangi*.

At first I did not understand what it was all about; only after
the unloading was finished did I gather from the oldest Sart that
they had been passengers on our steamer, and that when we had
disembarked these sacks of *tiangi* were found in the place which
we had occupied. Certain that we had forgotten them and having
learned where we were going, they decided to make haste to catch

---

[1] A *kobᶾir* is a kind of raft, the planks of which are fastened to *bourdiouks*,
that is, inflated goat skins.

up with us and give us back the *tiangi* we had obviously forgotten in the confusion. And he added: 'I decided to catch up with you without fail because the same thing happened to me once in my life and so I understand very well how disagreeable it is to arrive in a strange place without the necessary *tiangi*. And as for me, it makes no difference if I arrive in my village a week later; I shall regard it as if our steamer had run aground an extra time.'

I did not know how to reply or what to say to this queer fellow; it was just too unexpected for me and all I could do was pretend that I understood very little Sart and wait for the return of the professor. Meanwhile I offered him and his companions some vodka.

When I saw Skridlov returning, I quickly went ashore to meet him as if to help him carry the provisions, and told him all about it. We decided not to refuse the money, but to find out the address of this still unspoiled man, in order to send him a *pesh kesh* in gratitude for his trouble, and then to hand over the *tiangi* to the nearest Russian frontier post, giving the name of the boat and the date of its last trip and explaining in as much detail as possible all the facts which could serve to identify our fellow-traveller, the Sart, who had forgotten these sacks of money on the boat. And so we did.

Soon after this incident, which, in my opinion, could never have occurred among contemporary Europeans, we arrived at the famous town associated with the name of Alexander of Macedonia, which is now nothing more than an ordinary Afghan fort. Here we went ashore and, assuming the roles thought out beforehand, continued our journey on foot.

Passing from one valley to another and coming in contact with many different tribes, we finally came to the central settlement of the Afridis, in a region considered to be the heart of Kafiristan.

On the way, we did everything required of a dervish and a Seïd, that is to say, I sang religious verses in Persian, and the professor, after a fashion, beat out corresponding rhythms on the tambourine, in which he then collected alms.

I shall not describe the rest of our trip and the many extraordinary adventures connected with it, but will go on to the account of our accidental meeting with a certain man, not far from the aforementioned settlement—a meeting, the result of which gave quite another direction to our inner world, and thereby changed all our expectations, intentions and the plan itself of our future movements.

We left the settlement of the Afridis with the intention of proceeding towards Chitral. In the market of the next fairly large place I was accosted by an old man in native dress, who said to me softly in pure Greek: 'Please do not be alarmed. I quite accidentally learned that you are a Greek. I do not want to know who you are or why you are here, but it would be very pleasant for me to talk with you and see how a fellow-countryman breathes, for it is fifty years since I saw a man who was born in the land where I myself was born.'

By his voice and the expression of his eyes, this old man made such an impression on me that I was immediately filled with a perfect trust in him, as in my own father, and I answered him, also in Greek: 'To talk here now is, I think, very awkward. We, at least I, may run great danger, so we must think where we can talk freely without fear of undesirable consequences; perhaps one of us can think of some way or find some suitable place, and meanwhile I can only say that I myself will be unspeakably glad of this opportunity, for I am utterly weary of having to deal for so many months with people of alien blood.'

Without replying, he went on his way, and the professor and I went about our business. The next day another man, this time in the habit of a certain monastic order well known in Central Asia, placed in my hand, instead of alms, a note.

I read this note when we arrived at the *askhana* where we had lunch. It was written in Greek and I learned from its contents that the old man of the day before was also one of the, as they were called, 'self-freed' monks of this order, and that we would be allowed to come to their monastery since, regardless of nationality, all men were respected there, who strove towards the One God, Creator of all nations and races without distinction.

The next day the professor and I went to this monastery, where we were received by several monks, among them the same old man. After the customary greetings he led us to a hill some distance from the monastery, and there we sat down on the steep bank of a small stream and began to eat the food he had brought with him.

When we were seated, he said: 'Here no one will hear or see us and we can talk in perfect quiet about whatever pleases our hearts.'

In the course of conversation, it turned out that he was an Italian, but knew Greek because his mother was a Greek, and in his childhood, on her insistence, he had spoken this language almost exclusively.

He had formerly been a Christian missionary and had lived a long time in India. Once, when he had gone on some missionary work into Afghanistan, he was taken prisoner by Afridi tribesmen while travelling through a certain pass.

He was then passed from one to another as a slave, fell into the hands of various groups inhabiting these regions, and finally arrived in this place in the bondage of a certain man.

He had succeeded during his long stay in these isolated countries in gaining the reputation of being an impartial man who humbly recognized and submitted to all the local conditions of life, established by centuries. And so, through the efforts of this last master of his, to whom he had rendered some important service or other, he was given his full freedom and the promise that he could go wherever he pleased in these countries as though he were one of the local power-possessing inhabitants. But just at that time he accidentally came in contact with certain adepts of the 'World Brotherhood', who were striving for what he had dreamed of all his life, and, having been admitted to their brotherhood, he did not wish to go anywhere else but ever since then had lived with them in their monastery.

As our trust in this brother, Father Giovanni—which was the name we called him when we learned that he had once been a Catholic priest and had been called Giovanni in his own country —was growing all the time, we considered it necessary to tell him who we really were and why we were disguised.

Listening to us with great understanding and clearly wishing to encourage us in our strivings, he thought for a few moments and then, with a kindly, unforgettable smile, said:

'Very well then . . . in the hope that the results of your search will benefit my compatriots also, I will do everything I can to assist you to attain the aim you have set yourselves.'

The fulfilment of this promise of his began by his obtaining that same day, from the proper source, permission for us to stay at their monastery until we should become clear about our plans and decide what to do next in these regions and how. On the following day we moved into the living-quarters of the monastery and, first of all, took a good rest, which we really needed after so many months of tense life.

We lived there as we wished, and went everywhere in the monastery freely, except in one building where the chief sheik lived and to which were admitted each evening only those adepts who had attained preliminary liberation.

With Father Giovanni we went almost every day to the place where we had sat together the first time we came to the monastery, and there had long talks with him.

During these talks Father Giovanni told us a great deal about the inner life of the brethren there and about the principles of daily existence connected with this inner life; and once, speaking of the numerous brotherhoods organized many centuries ago in Asia, he explained to us a little more in detail about this World Brotherhood, which any man could enter, irrespective of the religion to which he had formerly belonged.

As we later ascertained, among the adepts of this monastery there were former Christians, Jews, Mohammedans, Buddhists, Lamaists, and even one Shamanist. All were united by God the Truth.

All the brethren of this monastery lived together in such amity that, in spite of the specific traits and properties of the representatives of the different religions, Professor Skridlov and I could never tell to which religion this or that brother had formerly belonged.

Father Giovanni said much to us also about faith and about the aim of all these various brotherhoods. He spoke so well, so clearly and so convincingly about truth, faith and the possibility of transmuting faith in oneself, that once Professor Skridlov, deeply stirred, could not contain himself and exclaimed in astonishment:

'Father Giovanni! I cannot understand how you can calmly stay here instead of returning to Europe, at least to your own country Italy, to give the people there if only a thousandth part of this all-penetrating faith which you are now inspiring in me.'

'Eh! my dear Professor,' replied Father Giovanni, 'it is evident that you do not understand man's psyche as well as you understand archaeology.

'Faith cannot be given to man. Faith arises in a man and increases in its action in him not as the result of automatic learning, that is, not from any automatic ascertainment of height, breadth, thickness, form and weight, or from the perception of anything by sight, hearing, touch, smell or taste, but from understanding.

'Understanding is the essence obtained from information intentionally learned and from all kinds of experiences personally experienced.

'For example, if my own beloved brother were to come to me here at this moment and urgently entreat me to give him merely a tenth part of my understanding, and if I myself wished with my whole being to do so, yet I could not, in spite of my most ardent desire, give him even the thousandth part of this understanding, as he has neither the knowledge nor the experience which I have quite accidentally acquired and lived through in my life.

'No, Professor, it is a hundred times easier, as it is said in the Gospels, "for a camel to pass through the eye of a needle" than for anyone to give to another the understanding formed in him about anything whatsoever.

'I formerly also thought as you do and even chose the activity of a missionary in order to teach everyone faith in Christ. I wanted to make everyone as happy as I myself felt from faith in the teachings of Jesus Christ. But to wish to do that by, so to say, grafting faith on by words is just like wishing to fill someone with bread merely by looking at him.

'Understanding is acquired, as I have already said, from the totality of information intentionally learned and from personal experiencings; whereas knowledge is only the automatic remembrance of words in a certain sequence.

'Not only is it impossible, even with all one's desire, to give to another one's own inner understanding, formed in the course of life from the said factors, but also, as I recently established with certain other brothers of our monastery, there exists a law that the quality of what is perceived by anyone when another person tells him something, either for his knowledge or his understanding, depends on the quality of the data formed in the person speaking.

'To help you understand what I have just said, I will cite as an example the fact which aroused in us the desire to make investigations and led us to the discovery of this law.

'I must tell you that in our brotherhood there are two very old brethren; one is called Brother Ahl and the other Brother Sez. These brethren have voluntarily undertaken the obligation of periodically visiting all the monasteries of our order and explaining various aspects of the essence of divinity.

'Our brotherhood has four monasteries, one of them ours, the second in the valley of the Pamir, the third in Tibet, and the fourth in India. And so these brethren, Ahl and Sez, constantly travel from one monastery to another and preach there.

'They come to us once or twice a year. Their arrival at our monastery is considered among us a very great event. On the days when either of them is here, the soul of every one of us experiences pure heavenly pleasure and tenderness.

'The sermons of these two brethren, who are to an almost equal degree holy men and who speak the same truths, have nevertheless a different effect on all our brethren and on me in particular.

'When Brother Sez speaks, it is indeed like the song of the birds in Paradise; from what he says one is quite, so to say, turned inside out; one becomes as though entranced. His speech "purls" like a stream and one no longer wishes anything else in life but to listen to the voice of Brother Sez.

'But Brother Ahl's speech has almost the opposite effect. He speaks badly and indistinctly, evidently because of his age. No one knows how old he is. Brother Sez is also very old—it is said three hundred years old—but he is still a hale old man, whereas in Brother Ahl the weakness of old age is clearly evident.

'The stronger the impression made at the moment by the words of Brother Sez, the more this impression evaporates, until there ultimately remains in the hearer nothing at all.

'But in the case of Brother Ahl, although at first what he says makes almost no impression, later, the gist of it takes on a definite form, more and more each day, and is instilled as a whole into the heart and remains there for ever.

'When we became aware of this and began trying to discover why it was so, we came to the unanimous conclusion that the sermons of Brother Sez proceeded only from his mind, and therefore acted on our minds, whereas those of Brother Ahl proceeded from his being and acted on our being.

'Yes, Professor, knowledge and understanding are quite different. Only understanding can lead to being, whereas knowledge is but a passing presence in it. New knowledge displaces the old and the result is, as it were, a pouring from the empty into the void.

'One must strive to understand; this alone can lead to our Lord God.

'And in order to be able to understand the phenomena of nature, according and not according to law, proceeding around us, one must first of all consciously perceive and assimilate a mass of information concerning objective truth and the real events which took place on earth in the past; and secondly, one must bear in oneself all the results of all kinds of voluntary and involuntary experiencings.'

We had many other similar never-to-be-forgotten talks with Father Giovanni.

Many extraordinary questions which never enter the heads of contemporary people were then aroused in us and elucidated by this rare man, Father Giovanni, the like of whom is scarcely ever met with in contemporary life. One of his explanations, which followed a question put to him by Professor Skridlov two days before we left the monastery, is of enormous interest for everyone, owing to the depth of the thoughts it contained and its possible significance for contemporary people who have already reached responsible age.

This question of Professor Skridlov was torn from him as from the depths of his being, when Father Giovanni had said that, before counting on really coming under the effects and influences of the higher forces, it was absolutely necessary to have a soul, which it was possible to acquire only through voluntary and involuntary experiencings and information intentionally learned about real events which had taken place in the past. He convincingly added that this in its turn was possible almost exclusively in youth, when the definite data received from Great Nature are not yet spent on unnecessary, fantastic aims, which appear to be good owing only to the abnormally established conditions of the life of people.

At these words Professor Skridlov sighed deeply and exclaimed in despair: 'What, then, can we do; how can we live on?'

In answer to this exclamation of Skridlov, Father Giovanni, having remained silent for a moment, expressed those remarkable thoughts which I consider it necessary to reproduce, in so far as possible, word for word.

I shall place them, as relating to the question of the soul, that is, the third independently formed part of the common presence of a man, in the chapter entitled 'The divine body of man, and its needs and possible manifestations according to law', but only in the third series of my writings, as complementary to two chapters of the same series which I have already decided and promised to devote—one to the words of the venerable Persian dervish concerning the body, that is, the first independently formed part in the common presence of a man, and the other to the elucidations of the old *ez-ezounavouran* concerning the second independently formed part of a man, namely, his spirit.

During our stay in this monastery, besides the talks with Father Giovanni, we had frequent conversation with other adepts of the brotherhood with whom we had also become friends, having made their acquaintance through Father Giovanni, who had taken us under his paternal protection.

We lived in this monastery about six months and left it, not because we could not have stayed there longer or did not wish to, but only because we were finally so over-filled with the totality of impressions we had received that it seemed as if even a little more would make us lose our minds.

Our stay there brought us so many answers to the psychological and archaeological questions which interested us, that it then seemed as if we had nothing more to seek, at least for a long time; so we abandoned our journey and returned to Russia by almost the same way as we had come.

After arriving in Tiflis the professor and I parted, he going to Piatigorsk, by the Georgian military road, to see his elder daughter, and I to Alexandropol to my family.

After this I did not see Professor Skridlov for rather a long time, but we corresponded regularly. I saw him for the last time in the second year of the World War, in Piatigorsk, where he was visiting his daughter.

I shall never forget the last conversation I had with him, on the summit of Mount Bechow. At that time I was living in Essentuki, and one day when we met at Kislovodsk he proposed that, in remembrance of the good old days, we should climb Mount Bechow, which was not far from Piatigorsk.

One fine morning about two weeks after this meeting, taking provisions with us, we did indeed set out on foot from Piatigorsk towards this mountain, and began the ascent up the rocks from the difficult side, that is, the side at the foot of which there is a well-known monastery.

This ascent is considered very difficult by everybody who has made it and it was indeed not easy, yet for both of us, after the mountains we had climbed up and down during our many travels together through the wilds of Central Asia, it was, as is said, child's play. Nevertheless we experienced great pleasure from this ascent and felt ourselves, after the monotonous life of the city, in an element which had already become almost natural to us.

Although it is not high, this mountain is so situated in relation to the surrounding countryside that from its summit we saw spread out before our eyes an extensive panorama of really extraordinary beauty.

Far to the south arose the majestic snow-capped peak of Elbrus, with the great chain of the Caucasian mountains outlined on both sides of it. Below us, as in miniature, could be seen the numerous settlements, towns and villages of almost the entire region of the Mineral Waters, and just below to the north stood out various parts of the town of Zheleznovodsk.

Silence reigned all around. No one was on the mountain, and no one was likely to come, as the usual easy road leading up from the northern side was visible for many miles and as clear as the palm of one's hand, and there was no one to be seen on it. And as for the southern face by which we had come, one rarely meets anybody daring enough to climb that!

On the summit of the mountain was a small hut, evidently for the sale of beer and tea, but that day there was no one there.

We sat down on a rock and began to eat. Each of us, spellbound by the grandeur of the scenery, silently thought his own thoughts.

Suddenly my glance rested on the face of Professor Skridlov and I saw that tears were streaming from his eyes.

'What's the matter, old fellow?' I asked him.

'Nothing,' he answered, drying his eyes, and then added: 'In general, during the last two or three years, my inability to control the automatic manifestations of my subconsciousness and my instinct is such that I have become almost like an hysterical woman.

'What has just happened, has happened to me many times during this period. It is very difficult to explain what takes place in me when I see or hear anything majestic which allows no doubt that it proceeds from the actualization of Our Maker Creator. Each time, my tears flow of themselves. I weep, that is to say, it weeps in me, not from grief, no, but as if from tenderness. I became so, gradually, after meeting Father Giovanni, whom you remember we met together in Kafiristan, to my worldly misfortune.

'After that meeting my whole inner and outer world became

for me quite different. In the definite views which had become rooted in me in the course of my whole life, there took place, as it were by itself, a revaluation of all values.

'Before that meeting, I was a man wholly engrossed in my own personal interests and pleasures, and also in the interests and pleasures of my children. I was always occupied with thoughts of how best to satisfy my needs and the needs of my children.

'Formerly, it may be said, my whole being was possessed by egoism. All my manifestations and experiencings flowed from my vanity. The meeting with Father Giovanni killed all this, and from then on there gradually arose in me that "something" which has brought the whole of me to the unshakeable conviction that, apart from the vanities of life, there exists a "something else" which must be the aim and ideal of every more or less thinking man, and that it is only this something else which may make a man really happy and give him real values, instead of the illusory "goods" with which in ordinary life he is always and in everything full.'

THE MATERIAL QUESTION

ON THE EIGHTH OF APRIL 1924, the day of the opening in New York of a branch of the Institute for the Harmonious Development of Man, a dinner in honour of Mr. Gurdjieff was arranged at one of the Russian restaurants there by his friends and by several pupils of the French branch.

After dinner most of those present went with Mr. Gurdjieff to the apartment of Mrs. R, at 49th Street. Here, over coffee served by the amiable hostess and liqueurs obtained somehow by Dr. B, conversation continued until breakfast of the following day.

Mr. Gurdjieff spoke mostly through interpreters, Mr. Lilyants and Mme Versilovsky, answering all kinds of questions that were put to him, chiefly of a philosophical character.

During a brief interruption, while we were eating water-melon—which came from Buenos Aires, and was a great rarity at that time of year even in New York—Dr. B, the proprietor of a large, fashionable sanatorium, who had the reputation of being a practical man, suddenly turned to Mr. Gurdjieff with the following question:

'Could you tell us, sir, what are the means by which your Institute exists and approximately what is its annual budget?'

To our surprise, Mr. Gurdjieff's answer to this question took the form of a long narrative.

As this story revealed an unsuspected aspect of the struggle he carried on throughout his life, I have undertaken to reproduce it, in so far as possible, exactly as it was told that day. I consulted other pupils who, like myself, had listened to the story with such interest and attention that they remembered it in almost all its details. And I verified my text by comparing it with the notes of Mr. F—the stenographer who took down all Mr. Gurdjieff's talks and lectures in America, so that people who asked questions which had been asked before could simply read through what Mr. Gurdjieff had already said on these subjects and thus economize his time.

Mr. Gurdjieff began as follows:

'The question you have put to me, esteemed Doctor, has always interested a great many of the people who have become more or less acquainted with me; but until now, not finding it necessary to initiate anyone into this personal affair of mine, I have either not answered at all or have turned it aside with a joke.

'Moreover, there have already sprung up about this subject all sorts of comical legends which clearly show the all-round idiocy of their inventors, and which are ever more and more embellished with new fantastic details as they circulate everywhere among parasites and idlers —no less idiotic—of both sexes. It is claimed, for example: that I receive money from some occult centre in India; or that the Institute is maintained by a black magic organization; or supported by the legendary Georgian Prince Mukransky; or that, among other things, I possess the secret of the philosophers' stone, and can make as much money as I wish by alchemical processes; or even, as many have recently said, that my funds are supplied by the Bolsheviks; and much else of the same sort.

'And, in fact, even the people closest to me do not know to this day exactly from where the money came for the colossal expenses I have borne for many years.

'I did not find it necessary to speak seriously about this question, that is, the material aspect of the existence of the Institute, because I had no illusions about the possibility of outside help and considered conversation on the subject simply a waste of time, or, as is said, a pouring from the empty into the void.

'But today, to this question which has been asked me so often and has already wearied me more than enough, I wish to reply, for some reason or other, not entirely jokingly, but somewhat more sincerely.

'My wish to reply more seriously today, is, it seems to me—and I am almost certain—due to the fact that, after having become by the will of fate (or rather through the stupidity of the power-possessors in Russia) poor as a church mouse, I have ventured to come to this "dollar-growing country", and here, breathing this air saturated with the vibrations of people who sow and reap dollars in a masterly fashion, I, like a thorough-bred hunting-dog, am on the scent of certain and good game. And I will not let the opportunity escape me.

'As I am now sitting here among you people who are fattened on what is called dollar-fat, and feel myself stimulated by the automatic absorption of these beneficent emanations, I intend by means of my reply, so to say, to "shear" some of you a little.

'Therefore, in the pleasant surroundings provided by a hostess of a hospitality so rare for the present day, I will take advantage of these fortunate circumstances to mobilize all the possibilities for the activity of my brain, as well as the capacities of my "talking-machine", and will reply to this question asked again today in such a way that each of you should begin to suspect that my pocket is, itself, a fertile soil for the sowing of dollar-seed, and that in sprouting there these dollars acquire the property of bringing the sowers what could be, in the objective sense, their real happiness in life.

'And so, my dear, for the time being, unconditionally respected dollar-holders! . . .

'Even long before I began putting my ideas into practice by means of my Institute, that is, when I was first thinking out the programme from every angle, I had carefully considered the material aspect, which, although secondary, was nevertheless very important.

'As I then expected to meet many obstacles in my effort to introduce into life the psychological ideas upon which this establishment, extraordinary for the present day, would be based, I felt it necessary to be independent, at least in the material sense; the more so, since experience had already shown me that wealthy people never become seriously enough interested in these questions to support a work of this kind, and that others, even with great interest and desire, cannot do much in this respect, as for such an enterprise a great deal of money is needed.

'That is why, if I wished to actualize in full what I had planned, it was necessary, before thinking of carrying out the psychological tasks, first of all to resolve this aspect of the problem. Therefore, with the aim of creating sufficient capital for this purpose within a set period, I began to devote much more time than before to earning money.

'What I have just said must in all probability arouse complete perplexity in most of you Americans, who at the present time everywhere on earth are considered excellent business men. You must be wondering how it was possible with such ease to earn these presumably large sums, and hence you must surely have received the impression of a certain sort of bragging on my part.

'Yes, indeed—this must even sound very strange to you!

'In order that you may understand, if only approximately, why and how I was able to do this and where I acquired such self-assurance, it is first of all necessary for me to explain that before this period of my life I had often been engaged in all sorts of commercial and financial undertakings, and was already considered by all who came in contact with me in this sphere a very astute business man.

'And further, I must tell you something of my early upbringing, which, from my experienced point of view, corresponds most nearly to the ideal formed in me on the subject of education. Owing to this upbringing I could then, and perhaps if required can still today, go one better than any business man whatever, and perhaps even than you American business men.

'It is particularly appropriate to tell you certain details of my education, since we are gathered today to celebrate the opening of an institution which has as its fundamental aim the correct, harmonious education of man. The more so, since this institution is based on experimental data accumulated over the course of many years and thoroughly verified by me—that very man who has sacrificed almost his whole personal life to the study of this vital question of education, so painful for the present day, and who, having been brought up by people with normally developed consciences, has been able to acquire the capacity, no matter what the circumstances, always to be impartial.

'The strongest intentional influence exerted upon me was that of my father, who understood education quite in his own way.

'I even intend at some time to write a whole book about all the direct and indirect methods of my father which ensued from his original views on education.

'As soon as there appeared in me the signs of a more or less correct comprehension, he began, among other things, to tell me all kinds of extraordinary tales, which always led up to a series of stories about a certain lame carpenter, named Mustapha, who knew how to do everything and one day even made a flying armchair.

'By this means and by other "persistent procedures" my father fostered in me, along with the desire to be like this expert carpenter, the irresistible urge always to be making something new. All my childhood games, even the most ordinary ones, were enriched by my imagining that I was someone who did everything not as it is usually done, but in quite a special way.

'This tendency, as yet ill defined, which my father inculcated in my nature from my earliest childhood in an indirect way, was later, in the first years of my youth, given a more definite form because the ideas of my first teacher about education turned out to be, in certain respects, in keeping with it; and so, in addition to the fulfilment of my scholastic duties, I practised various manual crafts and skills under his special instruction.

'The most characteristic educational procedure of my first teacher was that, as soon as he noticed that I was becoming familiar with any particular craft and was beginning to like it, he immediately made me give it up and pass on to another.

'As I understood much later, his aim was not that I should learn all sorts of crafts but should develop in myself the ability to surmount the difficulties presented by any kind of new work. And indeed, from that time on, work of every kind had sense and interest for me, not in itself, but only in so far as I did not know it and did not know how to do it.

'In short, owing to their original views on education, these two men, who consciously or even unconsciously—in the present case it does not matter—had taken upon themselves my preparation for responsible age, engendered in my nature a certain subjective property which developed gradually as the years passed and finally became fixed in the form of an urge frequently to change my occupation. As a result I acquired, even if only automatically, abilities of both a theoretical and practical nature for carrying on various manual and commercial occupations. My comprehension also was gradually increased as my horizon widened in various fields of knowledge.

'I will even add that, if I am recognized today in different countries as a representative of true knowledge in many fields of learning, I owe it in part to this early education of mine.

'Thanks to the resourcefulness, breadth of view and, above all, common sense, developed in me by correct education, I was able to grasp, from all the information I collected intentionally or accidentally in the subsequent course of my life, the very essence of each branch of learning, instead of being left with merely an accumulation of empty rubbish, which is the inevitable result among contemporary people of the general use of their famous educational method called learning by heart.

'And so, at an early age, I was already well equipped and able to earn sufficient money to provide for my immediate needs. However, as I had come to be interested, when still quite young, in those abstract questions which lead to an understanding of the sense and aim of life, and gave all my time and attention to this, I did not direct my capacities for earning money towards that self-sufficing aim of existence on which, owing to abnormal education, all the "conscious" and instinctive strivings of contemporary people, and particularly of you Americans, are concentrated. I turned to earning money only from time to time, and only in so far as it was needed for my ordinary existence, and to enable me to accomplish whatever was necessary for attaining the aim I had set myself.

'Coming from a poor family and not being materially secure, I had to resort rather often to earning this indeed despicable and maleficent money for unavoidable needs. However, the process itself of earning money never took much of my time, because, owing to the resourcefulness and common sense developed in me by correct education, I was already in all these life matters what might be called an expert, cunning old blade.

'As a very characteristic illustration of my capabilities in this direction I will relate an episode in my life when one day just offhand, for a small wager, I opened a very original workshop.

'The details of this episode will perhaps somewhat lengthen my present recital; nevertheless I think that, thanks to this marvellous liqueur—marvellous, by the way, because it was not made in the usual conditions established on earth, but at sea on an old barge off the coast of America—it will not seem too long or boring to you.

'Well then, it was not long before the last big expedition through the Pamir region and India organized by the society we had formed called the "Community of Truth Seekers", of which I had been a member from the very beginning.

'About two years before the departure of this expedition, the members of the community decided to make their rallying-point the town of Chardzhou in the Transcaspian region. All those intending to participate in the expedition were to meet there on the second of January of the year 1900, and from there first of all to move up along the course of the river Amu Darya.

'As quite a lot of time remained before this date, but not enough for a long journey, I, being then in Alexandropol on one of my customary short visits with my family, did not go far away as I usually did after spending the time I had reserved for them, but stayed on in the Caucasus, dividing my time between Alexandropol and Baku.

'I often went to Baku because there was a society there, composed mostly of Persians who were studying ancient magic, of which I had been an associate member for a long time.

'The events which led to the episode which I intend to relate to you took place just in this town of Baku.

'One Sunday I went to the bazaar.

'I must confess that I have always had a weakness for walking round in Eastern bazaars, and whenever I stayed in a place where there was a bazaar I would invariably go there. I very much liked to rummage about in the odds and ends, where I always hoped to come across something unusual.

'That day I bought some old embroidery, and was on my way out of the rag-fair when I saw a well-dressed but very sorrowful-looking young woman who had something to sell.

'I could see by everything about her that she was not a regular hawker, and was doubtless selling her wares from necessity. I went towards her and saw that she had an Edison phonograph for sale.

'The sad expression of the woman's eyes aroused pity in me, and, although I had very little money, without taking time to think about it, I bought this useless machine with all its appurtenances. I carried this burden back to the caravanserai where I was living, opened the box and found that it contained numerous rolls, most of which were damaged. Among those still intact only some were recorded, the others were blank.

'I stayed in Baku several days longer.

'My resources were coming to an end and I had to think about replenishing them. One overcast morning, I was sitting in bed, not yet dressed, pondering on how this was to be done, when I happened to glance at the phonograph. The idea of making use of it came into my head and I at once drew up a plan of action.

'I liquidated all my affairs there and that very day took the first boat leaving for the Transcaspian region. Five days later, in the town of Krasnovodsk, I set my phonograph going to make money for me.

'It must be said that the phonograph was still unknown in this region and it was the first time the local inhabitants had seen this marvel.

'As I have said, there were also some blank rolls with the phonograph. I quickly found a Tekin street musician, and got him to sing and play several of the favourite melodies of the local population, and on the remaining rolls I myself recorded a series of piquant anecdotes in Turkoman.

'Then I attached two additional ear-tubes to the four that were already on the machine—you may remember that the first Edison phonographs had ear-tubes—and set off with it to the bazaar, where I opened my original booth.

'I charged a price of five kopeks an ear-tube, and you will be able to imagine the result if I tell you that, during the whole time I was there, all day long, and particularly on market days, there was scarcely a moment when an ear-tube was free. At the end of each day the amount collected in five kopek pieces was probably not less than the profits of the biggest business in the town.

'After Krasnovodsk I went to Kizil-Arvat, and while there, I was invited several times to go with my machine to the houses of wealthy Turkomans in the neighbouring villages. For these "request performances" I received a considerable quantity of *tiangi* and once even two very good Tekin carpets.

'When I had made a good pile again here, I took the train with the intention of continuing this business in the town of Ashkhabad, but on the train I met one of the members of our community, with whom I made a wager thanks to which this phonographical career of mine came to an end.

'The comrade I met was the inimitable and fearless Mme Vitvitskaïa, who always wore men's clothes. She had participated in all our perilous expeditions into the depths of Asia, Africa and even Australia and its neighbouring islands.

'She also was to participate in the coming expedition and, having still a good many months free, had decided to go from Warsaw to Andijan to visit her sister—who was married to a representative of the textile firm of Poznansky—and to take a rest there before the date of our assembling at Chardzhou.

'On the way we talked a great deal, and, among other things, I told her about my recent enterprises.

'I do not remember how or for what reason a dispute arose between us, but the result was that it ended with a wager according to which, under very precise conditions and by a definite date, I was to make a certain sum of money.

'This wager interested Vitvitskaïa so seriously that she not only decided to stay with me to see how I would fulfil it, but even undertook to help me. So, instead of going on to Andijan, she got off the train with me at Ashkhabad.

'I must admit that the fulfilment of this accidentally arisen and complicated task which I had taken upon myself, interested me so much that I was fired with a passionate obstinacy to carry it out whatever the consequences, and even to surpass the set conditions.

'While still in the train I thought out a general plan of action, and as a first step I then and there drew up the following advertisement:

' "THE UNIVERSAL TRAVELLING WORKSHOP
IN ITS PASSAGE
WILL STOP HERE FOR A VERY SHORT TIME

' "Hurry, and give your orders and bring everything you have to be repaired or remodelled.

' "We repair sewing-machines, typewriters, bicycles, gramophones, music-boxes, electric, photographic, medical and other apparatus; gas and oil lamps; clocks; all kinds of musical instruments—accordions, guitars, violins, *taris* and so on.

' "We repair locks and weapons of all sorts.

' "We repair, remodel, upholster and refinish any piece of furniture whatever, either in our workshop or at your own house.

' "We repair, varnish and tune upright and grand pianos and harmoniums.

' "We install and repair electric lighting, bells and telephones.

' "We mend and re-cover umbrellas.

' "We repair children's toys and dolls, and rubber articles of all kinds.

' "We wash, clean and mend rugs, shawls, tapestries, furs, etc.

' "We remove all kinds of stains.

' "We restore pictures, porcelain and all kinds of antiques.

' "The workshop has a well-equipped galvano-plastic cabinet for gold-plating, silver-plating, nickel-plating, bronzing and oxidizing.

' "Any article relined with white metal; samovars relined and nickel-plated in twenty-four hours.

' "Orders taken for all kinds of embroidery—cross-stitch, satin-stitch, chenille, with beads, feathers, plush and so on.

' "We stamp anything you wish on wood, leather and cloth.

' "The workshop takes orders for all kinds of alabaster and plaster models such as: statuettes, domestic and wild animals, fruits, etc., etc., and also makes plaster masks of the dead.

' "We execute orders for artificial flowers in bread, wax, velvet and coloured paper, for wreaths, bouquets, ladies' hats and ushers' button-holes.

' "We write by hand, print, and decorate visiting cards, greeting and anniversary cards, and invitations.

' "We take orders for corsets and trusses and also make old ones into new.

' "We make ladies' hats from the latest Paris models.

' "Etc., etc."

'As soon as we arrived in Ashkhabad I found lodgings and obtained permission from the police to print and distribute the advertisements. The next day I rented, in the centre of the town, premises for the workshop, consisting of a large room opening on to the street for the shop, and two small rooms at the back; in addition, there was a small yard and a kind of shed.

'Having bought the most necessary tools and hastily set up a home-made Bunsen-battery and adapted some old wash-basins as vats for galvano-plastic work, I hung over the entrance a large sign with red letters on a white cloth, which said:

AMERICAN TRAVELLING WORKSHOP
HERE FOR A VERY SHORT TIME
MAKES, ALTERS AND REPAIRS EVERYTHING

'The next day, when the advertisements were ready, I pasted a great many of them on walls with the help of a street urchin and distributed the rest by hand. And then the fun began.

'From the very first day, a whole procession of Ashkhabadians brought their things to be repaired.

'Lord! What on earth did they not bring!

'Much of what they brought I not only had never seen before but had never even heard of. Indeed, there were the most unlikely things, such as an apparatus for plucking out grey hairs, a machine for stoning cherries for jam, a grinder for grinding copper sulphate to sprinkle on the sweat zones of the body, a special iron for ironing wigs, and so forth.

'In order to have a better picture of what went on there, you must be told, if only a little, about the local conditions.

'This part of the Transcaspian region and the part of Turkestan adjoining it had begun to be populated by foreigners only a few decades previously, and the new towns had grown up mostly on the outskirts of the old ones. Consequently almost all the towns of this region were composed of two parts: the old, as it was called, Asiatic town, and alongside it the new, Russian town—each living its own independent life.

'The population of these new towns consisted of Armenians, Jews, Georgians, Persians and others, but chiefly of Russians, most of whom were public officials or retired soldiers who had finished their terms of service in this region.

'Thanks to the natural riches of the country and the honesty of a local population as yet unspoiled by contemporary civilization, these newcomers quickly began to grow rich, but, in the absence of any cultural influences on the part of the ignorant officials who had happened to become their governors, they remained just as uncultivated as they had been before they migrated there. And so, along with a flourishing commerce, which had brought them material wealth, there was nothing to develop any aspect of their intellectuality or their technical knowledge.

'European civilization, which was rapidly spreading everywhere else, had scarcely touched the people of these places, and the little they learned about it through newspapers and magazines reached them in a completely distorted form, owing to the fantastic exaggerations of journalists, who in general—and particularly then in Russia—are quite incapable of even an approximate understanding of the real essence of what they are writing about.

'These newly-rich people, according to the inherency of all upstarts, imitated everything "cultured" and "fashionable"—in the given case everything European. But, drawing all their information about this culture and fashion only from Russian papers and magazines compiled by persons themselves ignorant in these matters, they presented to an impartial observer a comical and at the same time sad caricature.

'And so, in great material prosperity but without a single trace of even elementary culture, the inhabitants there were playing as children do at being civilized people.

'Nowhere was fashion more closely followed, everyone feeling obliged to be up to date in everything. Moreover, they eagerly bought, or ordered by post from everywhere, all sorts of new inventions and everything considered appropriate to the life of "the cultured gentle-man"—though of course only what they could find out about this from newspaper advertisements.

'Knowing this weakness of theirs, all the foreign tradesmen, especi-ally the Germans, unloaded a mass of useless merchandise on them, or goods which quickly got spoiled or worn out. The comedy went so far that you could even find among the objects advertised a special machine for lighting ordinary matches.

'As most of the articles they sent for were either worthless to begin with or went to pieces almost at once, and as there was not a single repair shop in the locality, each family accumulated stacks of broken things.

'There was still another reason why there turned out to be so many things for repair. At that epoch in the East, and particularly in Asiatic Russia, it was the custom never to part with anything once acquired, and never to sell it, even if it were no longer needed or had fallen apart. Moreover, even if one had wished to sell, there would have been no one to buy. And besides this, the practice was firmly entrenched of keeping things in remembrance of something or of someone.

'So, in every house the attics and sheds were filled with an amazing accumulation of useless things, which were even handed down from father to son.

'Consequently, when they learned that there was a workshop that repaired everything, they dragged to me devil knows what, in the hope of restoring and making use of things that had long lain useless, as, for example, grandfather's armchair and grandmother's spectacles, great-grandfather's balalaika, great-grandmother's watch, godfather's gift of a dressing-case, the blanket under which the bishop slept when he had stayed with them, an Order of the Star presented to father by the Shah of Persia, and so forth and so on.

'All these I repaired.

'Not once did I refuse anything or return it without repairing it.

'Even when I was offered too trifling a payment to justify the time spent on repairing some article or other, I nevertheless undertook to put it right if the thing was new to me, since in that case I was interested not in the money itself, but in the difficulty presented by a kind of work that was as yet unfamiliar to me.

'In addition to spoiled and really useless things they brought me quantities of brand-new things, not damaged at all, which they were unable to use merely because they did not know how to make them work, owing to their ignorance and lack of any even elementary technical knowledge, in short, owing to their stupidity.

'At that time the latest inventions, such as sewing-machines, bicycles, typewriters, etc., were spreading everywhere at a furious rate. All these things were enthusiastically ordered and bought, but then, owing, as I have already said, to the lack of even the simplest technical knowledge and in the absence of local workshops or specialists, as soon as the slightest thing went wrong with them, they were set aside as useless.

'I shall give you a few characteristic examples of this ignorance and naïveté, which I admit I then made use of quite deliberately, without experiencing any remorse of conscience whatsoever.

'I remember how one day a rich, fat Armenian, puffing and bathed in perspiration, accompanied by his daughter, dragged in a sewing-machine to be repaired, which he had bought for her trousseau when he was staying in Nijni Novgorod for the fair.

'At first this sewing-machine was, as he said, a treasure. It simply could not be praised too highly—it sewed so cleanly and so quickly; but all of a sudden for no rhyme or reason, and much to his vexation, it started going, as he expressed it, in reverse.

'Looking over the machine, I found it in perfectly good order.

'You may know that in certain sewing-machines, alongside the lever regulating the seam there is another lever for changing the direction of the feeder, and when this lever is shifted one changes the direction in which the material moves. Obviously someone had touched this lever unawares, and instead of the material being pushed forward, it was now being pulled backwards.

'I saw at once that to put the machine right I had only to shift the lever into place, and I could have done this then and there. But seeing that I was dealing with a crafty old rogue and learning from the conversation that he was a merchant of caracul skins, I felt sure, well knowing such types, that to cram his own pockets he had tricked more than one Tekki or Bukharian—who are as credulous as children—and I therefore decided to pay him back in his own coin. So I went into a long-winded story about what was wrong with his sewing-machine and told him that several pinions would have to be changed for the machine to work properly again, at the same time cursing by everything under the sun the rascally manufacturers of the day.

'In short, I skinned him for twelve roubles fifty kopeks, promising to put the machine right in three days; but, of course, he had scarcely reached the door when it was already put right, numbered and placed with the finished articles.

'I remember well how, on another occasion, an officer entered the workshop and said to me in a tone of great importance:

' "Go to the office of the regional commandant and tell the clerk in charge that I order him"—by the way, Russian officers of that period never spoke to anyone except to give orders—"to show you the typewriters. When you have looked at them let me know what is wrong with them."

'And off he went as he had come.

'His offhand, imperious tone astonished me and somehow infuriated me. So I decided to go there without fail, chiefly in order to find out what sort of a "bird" this officer was and perhaps also to find a way of putting one over on him, which I must admit, I always enjoyed doing, because, beneath an expression of naïve innocence, I knew how to punish such insolent persons very venomously.

'I went the same day to that office, announced myself to the head clerk and explained the reason of my visit. I discovered that it was the adjutant himself who had come to see me.

'While I was examining the typewriters, of which there were three, the loquacious clerk, whom I had already made my friend thanks to a cigarette and a piquant anecdote of officer life, explained to me the following:

'These machines, recently received from St. Petersburg, at first worked excellently; but soon one, then another, and then the third got out of order, all in the same way: the ribbon stopped unwinding. The adjutant, the quartermaster and others, all tried to put them in order, but, try as they might, no one succeeded, and for the last three days the office work had again to be written by hand.

'While the clerk was telling me all this, I had examined the typewriters and already knew what the trouble was.

'Some of you doubtless remember that, formerly, in certain makes of typewriters, the ribbon spools were unwound by the pressure of a spring placed in a special box in the lower part of the back of the machine, and were wound up by turning the box itself. As the ribbon moved slowly, the spring, being of considerable length, took quite a long time to run down, but from time to time it had to be wound up again.

The Material Question

'It was obvious that when the machines were delivered their springs had been fully wound up, and that, having run down in the course of time, they had only to be wound up again. But as there was no key or handle, it was difficult for people who had been given no instructions and lacked even the simplest technical notions, to discover how to rewind the spools.

'Of course, I did not say anything of this to the clerks, but accepted their invitation to dine with them, and, having eaten some good government cabbage soup and *kasha*, I went straight home on my antediluvian bicycle and what remained of its tires.

'That evening the adjutant came back to my workshop and in the same lofty tone asked: "Well, how about it? Have you found out yet why these brand new typewriters won't work?"

'Long before this, I had already become an old hand in the art of playing a role. So, assuming the expression called by real actors "respectful timidity and bashful deference", and employing special and pompous terms borrowed from various Russian technical works, I began to extol the perfections of this make of typewriter in every respect but one, in which unfortunately a change, though complicated and difficult to bring about, was absolutely necessary. As for the work to be done, I estimated that the charge would be almost a quarter of the cost of the machines themselves.

'The next day these perfectly good machines were solemnly brought to my workshop by almost a whole detachment of soldiers, headed by the adjutant.

'I accepted them immediately, then announced in a very serious manner that in no case could the machines be ready in less than ten days. The vexed adjutant begged me to finish them sooner if possible, as the work in the office was almost at a standstill.

'Finally, after much bargaining, I agreed to work at night and to deliver one machine in two days, but in return I begged him to be good enough to order his soldiers to bring the leavings of food from the mess for my three suckling pigs, which I had just bought and was keeping in my little yard.

'Two days later one of these quite faultless machines was "ready" and I promised the others for the end of the week.

'Besides the thanks and the eighteen roubles I received for repairing each machine, the soldiers brought food daily to my suckling pigs and took care of them themselves for the three months that I remained in

261

Ashkhabad, during which time my suckling pigs turned into full-grown porkers.

'Of course I explained to the clerks what had to be done when the springs ran down, but what my "repairing" had consisted of, they apparently never understood.

'The same kind of thing was repeated many times in the town of Merv, where I transferred my workshop and went on with the same sort of work for two more months.

'One day, the inspector of the local preparatory school there—I do not remember the name of the school—came to ask me to repair an electric machine for making experiments in physics.

'This was an ordinary electrostatic machine which, on the turning of discs, emits sparks, and which, for some reason or other, every school then—and it seems also even now—considered it its duty to possess. With this machine, in their famous so-called physics lessons, the teachers would pompously and as though performing a sacred ritual make instructive experiments, which consisted merely in turning the discs of the machine and compelling the children, one by one, to touch the little metal knobs of the Leyden jars. The grimaces of pain appearing on the faces of the children on touching these knobs always provoked uproarious laughter, which these pedagogues considered as "greatly assisting the digestion of food", and this was the usual finale of such a physics lesson.

'This inspector had ordered one of these machines and had received it unassembled from the German firm of Siemens & Halske in St. Petersburg. Although he and the other teachers, his colleagues, had assembled it according to the instructions, yet, try as they might, they could not obtain any sparks from it, and finally the inspector was compelled to apply to my workshop.

'I at once saw that everything was in good order except that the two discs composing the principal part of the machine were not quite correctly placed in relation to each other. It was simply necessary to loosen the nut on the axle and slightly shift one of the discs, and this I could have done in a minute. But I obliged this esteemed pedagogue, who taught others what he himself did not know, to come back to the workshop four times while I was, as it were, repairing his machine, and to pay me ten roubles seventy-five kopeks for supposedly charging the Leyden jars which needed no charging.

'Such cases were of almost daily occurrence throughout the existence of this workshop of mine. Always meeting the poor half-way, I did not consider it a sin to profit by the stupidity of those who undeservedly, only by virtue of positions acquired by chance, had become the local intelligentsia, but who on the scale of real intelligence actually stood much lower than the general population under their authority.

'But the most original and at the same time the most profitable affair turned out to be the corset business.

'That season, in Paris, the fashion in corsets had sharply changed; after having worn very high corsets fashionable women suddenly had begun to wear quite low ones.

'This new caprice of fashion soon became known in this region through the fashion magazines, but the corsets themselves were not yet on sale there, owing to the remoteness of these places; consequently many women began to bring me their old corsets to see if it was possible somehow to make them into fashionable ones.

'And on account of this corset business, I found myself on "Easy Street". This happened in the following way:

'Once I needed some whalebone for a certain stout Jewess's corset which I had to shorten and, incidentally, widen owing to the progressively increasing waist-line of the owner. After long and fruitless search, the assistant in a shop which, like so many others, did not have whalebone in stock, advised me to buy a whole out-of-date corset, since doubtless the proprietor would sell it at almost the price of the whalebone.

'I then went directly to the proprietor. But while I was bargaining with him, another plan ripened in my mind, and I bought from him not one corset, as I had intended, but all that he had in his shop—sixty-five old-fashioned corsets, at twenty kopeks apiece, instead of the usual price of four or five roubles. After which I hurried off to buy up corsets in all the other shops of Ashkhabad, paying even lower prices because everyone was glad to get rid of their stock of these quite useless articles.

'I did not stop at this, but the next day sent off the father of the two boys I employed, an old Jew, with instructions to buy up old-fashioned corsets in all the towns along the Central Asiatic Railway, while I myself, with pliers and scissors, set about making fashionable corsets.

'This was done very simply: the line where the corset had to be cut was traced in pencil, more having to be cut from the top and only a little from the lower part; then along this line the ends of the whalebone were broken off with pliers and the material cut off with scissors. Then the girls who worked with me under the direction of Vitvitskaïa ripped off the tapes binding the borders, cut them and sewed them on again around the shortened corset. All that remained to be done was to thread through half of the old laces, and a *mignon* corset of the latest Paris fashion was ready for sale—and as many as a hundred were made in a day.

'The most comical result was that the shop-owners, having learned of the metamorphosis of their old corsets, were obliged, in view of the great demand for them, to buy them back from me, with, as is said, gnashing of teeth, but now not for ten or twenty kopeks, but at the price of three and a half roubles a corset.

'In order to give you an idea of the outcome of all this, I need only say that I bought up and sold in the towns of Krasnovodsk, Kizil-Arvat, Ashkhabad, Merv, Chardzhou, Bukhara, Samarkand and Tashkent more than six thousand corsets.

'A material profit out of all proportion to the scale of the enterprise was achieved not merely owing to the ignorance and naïveté of the local, so to say, "variegated" inhabitants, or even to my well-developed astuteness and resourceful adaptability to all kinds of situations, but chiefly owing to my merciless attitude towards those weaknesses, present in me as in everyone, which, through repetition, form in man what is called laziness.

'It is interesting to note that, during that period, a change in the functioning of my common presence took place, inexplicable from the standpoint of ordinary science and repeated more than once in the course of my life. This was a change in the regulation of the tempo of the in-coming and out-going of energy which enabled me to sleep scarcely at all for several weeks, and even for months, yet at the same time to manifest an activity which, far from being reduced, was on the contrary even more intense than usual.

'The last time this state reappeared I was so interested in this phenomenon that it became for me, that is, for my self-cognizing parts, a question of equal significance to that of certain other questions which had arisen in me long before and the solution of which had, from then on, been the aim and sense of my life.

'I even intend, after arranging matters connected with the fundamental programme of the Institute, and when I shall again have the possibility of devoting half my time to my subjective interests, to give first place to the elucidation of this question.

'This as yet incomprehensible particularity of the general functioning of my organism may be seen very clearly in the situation which existed during the period I am describing.

'All day long an almost constant stream of customers, out-doing one another in loquacity, brought me their broken things for repair or came to pick up those already repaired, so that the greater part of my day was spent in receiving and returning orders. The intervals when there happened to be no customers gave barely enough time, even when I made exceptional haste, for going to buy new parts and the many and varied materials constantly required. Thus the work itself had to be done at night.

'During the entire period of existence of the workshop, I had to divide my time in this way—the day for customers and the whole night for working.

'I must say that I was greatly helped in all this work by Vitvitskaïa, who very soon became almost an expert at covering umbrellas, at remodelling corsets and ladies' hats, and especially at making artificial flowers. I was also helped by the two boys I had taken on at the very beginning, the sons of the old Jew; the elder cleaned and prepared the metal things for galvanizing and polished them afterwards, and the younger ran errands and kindled the fire in the forge and kept the bellows going. Towards the end I was also helped, and by no means badly, by six young girls from local patriarchal families, whose parents, desiring them to have a "complete education", sent them to my universal workshop to perfect themselves in fine needlework.

'Even at the beginning, when there were only four of us, the quantity of work done was indeed such that it gave the impression that behind the door leading to the back rooms, on which of course there was a notice "Entrance strictly forbidden to the public", at least several dozen expert craftsmen were working.

'The workshop was open in Ashkhabad three and a half months, and during that time I had made fifty thousand roubles. Do you know what such a sum then meant?

'For comparison, one must remember that at that time the salary of the average Russian public official was thirty-three roubles thirty-three kopeks a month, and that with this sum not only a single man, but one who had a family and even a crowd of children, contrived to live. The salary of a high-ranking officer, from forty-five to fifty roubles, was considered a great deal of money, and the dream of every young man was to earn this much.

'Meat then cost six kopeks a pound, bread two or three kopeks, good grapes two kopeks; and there were a hundred kopeks in a rouble.

'Fifty thousand roubles—that was considered a real fortune!

'During the existence of the workshop there were frequent opportunities for making greater profits by going into enterprises on the side. But one of the conditions of the wager was that the money was to be earned only by manual skills and by such small commercial transactions as would necessarily be connected with them, so I did not once yield to this temptation.

'The wager had long been won while still in Ashkhabad, and the agreed amount earned four times over; nevertheless, as I have said, I decided to go on with the same sort of work in another town.

'Almost everything had been liquidated. Vitvitskaïa had gone to her sister's, and I was getting ready to leave three days later for Merv.

'What I have already told you is, I think, sufficient for you to have some idea of what I wished to make clear by this story: namely, that that specific feature of the common psyche of man which is an ideal for you Americans and which you call the commercial fibre, may also exist—and be even more highly developed—along with other fibres which you Americans do not have, among people living on other continents. Nevertheless, to illustrate this further and to give a fuller picture of my activities in those days, I will tell you about one more commercial trick which I played just before I left Ashkhabad.

'I must tell you that just after I opened my workshop, I announced that I would buy all sorts of things. I did so for two reasons: firstly, I counted on finding parts needed for my repairs, as I had soon bought up in the shops and bazaars everything that could be of use to me for this purpose; and secondly, I hoped that among the old things brought in or offered for inspection at home I might—as often happened— chance upon something rare and valuable.

'In a word, I was also an antique dealer.

'A few days before my departure, I met at the bazaar a Georgian whom I had known before near Tiflis, where he had run the buffet at one of the stations of the Transcaucasian Railway. He was now a contractor for army provisions and he offered to sell me several old iron beds, of which he had a surplus.

'I went to his house that same evening and we went down into the cellar to look at the beds, but there was such an intolerable stench that it was almost impossible to stay there. Hastily examining the beds, I fled as quickly as possible, and began negotiations only after we reached the street. I learned then that the stench in the cellar came from herrings that were stored there, twenty barrels of them, which he had bought at Astrakhan for the local officers' mess. When the first two barrels were delivered and opened, the herrings were found to have gone bad and were rejected. The Georgian, fearing to lose his reputation, did not wish to offer them anywhere else, so he took them back and placed them temporarily in his cellar and then almost forgot about them. It was only now, after three months, when his whole house reeked of them, that he had made up his mind to get rid of them as soon as possible.

'What vexed him was not only that he had lost money on them, but that in addition he would even have to pay to have them carted to the dump-heap, as otherwise the sanitary commission might hear about it and fine him.

'While he was telling me all this, my thoughts began to work, according to the habit formed in me during this period, and I asked myself whether it might not be possible, by some combination or other, to derive profit even from this affair.

'I began to calculate:

' "He has twenty barrels of rotten herrings which must be thrown away. But the barrels themselves are worth at least a rouble apiece. If only I could get them emptied for nothing! Otherwise, carting them away would cost almost as much as they are worth . . ."

'Then suddenly it dawned on me that surely herrings—especially rotten ones—would make good manure. And I thought that a gardener, in order to get such good manure for nothing, would surely agree in return to fetch the barrels, empty them, rinse them out, and bring them to me at the workshop. After smoking them I would be able to sell them at once, as barrels were in great demand, and in this way in half an hour I should make twenty roubles. And nobody would lose anything, but on the contrary everybody would gain by this, even the Georgian who had lost on the merchandise, but would now at least save the expense of carting.

'Having thus thought things out, I said to the Georgian: "If you will take a little more off the beds, I will arrange for these barrels to be carted away without any cost to you."

'He agreed, and I promised to rid him of this source of infection the next morning.

'I paid for the beds, loaded them on my cart, and also took along one of the unopened barrels of herrings to show to a gardener. Back at the workshop we unloaded and put everything into the shed.

'Just at that time the old Jew, the father of the boys who were working for me, came in, as he usually did in the evenings to have a chat with his sons and sometimes even to help them with their work.

'I sat down in my little yard to smoke, and the thought suddenly entered my head to try the herrings on my pigs; perhaps they might eat them. Without explaining anything to the old man, I asked him to help me open the barrel.

'When the lid was raised, the old Jew bent over to inhale the odour, and immediately his face lit up and he exclaimed:

"Now that's what I call herrings! Herrings like these I have not seen for a long time, indeed not since I got into this damned country!"

'I was puzzled. Having lived mostly in Asia where they do not eat herrings, I could never tell good from bad even if I did happen to eat them. They all had the same nasty smell for me. So I was bound to give some credence to this emphatic announcement of the old Jew, the more so since formerly, when he lived in Russia in the town of Rostov, he had had a butcher shop where he also used to sell fish.

'However, I was still not entirely convinced and asked him whether he might not be mistaken, but he, offended to the core, replied: "What's that you're saying? These are genuine, preserved, such and such . . . herrings!" I do not remember what he called them.

'Still having some doubts, I told him that I had by chance bought up a whole consignment of these herrings, and that, among us, it was a good omen when any goods were opened if some were sold at once: it was a sign that the entire sale would be successful. So now we should at once, without waiting till morning, sell at least a few herrings. And I asked him to try to do this immediately.

'In this way I wanted to make sure that what the old man had said was true, and to act accordingly.

'Near my workshop lived many Jews, most of them tradespeople. As it was evening, most of the shops were closed. But just opposite the workshop lived a watchmaker, a certain Friedman. He was called on first and he instantly bought a whole dozen, paying, without any bargaining, fifteen kopeks a pair.

'The next buyer was the proprietor of the pharmacy on the corner, who at once bought fifty.

'From the delighted tone of these buyers I knew that the old man was right. The next morning, at daybreak, I hired carts and brought over to my place all the barrels except the two already opened, which were really quite spoiled and from which had come that terrible stench. These I immediately sent off to the town dump.

'The remaining eighteen barrels of herrings turned out to be not only good, but of the very best quality.

'Evidently, neither the buyer for the officers' mess nor the Georgian merchant, a native of Tiflis, where they do not eat herrings, knew any more about them than I did, that is, nothing at all; and from their peculiar smell they had considered them spoiled, and the Georgian had resigned himself to his loss.

'In three days, with the help of the old Jew, to whom I paid half a kopek per herring—which made him extremely happy—all the herrings were sold, wholesale and retail.

'By this time I had liquidated all my affairs, and on the eve of my departure I invited that Georgian, with my many other acquaintances, to a farewell supper. At table I related how well this affair had turned out for me, and, pulling the money out of my pocket, I offered to share my profits with him. But the Georgian, holding to a commercial principle firmly established among the old inhabitants of Transcaucasia and the Transcaspian region, refused to accept the money. He said that, when he had let me have the goods, he was certain they were quite worthless, and, if it had proved otherwise, it was a stroke of good luck for me and of bad luck for him, and therefore he considered it unfair to take advantage of my kindness. Moreover, the next day, when I left for Merv, I found among my things in the carriage a goat-skin of wine from this Georgian.

'After the episode of this peculiar workshop of mine, several years passed, in which, while working unceasingly to prepare all the conditions necessary for the accomplishment of the fundamental aim of my life, I had to occupy myself quite often with all kinds of money-making affairs.

'Although the many adventures and unexpected happenings of these years might be of great interest to you from both the psychological and the practical points of view, yet, not wishing to digress from the question raised this evening, I will not speak of them now, the more so since I intend to write an entire book about these years and similar periods of my life.

'I will only say that by the time I set myself the task of creating a definite amount of capital I had already acquired much experience and self-confidence. And therefore, when I directed all my faculties towards making money for this purpose, then—even though this aspect of human striving in itself had never been of interest to me—I carried it out in such a way that the results might have aroused the envy of even your best American dollar-business experts.

'I engaged in the most varied enterprises, sometimes very big ones. For instance: I carried out private and government contracts for the supply and construction of railways and roads; I opened a number of stores, restaurants and cinemas and sold them when I got them going well; I organized various rural enterprises and the driving of cattle into Russia from several countries, chiefly from Kashgar; I participated in oil-wells and fisheries; and sometimes I carried on several of these enterprises simultaneously. But the business I preferred above all others, which never required my specially devoting to it any definite time or needed any fixed place of residence, and which moreover was very profitable, was the trade in carpets and antiques of all kinds.

'Finally, after four or five years of, so to say, feverish activity, I liquidated all my affairs; and when, near the end of the year 1913, I went to Moscow to begin to actualize in practice what I had taken upon myself as a sacred task, I had amassed the m suof a million roubles and had acquired in addition two invaluable collections, one of old and rare carpets, and the other of porcelain and what is called Chinese cloisonné.

'It seemed then that with such a capital I would not have to think any more about financial matters, and would be free to put into practice the ideas which had already taken definite form in my consciousness and upon which my Institute would be based: namely, I wished to create around myself conditions in which a man would be continually reminded of the sense and aim of his existence by an unavoidable friction between his conscience and the automatic manifestations of his nature.

'That was about a year before the World War.

'In Moscow, and a little later in St. Petersburg, I arranged a series of lectures which attracted a number of intellectuals and men of science, and the circle of people interested in my ideas soon began to grow.

'Following my general plan, I then took steps towards the creation of my Institute.

'Little by little I began to prepare everything required for the accomplishment of my project. Among other things, I purchased an estate, ordered from different European countries whatever could not be obtained in Russia, and bought instruments and other necessary equipment. I even began to arrange for the publication of my own newspaper.

'In the thick of this work of organization, the war broke out, and I had to suspend everything, though in the hope of resuming as soon as the political situation became more settled.

'By this time, half the capital I had collected had already been spent on the preparatory organization.

'The war continued to gain ground, and, as hope of an early peace grew fainter and fainter, I was compelled to leave Moscow and go to the Caucasus to await the end of hostilities.

'In spite of the fact that political events filled everyone's mind, interest in my work continued to grow in certain circles of society. People really interested in my ideas began to collect at Essentuki, where I was then settled; they came not only from the immediate neighbourhood, but from St. Petersburg and Moscow, and, little by little, circumstances obliged me to form an organization there without waiting for the return to Moscow.

'But here too, events soon took such a turn that it became a problem not only to work but even to survive, no one ever knowing what the morrow would bring.

'The district of the Mineral Waters, where we were living, became a centre of civil war, and we found ourselves literally between two fires.

'Towns passed from hand to hand: one day to the Bolsheviks, the next day to the Cossacks, and the day after to the White Army or to some newly formed party.

'Sometimes on getting up in the morning we would not know under which government we were that day and only on going out into the street would discover what politics had to be professed.

'For me personally, of all that I went through in Russia, this was the period of most intense nervous strain.

'All the time I not only had to think and worry about obtaining the most immediate necessities of life, which had become almost unprocurable, but I was also constantly concerned about the lives of the hundred or so people who were in my care.

'What made me most anxious was the situation of about twenty of my pupils—as they began to call themselves—who were of military age. Young and even middle-aged men were being conscripted every day—one day by the Bolsheviks, the next day by the "Whites", the day after by some other faction.

'This constant tension could not be endured any longer; cost what it might, some way out had to be found.

'One night, when there was more shooting than usual, and echoes of the anxious conversations of my companions reached me from the adjoining rooms, I began to reflect very seriously.

'While I was considering ways out of the impasse, I remembered by association one of the sayings of the wise Mullah Nassr Eddin, which long before this had become for me a sort of fixed idea, namely: "In every circumstance of life always strive to combine the useful with the agreeable."

'I should mention here that for many years I had been interested in an archaeological question, and, in order to clarify certain details, I needed to find out as much as possible about the situation and pattern of arrangement of those monuments called dolmens, which have survived from very ancient times and can be found in our day in certain specific locations on almost every continent.

'I had definite information that such dolmens were to be found in many places in the Caucasus, and even knew the approximate location of some of them as indicated by official science. Although I had never had enough time for a systematic exploration of these places, nevertheless, during my frequent trips through the mountains of the Caucasus and Transcaucasia I had never missed an opportunity for going to see them, choosing for this the times least detrimental to the pursuit of my fundamental aim.

'As a result of what I had already discovered myself, it had become quite clear to me that in the regions between the eastern shores of the Black Sea and the chain of the Caucasus Mountains, especially in the neighbourhood of certain passes I had not as yet been over, dolmens were to be found, standing singly and also in little groups, of a particular type which would be of great interest to me.

'So, as I found myself cut off from the world, with my activities brought to a standstill by the situation which had arisen, I decided to use the time at my disposal for a special expedition to those regions of the Caucasus, in order to search for and examine these dolmens—and at the same time bring both myself and the people in my care into safety.

'The next morning I marshalled all my resources and, with the help of several persons who were more or less half-consciously or unconsciously devoted to me, and who had some kind of relationship with the various power-possessors of that moment, I set about trying to procure official permission for organizing a scientific expedition into the Caucasus Mountains.

'Having succeeded in getting this permission, I obtained by all sorts of devices everything necessary for a journey of this kind. I then chose a number of my pupils, chiefly those for whom it was most dangerous to stay in the district of the Mineral Waters. After I had provided for the others remaining behind, we set off in two parties, which were to meet at an agreed place.

'The first party of this scientific expedition, which started from the town of Piatigorsk, consisted of twelve persons, and the second, from the town of Essentuki, of twenty-one—of whom I was one.

'Officially, these two groups were considered quite independent of each other and as having nothing in common.

'Without really knowing the conditions then prevailing in this country, one must have a particularly fertile imagination to form even a rough idea of what it meant to organize a scientific expedition, moreover an official one, at such a time.

'From Essentuki I intended to go first through inhabited districts to Mount Indur, situated not far from Tuapse, and from there to begin searching in a south-easterly direction, along a line from twenty-five to sixty miles distant from the shores of the Black Sea. For the first part of the journey I managed, after great difficulties, to procure from the Bolshevik Government, which was then in power, two railway wagons, and this I did at a time when, owing to the constant movement of troops, it was almost unthinkable even for one man without luggage to travel by rail.

'Having squeezed into these wagons all twenty-one persons, two horses, two mules and three two-wheeled carts, not to mention the great quantity of equipment bought for the expedition, such as tents, provisions, and various instruments and weapons, we started off.

'We travelled this way as far as Maikop. But since almost the whole road-bed of the railway beyond this town had been destroyed the previous day by a newly formed group of rebels who called themselves by some such title as the Greens, our expedition was compelled to continue further on foot and by cart, and not in the direction of Tuapse, as I had originally intended, but towards what is known as the White River Pass.

'In order to reach uninhabited territory, we had to pass through populated districts and to cross the Bolshevik and White Army lines no fewer than five times.

'Whenever I recall all those almost indescribable difficulties, even now that it is all over and only a memory of the past, there arises in me a feeling of real satisfaction that I succeeded in surmounting them. It was indeed as if, during that whole period, miracles were being performed for us.

'The epidemic of fanaticism and mutual hatred, which had seized all the people around us, did not touch us at all: one might have said that I and my companions moved under supernatural protection.

'Just as our attitude towards each side was impartial, as if we were not of this world, so their attitude towards us was the same—they considered us completely neutral, as in truth we were.

'Surrounded by infuriated beasts of people, ready to tear one another apart for the slightest booty, I moved amid this chaos quite openly and fearlessly, without concealing anything or resorting to any subterfuge. And in spite of the fact that "requisitionary" pillaging was in full swing, nothing was taken from us, not even the two casks of alcohol which, on account of great scarcity, were the envy of all.

'In telling you about this now, a feeling of justice, that very justice which comes from my understanding of the psyche of people subjected to such events, obliges me to pay a tribute to those of the Bolsheviks and White Army volunteers—most of them perhaps no longer alive—whose attitude of good will towards my activities, even though adopted unconsciously and purely instinctively, assisted the fortunate outcome of this dangerous enterprise of mine.

'Indeed, if I did manage to get safely out of that hell, in the full sense of the word, it was not due entirely to my well-developed ability to discern and play upon the slightest changes in the weaknesses of the psyche of people in a psychosis of this kind. In the conditions in which these events were taking place I would not have been able, even by maintaining the most active vigilance day and night, to foresee all the unexpected things that happened and to take corresponding measures.

'In my opinion, we got out safely because in the common presences of these people—although in the grip of a psychic state in which the last grain of reasonableness vanishes—the instinct inherent in all human beings for distinguishing good from evil in the objective sense was not completely lacking. And therefore, instinctively sensing in my activities the living germ of that sacred impulse which alone is capable of bringing genuine happiness to humanity, they furthered in whatever way they could the process of accomplishment of that which I had undertaken long before this war.

'In all our dealings with them there was never once a situation, either with the Bolsheviks or the White Army volunteers, from which I could not find some way out.

'Here I will add, by the way, that if at some time in the future the life of people should flow normally, and if there should then be specialists for investigating events similar to those which occurred in Russia, the various documents I have kept, which were issued to me by the two opposing sides for the protection of my interests and possessions, would furnish very instructive evidence of the extraordinary incidents that can occur during such mass psychoses.

'For example, among these numerous documents, there is one paper on one side of which is written:

> The bearer, Citizen Gurdjieff, has the right to carry everywhere a revolver—calibre....number....
> Certified by signature and seal affixed:

	The President of the Soldiers'
Secretary:	and Workmen's Deputies:
SHANDAROVSKY	ROUKHADZE
	Place of issue: Essentuki
	Date of issue:....

'On the back of this paper is written:

> A certain Gurdjieff is authorized to carry a revolver numbered as indicated on the reverse side.
> Certified by signature and seal affixed:

	For General Denikin:
	GENERAL HEYMAN
Chief of Staff:	
GENERAL DAVIDOVITCH NASCHINSKI	
	Issued in Maikop.
	Date:....

'After tremendous efforts, surmounting numerous unexpected obstacles, we went through devastated Cossack villages, and finally got to Kumichki, the last inhabited place before the wilderness of the

Caucasus Mountains. Beyond this point there were no passable roads.

'In Kumichki we made haste to procure whatever provisions were still obtainable, abandoned our carts to their fate, loaded most of our things on the horses and mules, and carrying the rest ourselves, began to climb up the everlasting mountains.

'Only after crossing the first pass did we at last breathe freely, feeling that the greatest dangers were behind us; but it was just here that the real difficulties of the journey began.

'About this part of the expedition from Kumichki over the White River pass to Sochi, across the wilds of the Caucasian range, a journey which lasted about two months, filled with strange and even extraordinary adventures, I will not say anything. And this is because, according to information which has reached me, a description of this escape of ours from the "centre of hell to its edge" through the almost impassable wilds of these mountains, as well as of our successful investigation of dolmens and of all the visible and hidden riches of this region, has already been written and will doubtless soon be published by certain members of this singular scientific expedition, who subsequently returned to Russia and are now cut off from the rest of the world.

'The group of people round me on this journey happened quite unexpectedly to be of such diverse types and education as could not have been more suitable for the aims of our expedition, and they very effectively helped me to resolve the problem of the dolmens. Among them were very good technicians and specialists in various branches of science—mining and other engineers, as well as specialists in archaeology, astronomy, zoology, medicine and other fields of knowledge.

'I will only add that, of all my impressions during this journey, the most outstanding is of the beauty of the regions between Kumichki and Sochi, especially of those from the pass down to the sea; which indeed deserve the high-sounding name of "terrestrial paradise", often attributed to other parts of the Caucasus by the so-called intelligentsia.

'Although these regions would be quite suitable for agriculture as well as for watering-places, and are not very far from populated centres, yet, in spite of the growing need for land of this sort, they remain, for some reason or other, uninhabited and undeveloped.

'They were formerly populated by Cherkesses, who migrated to Turkey forty or fifty years ago; since then they have been abandoned and no man's foot has trod them.

'On our way we sometimes came across formerly well-cultivated lands and excellent orchards, which, though overgrown and wild, were still yielding enough fruit to feed thousands.

'Well then, only at the end of about two months, worn out with fatigue and with our provisions almost gone, did we succeed in reaching the town of Sochi on the shores of the Black Sea.

'Here, because certain members of the expedition, during what might be called our "Way of Golgotha", were not equal to the situation, but manifested properties not corresponding at all to the high aim we had in view, I decided to part with them and went on with the others. We travelled now by ordinary roads to the town of Tiflis, where there was still, for that tumultuous time, a relative degree of order under the rule of the Menshevik democrats of Georgian nationality.

'Four years had passed from the beginning of the organization of the Institute in Moscow up to the time of our arrival in Tiflis. Together with time had gone money, and all the more rapidly because, towards the end of this period, money had had to be spent not only for the work of the Institute itself, but on much else besides which had not been foreseen in the original calculations.

'The trouble was that the catastrophic events in Russia, the colossal upheavals, the war and civil war, had shaken people out of their usual grooves, and everything was so mixed up and turned upside down that the wealthy and secure of yesterday found themselves the totally destitute of today. This was the situation of many of those who had left everything to follow my ideas, and who during this period, through their sincerity and corresponding manifestations, had become like next of kin to me; and so I had now to provide a means of livelihood for nearly two hundred people.

'My difficulty in this respect was complicated by the fact that many of my relatives were in a still worse position than the others, and I had not only to support them financially, but to provide shelter for them and all their families, since most of them had been living in places in Transcaucasia which had been completely devastated and pillaged in the civil war and by the Turks.

'In order that you may picture to yourselves the generally prevailing horror, I will describe one of the many scenes I witnessed.

'This was at the time when I was in Essentuki, and life there was still relatively calm.

'I was maintaining two "community houses" for my relatives and the followers of my ideas, one for eighty-five people in Essentuki, and the other for sixty people in Piatigorsk.

'The already high cost of living was rising daily. It was becoming more and more difficult, even with large sums of money, to obtain food for the two houses and I barely succeeded in making both ends meet.

'One rainy morning, while sitting at the window looking out at the street and thinking how to obtain this, that and the other, I saw two odd-looking conveyances pull up at my door, from which a number of shadowy forms slowly emerged.

'At first it was even difficult for me to make out what they were, but, as my agitated thoughts grew a little calmer, I gradually began to realize that these were people, or more exactly skeletons of people, with only their burning eyes alive, clad in rags and tatters, their bare feet covered with wounds and sores. There were twenty-eight in all, among them eleven children between the ages of one and nine.

'These people turned out to be relatives of mine, among them my own sister with her six little children.

'They had been living in Alexandropol, which, among other places, had been attacked by the Turks two months before. As neither the post nor the telegraph service were working and the towns were cut off from each other, the inhabitants of Alexandropol only learned of the approaching attack when the Turks were about three miles from the city. This news gave rise to an indescribable panic.

'Just picture to yourselves how people must feel when, worn out and strained to the extreme limit, they realize that the enemy, stronger and better armed than their own troops, will inevitably enter the city and will mercilessly and indiscriminately massacre not only the men, but the women, the aged and the children, as was the order of things there.

'And so my relatives, like all the rest, learned of the approach of the Turks only about an hour beforehand, and, seized with this panic, fled in terror just as they were, without stopping to take anything with them.

'Quite bewildered and dashing off at random, they first even ran in the wrong direction. It was only when they were too exhausted to go further that they came to themselves a little, realized their mistake and took the direction of Tiflis.

'After twenty long, painful days of walking over the mountains through almost impassable places, sometimes even crawling on hands and knees, hungry and cold, they finally arrived in Tiflis barely alive.

'Having learned there that I was living in Essentuki and that communications with that town were then open, they managed with the help of friends to hire two covered carts; and, barely moving along what was called the Georgian military road, they finally landed at my door, as I have just said, in such a state that they were not even recognizable.

'Imagine the situation of a man who sees such a picture and who, in spite of the extreme difficulties of the moment, considers himself to be, and in fact is, the only one able to shelter them, clothe them, care for them and, in short, set them on their feet.

'All these unforeseen expenses, as well as the cost of the expedition and the money left to provide for those who stayed behind in the Mineral Water towns, had used up all my reserves by the time I arrived, with a whole following, in Tiflis. Not only was my ready money gone, but also those valuables which my wife and I, during our constant moving about, had been able to carry with us.

'As for the other valuable things I had collected for many years, although a few had been disposed of, at the very beginning of the chaotic events in Russia, by some of my pupils from the two capitals who afterwards came with their families to be near me in Essentuki, all the rest, including the two unique collections I have mentioned, remained partly in Petrograd and partly in Moscow, and I had no idea what had become of them.

'By the second day after my arrival in Tiflis, matters had come to such a pass that I found myself without a single cent in my pocket. I had to beg the wife of one of my people to lend, or simply give me, her last ring, containing a small diamond of approximately one and a quarter carats, which I immediately sold so that everyone might eat that evening.

'Things were made still more difficult by the illness I had contracted while crossing the Caucasus Mountains, where one is subjected to enormous differences of temperature between the day and night. My condition became worse, since I could not lie in bed, but, with a temperature as high as 104°, was compelled to run about the city in order to find at any cost some way out of this desperate situation.

'I acquainted myself with all the prospects of the local business world and, having seen that, in spite of the general depression throughout Transcaucasia, the trade in both new and old Oriental carpets was still flourishing, I at once decided to occupy myself with this business.

'I chose several qualified persons from those who had come there with me and also from those of my relatives who had lived there a long time, and, having taught them how to assist me, I very quickly organized a serious business in carpets.

'Some of my assistants went round in Tiflis and the neighbouring towns and searched for and bought up all sorts of carpets; a second group washed and cleaned them, while a third repaired them. The carpets were then sorted out and some of them were sold retail, and the others wholesale—either for the local trade or for export to Constantinople.

'By the third week this carpet business had begun to bring in such an income that there was not only sufficient money for all to live on, but a great deal left over. In view of these profits and the obviously still greater prospects of this business, the desire arose in me to establish my Institute on a temporary basis there, without waiting for peace and my return to Moscow; the more so as I had always intended to open a branch of the Institute in Tiflis.

'While continuing the carpet business I therefore set about organizing the Institute; but it soon became clear, in view of the great housing crisis in Tiflis at the time, that it would be impossible for me to find quarters suitable for my purpose unaided, and I applied to the Georgian government for assistance.

'The Georgian government met me half-way, and directed the mayor of Tiflis to assist me in every way to find a building "worthy of such an important establishment of general public significance", and to place it entirely at my disposal. The mayor himself, and several members of the municipal council who were interested in my work, were indeed very assiduous in searching for the necessary building. But in spite of all their good will they could not find anything suitable, and offered me temporary quarters, promising to change them shortly for something permanent and more adequate.

'Thus, for the third time, I began the organization of the Institute, and first of all set about the same inevitable business of acquiring the necessary furnishings and equipment.

'Here, among the inhabitants of Tiflis, many people had been deeply affected by the change in their conditions of life and felt the need to turn towards other values. As a consequence, within a week after the opening of my Institute, all the special classes which had been started in these temporary premises were filled up, and there were also waiting-lists of two or three times as many people for the classes I expected to start as soon as we had a larger building.

'In these temporary premises which were unsuitable in every respect, and under exceedingly trying conditions, "work on oneself" began to come to life. Studies were carried on for several months by dividing the pupils into separate groups and by arranging working hours in the morning, afternoon and evening, and even late at night.

'But the government kept putting off the question of the promised building week after week, and it became more and more impossible to continue the work in our inadequate premises. And when, owing to the Bolsheviks' advance into Georgia, all the harassing difficulties of daily living increased and the Georgian government itself was shaken, I finally gave up wasting my time and energy in the struggle with the conditions round me. I decided not only to liquidate everything in Tiflis, but even to break with everything that up till then had tied me to Russia, and to emigrate beyond its borders and found my Institute in some other country.

'I sold for a mere song everything acquired for the Institute in Tiflis and, providing as well as possible for those of us who remained behind, I left under great difficulties for Constantinople, taking with me thirty people.

'At the time of my departure from Tiflis, the sale of carpets had brought me a considerable sum of money. I calculated that, even after providing for the people remaining behind and allowing for the expenses of the journey, there would still be enough on arriving in Constantinople to last for a fairly long period.

'Alas, we had counted without the Georgians! Thanks to them we were not able to make use of this money which had been earned, literally, by the sweat of our brows.

'This happened because the local currency at that time had no value outside the country and could not be exchanged anywhere, so those who went abroad took with them, instead of currency, diamonds or rugs. I likewise decided to take, instead of money, several precious stones and twenty rare carpets and, having fulfilled all the official requirements for their export, I distributed them among my companions.

'Yet on leaving Batum, although we had the documents certifying that we had paid all the duties and taxes, the so-called Special Georgian Detachment, quibbling about something or other, confiscated quite illegally, supposedly only temporarily, almost all the carpets I had distributed among the people accompanying me. Later, at Constantinople, when we took steps to recover them, Batum had been occupied by the Bolsheviks, the scoundrelly Detachment with its chiefs had dispersed, and, of course, there was no trace of the rugs. Of the twenty, only two were saved, having come via the diplomatic bag entrusted by the Finnish consul to a Finnish member of the Institute.

'And so I found myself in Constantinople in almost the same situation as on arriving in Tiflis.

'I had at my disposal only two small diamonds and the two remaining rugs. From the sale of these, even at a good price, I could not count on enough money to provide for such a crowd of people for more than a very short time, especially since all of us needed clothes. When we were living in Tiflis there were no clothes to be had, and all our things were so ragged that it was impossible to go about in them in this city, where life was more or less normal.

'But luck was with me; I immediately ran across several fortunate business transactions.

'Among other things, I collaborated with an old friend and countryman of mine in the resale of large consignments of caviar; in addition, I participated in the sale of a certain ship. And my finances improved once more.

'While still in Tiflis I had renounced once and for all the idea of making Russia the permanent centre of the activities of my Institute, but I did not then know the conditions of life in Europe well enough to have any definite plan as to where to settle. On thinking it over, however, it seemed to me that Germany, owing to its central geographical position and its cultural level, about which I had heard so much, would be the country most suitable for my purposes.

'But, having been held up in Constantinople because of the eternal question of money, so painful for all those who have no uncle in America, I had to occupy myself there for several months longer with all sorts of business deals in order to have enough cash to go on further. Meanwhile, so that the people who had accompanied me should, as is said, continue with "the work", I rented the only large premises I could find in the part of Constantinople called Pera, where almost all the Europeans live. And whenever I was free from my commercial affairs, I directed the class in movements which had been begun in Tiflis, arranging public demonstrations on every Saturday to accustom the pupils not to be embarrassed in the presence of strangers.

'The local Turks and Greeks, who assembled in large numbers to watch these demonstrations, showed a great interest in the movements and in the music which I had composed specially for them, as well as in the various activities carried on by my people in preparation for the future work of the Institute in Germany; and I received an ever-growing number of requests from the visitors to be allowed to take part. At the same time the generally unstable situation in Europe continued to threaten all my projects, since the mutual distrust between governments made the obtaining of visas for foreign countries very difficult, and there were also great fluctuations of the rates of exchange from day to day.

'I decided therefore that I would extend the range of my activities there in Constantinople by organizing public lectures to elucidate various aspects of my fundamental ideas, and by opening courses for the study of three fields of human manifestation, namely, movements, music and painting, considered in their relationship to objective science.

'And so once again I plunged headlong into feverish activity, continuing to make money by every possible means in Constantinople itself, as well as in Kadiköy on the opposite side of the Bosphorus, to which I had to cross over by boat almost every day. All the rest of my time I devoted to the classes I had organized, in which a great many new pupils were now participating—so that the only moments I could find to draft the synopsis of the series of lectures, which were to be read by certain specially prepared pupils, were during my trips to and fro on the ferry and in tram-cars.

'I lived in this feverish activity for about a year, until the long-awaited visas arrived, by which time the chronic hole in my pocket, made by the rapid flow of money through it, had finally become somewhat stopped up and something had even begun to accumulate in the folds.

'Since at that time the wiseacring of the Young Turks began to have a particular smell, I decided—without waiting for the various delights which were bound to develop in connection with these wiseacrings— to get away with my people as quickly as possible, with our skins whole. So, having speedily transferred my classes to Kadiköy and placed at their head some of the most qualified of my new pupils, I left for Germany.

'Arriving in Berlin, I obtained lodging in various hotels for all the people who had travelled with me and rented, in a part of Berlin called Schmargendorf, a large hall for continuing the interrupted work. And then I immediately began to travel about Germany, going to different places where various acquaintances had found possible buildings for the Institute.

'After seeing a certain number of them, I finally chose, in Hellerau near the city of Dresden, a house which had been specially designed and equipped on a rather grand scale for a new cultural movement, recently much talked about, called the Dalcroze system.

'Finding this house and its installations more or less suitable for the founding and further development of the headquarters of the Institute, I resolved to acquire the complete establishment. But while carrying on negotiations with the owner, a proposition was made to me, by a group of English people who had become interested in my ideas, to open the main Institute in London; and they offered to undertake all the expenses and problems of organization.

'In view of the precarious financial situation brought about by the continuing crisis in every country, affecting both myself and those with whom I had dealings, I was tempted by this offer, and went to London to see for myself the state of affairs there, on the spot.

'As the progress of the work in Berlin under my direction was of great importance to me, and any prolonged absence would have been detrimental, and as I could not work out all the questions connected with the English proposal in a short time, I decided to travel to London every two or three weeks for several days; and, each time, I went by a different route in order to become acquainted with other European countries.

'As a result of my observations during these journeys, I came to the definite conclusion that the best place for the foundation of the Institute would be neither Germany nor England, but France.

'France gave me the impression of a country which was then politically and economically more stable than the others; and although less central geographically than Germany, yet its capital, Paris, was considered the capital of the world, so France seemed to be a sort of cross-roads of all the races and nationalities on earth. Consequently to my eyes it appeared to be the most suitable base for the diffusion of my ideas.

'England, owing to its insular situation, would not have allowed any development in this respect; an Institute founded there would have taken on the narrow character of a local institution.

'That is why, on one of my journeys to London, I definitely refused to found the central establishment there; but I agreed to send over instructors specially prepared by me and also a certain number of my pupils, who were to be maintained there until the opening of an English branch of the main Institute.

'In short, we arrived in France during the summer of 1922.

'There I found that, after having paid all the expenses of the journey, I had at my disposal only one hundred thousand francs.

'Having arranged in Paris a temporary lodging house for my pupils, I rented the Dalcroze School as a temporary hall for the continuation of our work, and began to look for a house, and also for funds, to establish the Institute.

'After a long search, the most suitable of the many properties I inspected near Paris proved to be an estate named the Château du Prieuré, situated not far from the famous Château de Fontainebleau.

'The owner of this château, who had inherited it from a celebrated lawyer, and who wished to be rid of it as soon as possible owing to the great expense of its upkeep, preferred to sell rather than rent. Having several buyers in view, she dragged out negotiations with me, manifesting thereby the tendency which contemporary meteorologists would formulate in the words: "either snow or rain or something or other". On my side, as you well understand, the depleted state of my exchequer at that time gave me no possibility of buying it.

'Finally, after much beating about the bush and many stipulations, the owner consented to postpone the sale of the property for a year, and to rent it to me for this period for sixty-five thousand francs, giving me six months to decide whether I would buy; after which she would have the right to sell the property to another party and I would be obliged to vacate without delay.

'Having leased the Château du Prieuré under these conditions, I moved to this estate the next day with fifty pupils. This was on the first of October 1922. From that day on, under specifically European conditions quite foreign to me, there began one of the maddest periods of my life.

'When I walked through the gates of the Château du Prieuré, it was as though, right behind the old porter, I was greeted by Mrs. Serious

Problem. My one hundred thousand francs, down to the last sou, had already been scattered to the winds, partly in paying the rent of the property and partly in the expenses of living for three months in Paris with so many people. And now, besides continuing to maintain such a crowd of people, I had to face the immediate prospect of spending another large sum of money on furnishings and equipment, since neither the furniture, nor other household articles in the place had been planned for such a number of residents—with a further large number coming from England, as the branch in London had not been opened.

'My situation was further complicated by the fact that when I arrived in Paris I spoke no Western European language.

'On my departure from Batum this question of languages had begun to disturb me. But in Constantinople I had nothing to worry about, since the languages chiefly used there were Turkish, Greek and Armenian, all of which I knew well. As soon as I left Constantinople, however, and arrived in Berlin, great difficulties in this respect began to appear for me. And now here in Paris, faced with the necessity of again finding means to cover colossal expenses, I felt more than ever the need to know European languages, while at the same time I did not have a minute in which to apply myself to learning them.

'To do business through interpreters was next to impossible, especially for commercial transactions, where one needs to catch the mood of the man one is dealing with and to play on his psyche. Even with a good interpreter, the long pauses necessary for the translation destroy all the effect one has made, not to mention the difficulty of rendering the intonations, always so important in such negotiations.

'And I did not even have a good interpreter, since all the people who might have helped me in this problem came from other countries and knew French as foreigners usually do, and Russians in particular, that is to say, just enough for what is called drawing-room conversation—and even then not in France—while all this time I needed sound French for serious commercial negotiations.

'The amount of nervous energy I wasted during those first two years in France, at the moments when I felt that what I had said was not being translated correctly, would doubtless have been quite sufficient for a hundred of your novice brokers on the floor of the New York Stock Exchange.

'In view of the fact that on arriving at the Château du Prieuré a considerable sum was urgently needed for furnishings, which would be impossible to earn at once, I began to look about for a possibility of obtaining a loan to cover the most pressing needs. My intention was to organize the work of the Institute for the time being in such a way that I could devote half of my time to earning money, and thus gradually pay off what I had borrowed.

'I succeeded in arranging this loan in London, where I borrowed from various persons interested in the Institute. This was the first time I departed from the fundamental principle I had imposed upon myself fifteen years before: namely, to take on myself sole responsibility for the accomplishment of my work, without accepting any material help from the outside.

'I can categorically affirm that until then, in spite of the enormous expenses, and the failures and losses brought about through no fault of mine but through the political and economic circumstances of the preceding years, I did not owe a cent to anyone: everything was the result of my own labour. Friends, and people who had interest in or sympathy for my ideas, had many times offered me money, but I had always refused, even at difficult moments, preferring to surmount the obstacles by my own efforts rather than betray my principles.

'Having alleviated the immediate difficulty at the Prieuré by this loan, I set myself red-hot to work. My task at this period was, one can indeed say, superhuman. Sometimes I had to work literally twenty-four hours a day: all night long at Fontainebleau and the whole day in Paris, or vice versa. Even the time of travelling back and forth by train was taken up with correspondence or negotiations.

'The work went well, but the excessive pressure of these months, immediately following eight years of uninterrupted labours, fatigued me to such a point that my health was severely shaken, and despite all my desire and effort I could no longer maintain the same intensity.

'In spite of the obstacles which hindered and restricted my work— the poor state of my health, the difficulty of carrying on business negotiations without knowing the language, and the number of my enemies, which increased, as has long ago become a law, proportionately with the number of friends—I nevertheless managed to accomplish within the first six months most of what I had planned to do.

'Since for most of you Americans, particularly in modern times, the only effective stimulus for the flow of thoughts is the familiar image of a balance-sheet, I wish at least to enumerate for you, quite simply, the expenses that I succeeded in meeting from the time of my entering the Château du Prieuré up to my departure for your America.

'The following is approximately what was paid:

Half the cost of a large property plus a substantial sum towards the purchase of a small adjacent property.

The entire cost of the initial outfitting and installation of the Institute including:

Repairs, alterations, and putting of the property into shape.

Purchase of miscellaneous materials, tools and agricultural machinery; instruments and apparatus for the medical section, etc.

Purchase of live-stock—horses, cows, sheep, pigs, poultry, etc.

To all this was added the considerable cost of the construction, fitting out and decoration of a building intended among other things for the exercises of movements and for demonstrations—a building called by some the Study House and by others the Theatre.

Finally, I succeeded during this period, even while providing for the needs of guests and pupils of the Institute, in paying back part of the loan I had contracted.

'One of the best sources of income during these months was the psychological treatment of certain difficult cases of alcoholism and drug addiction. I was widely considered one of the best specialists in this field, and the families of these unfortunates sometimes offered me very substantial sums for giving up my time to them.

'I remember especially a rich American couple who entrusted me with their son, judged to be incurable, and who spontaneously doubled the agreed fee in their joy at his cure.

'In addition, I went into partnership with some business men, and undertook with them a number of financial ventures. I made a considerable profit, for instance, from the resale, at an unexpectedly good price, of a whole block of oil shares.

'I made two profitable business deals with a partner by opening, one after the other, two restaurants in Montmartre, which I organized in a few weeks and sold as soon as they were well launched.

'It even seems strange to me how easily I can now enumerate the results of my efforts during that period, when I remember how they were always accompanied by inner experiences disturbing the whole of me and demanding an incredible tension of my forces.

'During these months I had to be at work at eight in the morning and only finished at ten or eleven in the evening; I spent the rest of the night at Montmartre, not only for my restaurant business, but also for the treatment of an alcoholic who got drunk every night in that quarter, and who gave me a great deal of difficulty because he did not wish to be cured.

'It is worth mentioning that my external life at this period, when I was spending every night in Montmartre, provided many of those who knew me, or had seen or heard about me, with rich material for gossip. Some envied my opportunities for gay revels, others condemned me. As for me, I would not have wished such revels even for my bitterest enemy.

'In short, the urgent necessity of finding a stable solution for the financial problem of the Prieuré, the hope of finally freeing myself from these chronic material cares and the wish to be able to devote myself entirely to my real work, that is, to the teaching of the ideas and methods on which the Institute was based—a wish postponed in its fulfilment from year to year owing to circumstances over which I had no control—all led me to make superhuman efforts, regardless of the disastrous consequences that might ensue for me.

'But in spite of all my reluctance to stop, as is said, half-way, I was compelled again to interrupt everything just before completing the preparation of those conditions which alone would have made it possible to accomplish the fundamental tasks of the Institute.

'During the last months of this period the state of my health had indeed become so poor that I was compelled to reduce my hours of work. And then, when I began to be affected by certain ailments I had never had before in my life, I confess I became worried and decided to cease all active work, both mental and physical; however, I continually put off doing so up to the day when a bad chill forced me, willy-nilly, to stop everything.

'The circumstances are worth describing:

'One evening I finished my work in Paris earlier than usual, at about ten o'clock, and as I had to be at the Prieuré without fail the next morning, where an engineer was coming to discuss plans and estimates for a special steam-bath I intended to construct, I decided to go there at once, go to bed early and have a good sleep. So, without stopping anywhere, not even at my apartment in town, I started off for Fontaine-bleau.

'The weather was damp; I closed the windows of my car; and during the trip I was feeling so well that I even began to make plans in my mind for a pottery kiln which I intended to construct before long, at the Institute, in the ancient Persian style.

'On approaching the Fontainebleau forest, I was thinking to myself that I would soon be coming to a place where in damp weather there was often fog late at night. I looked at my watch—it was a quarter past eleven. I put on the large headlights and accelerated the car in order to pass this damp place more quickly.

'From that moment on I remembered nothing, neither how I drove, nor what happened.

'When I came to myself I saw the following picture: I was sitting in the car, which stood right there on the roadway; around me was the forest; the sun was shining brightly; a big wagon loaded with hay had stopped in front of the car and the driver was standing at my window tapping on it with his whip, and it was this which had awakened me.

'It seems that in the evening, after looking at my watch, I must have gone on about a kilometre and then fallen asleep against my will, which had never happened to me in my life before. I had slept on until ten o'clock in the morning.

'Luckily the car had stopped nearly where it should have been according to French traffic regulations, and all the morning traffic must have passed me without disturbing my sleep. But this wagon-load was too big to pass, and the driver had to wake me.

'Although I had slept very well in these strange conditions, the chill I caught that night was so severe that even now I can feel its effects.

'From then on it became very difficult for me, even with violence to myself, to demand from my body too strenuous an effort.

'Willy-nilly, I had to stop all my business. The situation of the Institute therefore became critical in the extreme. Not only was it impossible to complete indispensable tasks, but everything already accomplished was threatened with ruin because bills were coming due and no one was equal to taking care of them in my place.

'I would have to contrive something.

'One day, when I was sitting on the terrace of the Grand Café, famous among foreigners, thinking about my current affairs and how they were affected by my state of health, I reflected as follows:

The Material Question

' "As in my present condition I cannot, and at least for a certain time must not, work with the intensity which is required for such a great task, but must on the contrary allow myself a complete rest, even if only temporarily, why should I not immediately carry out the plan I have made to go to America, without waiting to complete the preparations for the trip?

' "A tour through the different states of North America, with constant travelling and change of environment, far from the usual surroundings and consequently always with new impressions, will create the necessary conditions—in accordance with my established subjectivity—for a complete rest.

' "All the more so, because I will be far away from the place where my present interests are concentrated, and free for a while from a certain feature of my character which I know only too well from repeated experiences during my frequent travels through wild countries. Each time I have been subjected to the 'kind manifestations' of God's creatures, quadruped as well as biped, and however badly I have been battered by them, as soon as I am even slightly better this feature always impels me to somehow struggle back on my feet and plunge at once into the enterprise in hand."

'In order that you may understand what I mean by not waiting to complete the preparations for the trip to America, I must tell you that when the Institute in France was first organized, I began to prepare material for a series of lectures which would make known to the public the fundamental ideas of the Institute and their application to different domains, such as psychology, medicine, archaeology, art, architecture, and even to the various, as they are called, supernatural phenomena.

'In addition I had begun to prepare pupils for a series of demonstrations which I wished to present on a tour through Europe and America. My aim was to introduce, in this way, into the process of the everyday life of people the significance of these ideas, and to show the practical results to which they could lead—ideas based on material I had collected in different parts of Asia inaccessible to the average man.

'As a result of these reflections on the terrace of the Grand Café, I decided to take the risk of leaving at once, simply with the material which had already been prepared.

'I even gave myself my word not to work on anything serious whatsoever, from the moment of leaving France until returning there, but to eat well, sleep a great deal and read only books whose contents and style were in keeping with the spirit and character of the stories of Mullah Nassr Eddin.

'I was ready to run the risk of this venture because I was beginning to hope that my pupils would now be capable of organizing various lectures and demonstrations in America by themselves, without my participation.

'One of the chief dangers of carrying out this sudden decision, which I had made for the two purposes of restoring my health and adjusting the finances of my Institute—this child I had conceived and had borne with incredible difficulties and which was only just beginning to live an independent life—stemmed from the fact that in order to succeed it was necessary to take with me no less than forty-six people, who in America, as in France, would be of course entirely in my care. It was the only way to resolve the agonizing material problem, but it was impossible not to take into account that, in the event of failure, the general situation would be still worse and could even lead to complete catastrophe.

'What a trip to America with forty-six people meant financially, you, with your passion for making frequent trips from this continent to Europe, will easily comprehend, even without any of your discussions. And you can better weigh the gravity of this madcap step if you will take into consideration the simple fact that for your trips you change your dollars into francs, whereas I, on the contrary, had to change my francs into dollars.

'At the moment of deciding to go, the only money I had in reserve was the three hundred thousand francs which I had collected and set aside for the payment due on the fifteenth of February, the day when the deed of purchase of the Château du Prieuré was finally to be signed. I none the less resolved to risk spending this money on the trip and hurriedly began to prepare for our departure.

'While proceeding with the preparations necessary for such an expedition, that is, buying tickets, arranging visas, purchasing clothing, making costumes for the demonstrations of dances and so forth, I concentrated all my attention on the classes of movements and increased the number of rehearsals held in the now completed Study House. Noticing once again how embarrassed the participants were in the presence of strangers, I decided to give, just before sailing, several public demonstrations at the Théâtre des Champs-Élysées in Paris.

'Although I knew that this last-minute undertaking of mine would cost a pretty penny, I did not in the least expect that the total would soar to such fantastic heights.

'And indeed, the Paris demonstrations, the steamship tickets, the paying of the most urgent bills, the provision of money for those who were staying in Europe, as well as certain unforeseen expenses which made their appearance almost imperceptibly, swallowed up the whole of the three hundred thousand francs even before my departure.

'And so I found myself at the last minute in a super-unique tragi-comic situation. Everything was ready for our departure but I could not sail. To set out on such a long journey with such a number of people and not have any reserve cash for an emergency was, of course, unthinkable.

'This situation revealed itself in all its splendour three days before the sailing of the boat.

'And then, as has happened to me more than once in critical moments of my life, there occurred an entirely unexpected event.

'What occurred was one of those interventions that people who are capable of thinking consciously—in our times and particularly in past epochs—have always considered a sign of the just providence of the Higher Powers. As for me, I would say that it was the law-conformable result of a man's unflinching perseverance in bringing all his manifesta-tions into accordance with the principles he has consciously set himself in life for the attainment of a definite aim.

'This event took place as follows:

'I was sitting in my room at the Prieuré searching in my mind for a way out of the incredible situation that had arisen, when suddenly the door opened and my old mother came in. She had arrived only a few days before with several members of my family who had stayed on in the Caucasus after my departure from Russia; and it was only recently that I had succeeded, after a great deal of trouble, in getting them to France.

'My mother came over to me and handed me a small packet, saying:

' "Please, relieve me of this thing: I am so tired of always carrying it around."

'At first I did not understand what she was talking about and automatically untied the packet. But when I saw what was in it, I almost jumped up and danced for joy.

'To explain to you what this thing was, which at this desperate moment could arouse in me such a feeling of gladness, I must first tell you that, when I went to live in Essentuki, the agitation of minds which had spread everywhere in Russia evoked in the consciousness of every more or less sensible person a foreboding of ominous events to come, and I therefore sent for my old mother, then at Alexandropol, to come and live with me. And later, when I went off on the scientific expedition I have mentioned, I entrusted her to those who remained behind in Essentuki.

'Then, I must tell you that in that year, 1918, in the Caucasus as in all of Russia, the value of the rouble was declining daily, and everyone who had money bought objects of universal use and more stable value, such as precious stones, precious metals, rare antiques and so on. I also converted all my capital into valuables which I always carried on my person.

'But at the time of the departure of the expedition from Essentuki, since pillaging raged everywhere under the guise of search and requisition, I would have incurred a great risk in carrying all these valuables myself. So I distributed part of them among my companions in the hope that, even if we did not escape the pillaging, there would nevertheless be a chance for some of us to save something; and the rest I divided among those who remained in Essentuki and Piatigorsk, among whom was my mother.

'One of the things I gave my mother was a brooch which I had bought shortly before in Essentuki from a certain grand duchess who was in great need of money, and, on giving it to my mother, I told her that she should take particular care of it as it was very valuable.

'I was sure that, constrained by necessity, my family must have sold this brooch soon after my departure; or, if not, that it had been stolen during their constant moving from place to place, because each town at that time was at the mercy of a band of pillagers without respect for anyone or anything; or finally, that it had been lost on the journey twenty times over.

'In short, I had completely forgotten about this brooch and the thought of bringing it into my calculations could never have arisen in any corner of my brain.

'But it seems that when I entrusted the brooch to my mother and asked her to take particular care of it, she thought that it must be very valuable to me personally as a remembrance, and had to be returned to me. All these years she had guarded it as the apple of her eye, had avoided showing it to any of her family, and had always carried it about with her like a talisman, sewn up in a little bag. And now, she was glad to be able to return it to me at last, and to be rid of something that had been a constant worry to her.

'Can you imagine my relief when I recognized this brooch and realized at once how I could make use of it?

'On the following day, with this brooch in my pocket, I was in a position to borrow two thousand dollars from a friend; but I took this valuable to America with me, since in Paris I was offered only one hundred and twenty-five thousand francs for it, whereas in my opinion it was worth much more—and I found I was not mistaken when I sold it here in New York.'

At this point in his narrative Mr. Gurdjieff paused, and, with his particular smile, began to smoke a cigarette. In the silence reigning in the room, Mr. H rose from his place, went over to Mr. Gurdjieff, and said:

'Mr. Gurdjieff, I really do not know, after all the joking remarks you have seen fit to make about the material question, whether it is due to the particular order in which you have told your story today, or to my naïveté or suggestibility, but, beyond all doubt, at this moment I am ready with my whole being to do anything to lighten the enormous burden you have voluntarily taken upon yourself.

'And I shall perhaps be even nearer the truth if I tell you that this impulse has arisen in me owing to the distinct impression I received throughout your narrative: that in taking upon yourself this high task, a task beyond the limits of strength of an ordinary man, you have always up till now been absolutely alone.

'Allow me to put into your hands this cheque which represents all that I have at my disposal at this moment. At the same time, in the presence of all those here, I pledge myself to deliver the same sum to you every year for the rest of my life, wherever you may be and whatever may be your circumstances!'

When Mr. H had finished speaking and, visibly moved, was wiping his forehead with his handkerchief, Mr. Gurdjieff stood up and, placing a hand on his shoulder, looked at him with that penetrating, kind and grateful look of his, which I personally can never forget, and said simply:

'Thank you—my, from today, God-given brother.'

But the strongest proof of the great impression produced by the narrative of Mr. Gurdjieff was the declaration of a certain Lady L, who was visiting in New York, and was present that evening as the guest of Mr. R. She suddenly said, with great sincerity:

'Mr. Gurdjieff, it is somewhat by chance that I am present at this meeting in honour of the opening of a branch of your Institute in New York, and that I have been able to hear your story, which has intensely interested me. But before this, I have more than once had the opportunity to hear something of your activities and of the beneficent ideas to which your Institute has given life; and I have even had the good fortune to be admitted to one of the demonstrations which you organized every week in the Study House in the park of the Prieuré, and to see with my own eyes certain other striking examples of your achievements. It will not surprise you, therefore, if I tell you that I have thought of your work many times and have always felt a desire to be useful to you in some way. And now, after having heard the story of your indefatigable efforts, and felt with a woman's intuition the truth of what you are bringing to humanity, I understand how greatly your activities are paralysed by the lack of that which has become today the motive power in the life of people—I mean money; and so I also wish to bring my contribution to your Great Work.

'In comparison with most people, my resources are certainly not small and should permit me to offer you a rather large sum. In reality, they just suffice to meet the established requirements of life according to my social position. I have been thinking all evening what I could do for you, and I have thought of the money which little by little I have laid aside and deposited in a bank for a rainy day. Until I can do better, I have decided to put half of this temporarily at your disposal, without interest, until such time as—God forbid—some serious occurrence might require me to make use of these savings, as one never knows what the future may hold!'

During Lady L's heartfelt speech Mr. Gurdjieff listened to her attentively with a kindly and serious expression. Then he replied:

'Thank you, esteemed Lady L. I particularly appreciate your frankness, and if I accept this sum of money, which will be of great assistance to me in my present activities, I, in my turn, must speak frankly to you. Lifting for once the veil of the future, I can tell you with special gratitude that I shall be able to return this sum to you in exactly eight years, at a time when, although in perfect health, you will have the greatest need of what constitutes today, as you have so correctly said, the motive force of the entire process of the life of man.'

Mr. Gurdjieff remained silent a long time, as though immersed in heavy thoughts. Suddenly he looked tired. His eyes rested for a moment on each one of us.

*   *   *

I am now revising this manuscript from notes of my pupils, sitting in a restaurant in the city of New York, named Childs, at the corner of Fifth Avenue and 56th Street—in the same conditions in which I have always done my writing during the past six years, that is, in various public places, such as cafés, restaurants, clubs or dance-halls; since the manifestations, contrary to my nature and unworthy of man, which are usual in places of this kind, apparently have a beneficial influence on the productivity of my work. And I do not find it superfluous to point out a singular fact, which you are at liberty to consider pure coincidence or even the effect of supernatural providence: namely, that without any intention on my part, but perhaps simply because in my work as a writer I always conform to an exact order, I have finished the revision of this text today in this same city, exactly seven years to the very day since the evening which has just been described.

In order to complete this narrative I will simply add, on the subject of my first trip to America, that although the undertaking was risky to say the least—with a troupe of people not having a cent in their pockets and not speaking a word of the local language, with the programme of the proposed demonstrations not yet completed, and without any advance publicity such as is usual, particularly in America —the success of this tour of demonstrations for the purpose of making known the results of the work of the Institute far outstripped my expectations.

I may boldly state that, if I had not had a serious accident a few days after my return to France which prevented me from going back to America six months later as I had intended, everything I had accomplished on this continent, with the help of those who had accompanied me, would have allowed me not only to repay all my debts, but even to ensure for the future the existence of all the branches of the Institute for the Harmonious Development of Man, both those already in activity and those I intended to open the following year.

But is it worth talking about now?

In writing about this period of my life, there involuntarily arises in my memory that saying of our dear Mullah Nassr Eddin: 'Do not recall with grief the beautiful hair of the convict's head!'

As I was writing these last words someone came and sat down at my table.

All my acquaintances without exception know the condition imposed on everyone who comes to talk to me, which is to wait until I have finished writing and begin the conversation myself. Let it be said in passing that, although they have always respected this condition, I have nevertheless very often sensed that, while fulfilling the requirement scrupulously, some of them were grinding their teeth as if ready to drown me in a spoonful of the latest fashionable medicine.

When I had finished writing I turned to the newcomer and, from the first words he spoke, a series of reflections and deductions was started in me, the whole of which brought me to a categorical decision. If, just as I am concluding, I would now refrain from speaking about this categorical decision and the reflections which brought it into being, I would be acting contrary to the fundamental principles which run like a red thread all through this narrative.

To understand my situation at this moment, you must know that the person who came to sit at my table, and who left after receiving the requisite instructions from me, was no other than my secret partner in the wholesale trade in antiques. I say 'secret' because no one, not even any of the people nearest to me, knows about these business relations of mine.

I had entered into these relations with him six years previously, a few months after my accident. I was then still very weak physically but, with my customary faculty of thinking re-established, I began to cognize in all its nakedness my material situation of that date, due partly to the enormous expenses of the trip to America and partly to the expenses incurred on account of the serious illnesses of my mother and my wife. As prolonged lying in bed was becoming an increasingly unbearable moral torment for me, I began taking trips by car to try to relieve this suffering by taking in different impressions, and also in order to get wind of some business deal suitable for my condition at the time. Accompanied by several people who were constantly with me, I began to go about everywhere, chiefly to the gathering places of Russian refugees in Paris.

It was thus that one day in one of the famous cafés in Paris a man came over to me whom I did not immediately recognize. It was only during the course of conversation that I remembered having met him many times in various towns of the Caucasus, Transcaucasia and the Transcaspian region. Travelling from town to town through these countries, he had been engaged in trading in all kinds of antiques, and had met me because almost everywhere in Asia I was known as an expert on antiques and as a very good dealer in rugs, Chinese porcelain, and cloisonné.

He told me, among other things, that he had managed to salvage a certain capital from the disaster in Russia and that, making use of his knowledge of English, he was engaged in the same business in Europe.

In telling me about his affairs he complained that the chief difficulty was that in Europe the market was flooded with all kinds of imitations, and suddenly he asked me:

'By the way, my dear fellow-countryman, how about going into partnership with me, if only for the appraisal and valuation of the antiques?'

The result of our talk was that we drew up an agreement which brought about my participation in his business for four years. Before purchasing any of the antiques, he was to bring them to me for my appraisal. Or if they happened to be in places which more or less fitted in with the itinerary of the trips I had to take for many reasons during my activities as a writer, I would go myself to inspect them and communicate my opinion to him in a way agreed upon.

So it continued for a certain time. He would spend the whole year travelling about Europe unearthing and buying all sorts of rare pieces, which he would bring here to America and sell to antique dealers, chiefly in New York. As for me, I was only a partner for appraising the antiques.

However, last year, when the crisis in my material situation reached its zenith, while at the same time this business continued to do well since numerous outlets had been found and Europe was overflowing with merchandise of this kind, I had the idea of restoring my finances by this means; and I decided that the scale of operations carried on by my partner should be expanded as much as possible.

With this aim, instead of allowing myself some rest before and after my tiring journeys, as had been my habit in recent years, I began to devote all my available time to making arrangements for borrowing money from various people who trusted me and with whom I was in contact for one reason or another. Having thus collected a sum of several million francs, I invested all of it in this business.

Encouraged by the development of our enterprise and the prospect of substantial profits, my partner worked to procure merchandise without sparing his strength, and, as agreed upon, he arrived in America this year with his whole collection six weeks before I came here myself.

Unfortunately, however, a general economic depression had meanwhile come about, particularly affecting this trade, and we could no longer count on any profit, nor even hope for the recovery of our capital. And this was precisely what he came to tell me.

What words should I use this time to describe the unexpected material situation in which I now found myself, when I have just referred to the crisis of last year as having reached its zenith?

I cannot find a better expression than that of Mullah Nassr Eddin which I have just this moment remembered: 'Ah, it's no great wonder that a bald daughter should be born to the oldest spinster of the village by that rascal of a mullah! But now if an elephant's head and a monkey's tail should grow on a bed-bug, that indeed would be astonishing!'

And to understand why my material situation had again passed through such a crisis, it is not necessary to have a college education.

Last year, when I first had the idea of developing my antique business in America on a large scale, I estimated and was fully convinced that this project of mine would yield a profit that would suffice not only to pay off all my accumulated debts, but would also enable me, without depending on anyone, to publish the first series of my writings— which I counted on having finished by then—and after that to give all my time to the second series. But unfortunately this unforeseen American crisis has plunged me, as Mullah Nassr Eddin would say, into such a 'deep galosh' that today I can scarcely see a single streak of daylight out of it.

For six years, for the purpose of preparing the material for the three series of books I intended to write, I had always and everywhere, in all conditions and circumstances, to 'remember myself' and to remember the task I had set myself, by the fulfilment of which I wished and still wish to justify the sense and aim of my life.

I had to hold myself without weakening, while experiencing all kinds of feelings, to an extremely intense level of inner activity in order not to identify myself with anything. And I had to resist, with a merciless attitude towards myself, any change in the automatically flowing process of mental and emotional associations demanded for the themes of thought which I had been working out during this time. And, finally, I had to force myself not to neglect or omit anything which might be related to, logically correspond to, or contradict any of the innumerable series of separate ideas which in their totality constitute the substance of my writings.

In my concern to express my thoughts in a form accessible to others, my psychic concentration, time and again, reached such a point that for unusually long periods I forgot even my most essential needs.

But the objective injustice most painful to me in all this was that, during this inner concentration of the whole of my force for the purpose of transmitting true knowledge to people, both now and of the future, I had frequently to tear myself away from this state, and, at the cost of my last reserves of energy accumulated with much difficulty during short intervals between the hours of intensive work, to think out various complicated arrangements for postponing this or that payment or settling one or another of my debts.

During these six years, I grew tired to the point of exhaustion not from writing, rewriting, and again revising the many manuscripts piled in a cellar arranged especially for my archives, but from this periodic necessity to turn over and over in my head all possible combinations for dealing with these ever-increasing debts.

Until these last years, whenever I needed the support of others for a material problem, of little importance compared to that for which my time was necessary—support concretely expressed by the word 'money'—and when I did not receive it, I could still be resigned to this, as I understood that the significance of my activities could not be clear to everyone. But now that the significance and aim of my activities, thanks to what I have actualized during the last six years, may be recognized by all, I do not intend to resign myself to this any longer; but on the contrary I consider myself justified, with an entirely clear conscience, in requiring that every person who approaches me, without distinction of race, faith, or material or social position, shall protect me as the apple of his eye, in order that my force and time may be spared for the activities corresponding to my individuality.

Well then, the aforementioned categorical decision, which was the result of these serious reflections after my secret partner left Childs Restaurant, and which I made according to principle, is as follows:

While I am here among people who have not undergone the catastrophic consequences of the last great war, and through whom I shall suffer considerable losses—of course without intention on their part— I will once again, by myself alone, without other people taking the initiative and, of course, without resorting to any means which could one day give rise in me to remorse of conscience, make use of certain capacities formed in me thanks to correct education in my childhood to acquire such a sum of money as will clear up all my debts and in addition enable me to return to the continent of Europe and live without want for two or three months.

And in doing this I shall experience again the highest satisfaction foreordained for man by Our Common Father, formulated in ancient times by the Egyptian priest who was the first teacher of Saint Moses in the words: *Satisfaction-of-self arising from the resourceful attainment of one's set aim in the cognizance of a clear conscience.*

Today is the tenth of January. Three days from now, by the old style calendar, the New Year will be welcomed in at midnight, an hour which is memorable for me as the time of my coming into the world.

According to a custom established since childhood, I have always begun, from that hour, to conform my life to a new programme thought out beforehand and invariably based on a definite principle, which is to remember myself as much as possible in everything, and voluntarily to direct my manifestations and also my reactions to the manifestations of others in such a way as to attain the aims chosen by me for the coming year. This year I will set myself the task of concentrating all the capacities present in my individuality towards being able to acquire, by my own means, before my proposed departure from America about the middle of March, the sum of money needed for clearing up all my debts.

Then, on my return to France, I shall begin again to write, but on the sole condition that henceforth I be relieved of all concern about the material conditions necessary for my mode of life, already established on a certain scale.

The Material Question

But if, for some reason or other, I fail to accomplish the task I have set myself, then I will be forced to recognize the illusory nature of all the ideas expounded in this narrative, as well as my own extravagant imagination; and, true to my principles, I will have to creep with my tail between my legs, as Mullah Nassr Eddin would say, 'into the deepest old galoshes that have ever been worn on sweaty feet'.

And if this should be the case, I would then categorically decide to do as follows:

To give for publication only the manuscripts I have just revised in final form, that is, the first series of my writings and two chapters of the second; to cease writing for ever; and, on returning home, to light in the middle of the lawn before my windows a huge bonfire and throw on it all the rest of my writings.

After which I will begin a new life by using the capacities I possess for the sole purpose of satisfying my personal egoism.

A plan is already outlining itself in my madcap brain for my activities in such a life.

I picture myself organizing a new 'Institute' with many branches, only this time not for the Harmonious Development of Man but for instruction in hitherto undiscovered means of self-satisfaction.

And there is no doubt that a business like that would run as if on greased wheels.

PENGUIN

ARKANA

NEW AGE BOOKS FOR MIND, BODY & SPIRIT

With over 200 titles currently in print, Arkana is the leading name in quality books for mind, body and spirit. Arkana encompasses the spirituality of both East and West, ancient and new. A vast range of interests is covered, including Psychology and Transformation, Health, Science and Mysticism, Women's Spirituality, Zen, Western Traditions and Astrology.

If you would like a catalogue of Arkana books, please write to:

Sales Department – Arkana
Penguin Books USA Inc.
375 Hudson Street
New York, NY 10014

Arkana Marketing Department
Penguin Books Ltd
27 Wrights Lane
London W8 5TZ

Available while stocks last.

PENGUIN

ARKANA

NEW AGE BOOKS FOR MIND, BODY & SPIRIT

A SELECTION OF TITLES

The Dreambody in Relationships   Arnold Mindell

All of us communicate on several levels at once, and Mindell shows how much of our silent language conflicts with overt behaviour. He argues that bringing all the hidden parts of ourselves to awareness as they affect us is important for the well-being not only of our relationships but also of the community – indeed, the world – in which we live.

The Sacred Yew   Anand Chetan and Diana Brueton

Recently it has been discovered that the yew can live for many thousands of years. *The Sacred Yew* is the inspiring story of one man's crusade to preserve this revered yet threatened tree and explain its importance to all our lives.

Be As You Are   Sri Ramana Maharshi

'The ultimate truth is so simple.' This is the message of Sri Ramana Maharshi, one of India's most revered spiritual masters whose teachings, forty years after his death, are speaking to growing audiences worldwide. 'That sense of presence, of the direct communication of the truth so far as it can be put into words, is there on every page' – *Parabola*

In Search of the Miraculous: Fragments of an Unknown Teaching   P. D. Ouspensky

Ouspensky's renowned, vivid and characteristically honest account of his work with Gurdjieff from 1915 to 1918. 'Undoubtedly a *tour de force*. To put entirely new and very complex cosmology and psychology into fewer than 400 pages, and to do this with a simplicity and vividness that makes the book accessible to any educated reader, is in itself something of an achievement' – *The Times Literary Supplement*

PENGUIN

ARKANA

NEW AGE BOOKS FOR MIND, BODY & SPIRIT

A SELECTION OF TITLES

Herbal Medicine for Everyone Michael McIntyre

'The doctor treats but nature heals.' With an increasing consciousness of ecology and a move towards holistic treatment, the value of herbal medicine is now being fully recognized. Discussing the history and principles of herbal medicine and its application to a wide range of diseases and ailments, this illuminating book will prove a source of great wisdom.

The Cult of the Black Virgin Ean Begg

Why are over 500 of the world's images of the madonna 'black' or 'dark'? And why are they so little known? A resurfacing of the powerful pagan goddesses of sexuality, the underworld and earth-wisdom, the Black Virgins are symbols of power and majesty, the other aspect of the traditional Madonna's maidenhood or tender maternity.

Views from the Real World G. I. Gurdjieff

Only through self-observation and self-exploration, Gurdjieff asserted, could man develop his consciousness. To this end he evolved exercises through which awareness could be heightened and enlightenment attained. *Views from the Real World* contains the talks and lectures he gave on this theme as he travelled from city to city with his pupils. What emerges is his immensely human approach to self-improvement.

Riding the Horse Backwards Arnold and Amy Mindell

Arnold Mindell is the originator of perhaps the most inspiring 'school' of healing we have in the West now, process work, and in this running narrative of one of his workshops, which he gave with Amy Mindell at the Esalen community in the United States, we're taken to the heart of the magic.